THE BRITISH CAMPAIGN
IN FRANCE AND FLANDERS
JULY TO NOVEMBER
1918

BOOKS BY A. CONAN DOYLE

THE FIRM OF GIRDLESTONE.
THE WHITE COMPANY.
THE MYSTERY OF CLOOMBER.
MICAH CLARKE.
THE REFUGEES.
THE CAPTAIN OF THE "POLESTAR."
THE DOINGS OF RAFFLES HAW.
THE GREAT SHADOW.
THE PARASITE.
A STUDY IN SCARLET.
THE SIGN OF FOUR.
THE ADVENTURES OF SHERLOCK HOLMES.
THE MEMOIRS OF SHERLOCK HOLMES.
THE RETURN OF SHERLOCK HOLMES.
ROUND THE RED LAMP.
THE EXPLOITS OF BRIGADIER GERARD.
THE STARK-MUNRO LETTERS.
RODNEY STONE.
THE TRAGEDY OF THE KOROSKO.
UNCLE BERNAC.
THE GREEN FLAG.
SONGS OF ACTION.
SONGS OF THE ROAD.
THE GREAT BOER WAR.
A DUET, WITH AN OCCASIONAL CHORUS.
THE HOUND OF THE BASKERVILLES.
THE ADVENTURES OF GERARD.
SIR NIGEL.
THE VALLEY OF FEAR.
THE LAST GALLEY.
DANGER.
THE NEW REVELATION.
THE VITAL MESSAGE.

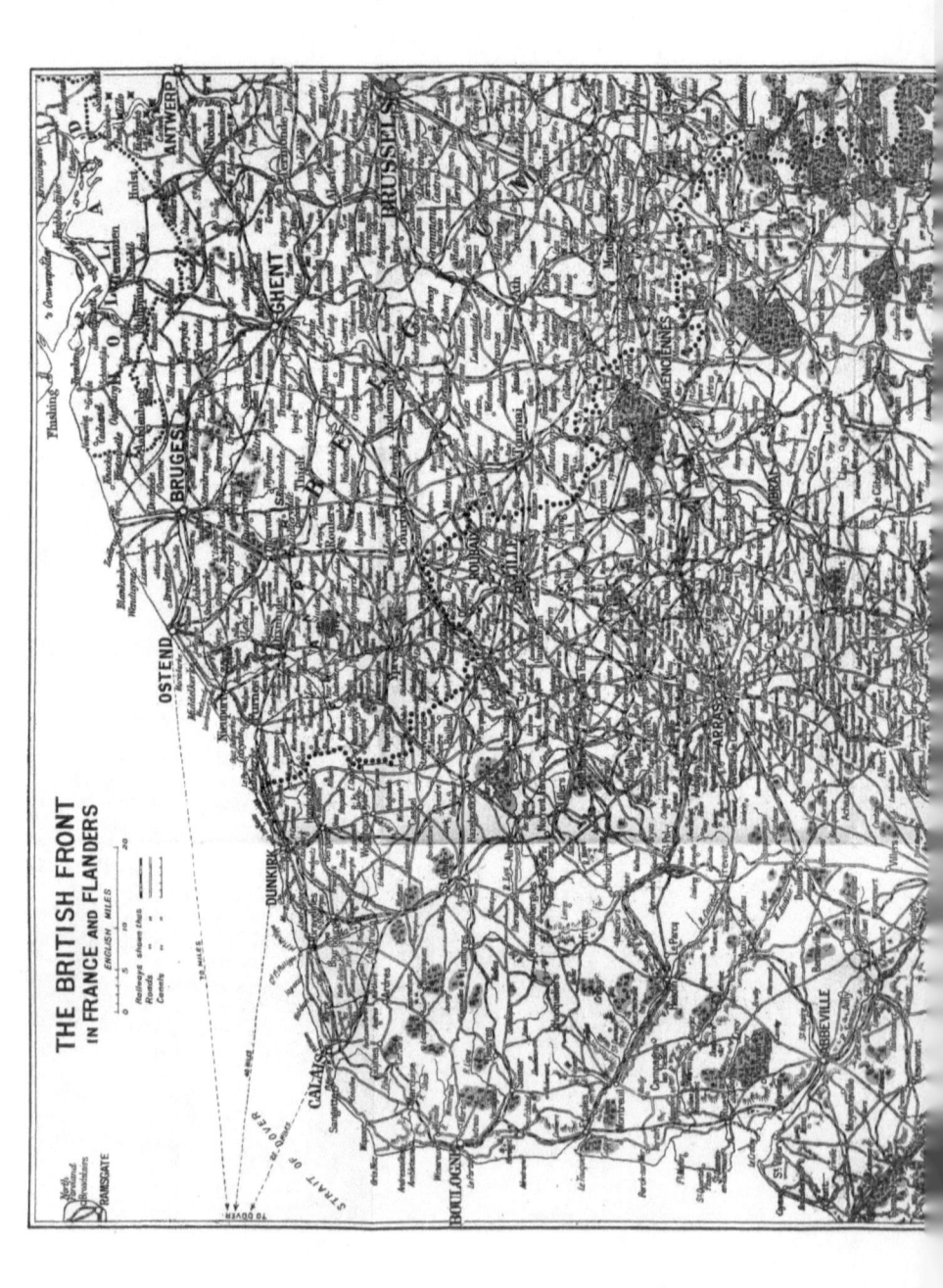

THE BRITISH CAMPAIGN

IN FRANCE AND FLANDERS

JULY TO NOVEMBER
1918

BY

ARTHUR CONAN DOYLE
AUTHOR OF
'THE GREAT BOER WAR,' ETC.

The Naval & Military Press Ltd

Published by

The Naval & Military Press Ltd
Unit 10 Ridgewood Industrial Park,
Uckfield, East Sussex,
TN22 5QE England

Tel: +44 (0) 1825 749494
Fax: +44 (0) 1825 765701

www.naval-military-press.com
www.military-genealogy.com

In reprinting in facsimile from the original, any imperfections are inevitably reproduced and the quality may fall short of modern type and cartographic standards.

CONTENTS

CHAPTER I

THE OPENING OPERATIONS

From July 1 to August 8, 1918

The general position—German attack of July 16—French counter-attack of July 18—Turn of the tide—Fifty-first and Sixty-second Divisions on the Ardres—Desperate fighting—The Fifteenth Scots Division at Buzancy—Le Glorieux Chardon d'Écosse—Nicholson's Thirty-fourth Division at Oulchy-le-Château—The campaigns on the periphery 1

CHAPTER II

ATTACK OF RAWLINSON'S FOURTH ARMY

The Battle of Amiens, August 8-22

Great British victory—Advance of the Canadians—Of the Australians—Of the Third Corps—Hard struggle at Chipilly—American assistance—Continuance of the operations—Great importance of the battle 24

CHAPTER III

CONTINUATION OF THE OPERATIONS OF RAWLINSON'S FOURTH ARMY

From August 22 to the Battle of the Hindenburg Line, September 29

Further advance of the Australians—Of the Third Corps—Capture of Albert—Advance across the old Somme battlefield—Capture of Mont St. Quentin—Splendid Australian exploit—Fall of Peronne—Debut of the Yeomanry (Seventy-fourth) Division—Attack on the outliers of the Hindenburg Line—Appearance of the Ninth Corps—Eve of the Judgment 43

CHAPTER IV

THE ATTACK OF BYNG'S THIRD ARMY

August 21, 1918, to September 29, 1918

Advance of Shute's Fifth Corps—Great feat in crossing the Ancre—Across the old battlefield—Final position of Fifth Corps opposite Hindenburg's Main Line—Advance of Haldane's Sixth Corps—Severe fighting—Arrival of the Fifty-second Division—Formation of Fergusson's Seventeenth Corps—Recapture of Havrincourt—Advance of Harper's Fourth Corps—Great tenacity of the troops—The New Zealanders and the Jaeger—Final position before the decisive battle 80

CHAPTER V

THE ADVANCE OF HORNE'S FIRST ARMY

From August 26 to September 27

The indefatigable Fifty-first Division—Capture of Greenland Hill—Fine advance of the Canadians—Breaking of the Drocourt-Quéant line—Fine work of the Sixty-third Naval Division—Great day for the Dominion—Demeanour of German prisoners . . . 138

CHAPTER VI

THE OPERATIONS OF RAWLINSON'S FOURTH ARMY

From the Battle of the Hindenburg Line (September 29) to the Battle of the Selle, October 17

The first American operations—The rupture of the Hindenburg Line—Predicament of Twenty-seventh American Division—Their gallant resistance—Great Australian attack—Remarkable feat by the Forty-sixth North Midland Territorial Division—Exeunt the Third Corps and the Australians—Entrance of the Thirteenth Corps—Rupture of the Beaurevoir line—Advance to the Selle River . 149

CHAPTER VII

THE OPERATIONS OF RAWLINSON'S FOURTH ARMY

From the Battle of the Selle, October 17, to the end

Attack upon the line of the Selle River—Stubborn work by the Second American Corps—Success of the Ninth Corps—Hard fighting at Le Cateau—Great feat of the South Africans—Continued advance—Delay-action mines—Capture of Landrecies—Dramatic exit of the German machine-gunner—Splendid work of the First Division 182

CONTENTS

CHAPTER VIII
OPERATIONS OF BYNG'S THIRD ARMY
From the Battle of the Hindenburg Line (September 29) to the Battle of the Selle (October 17)

Fighting at L'Escaut Canal—Dash of the New Zealanders—The Guards in a hot corner—Crossing of the Canal—Back on the old ground—Great work by all four Corps of the Third Army . . . 207

CHAPTER IX
OPERATIONS OF BYNG'S THIRD ARMY
From the Battle of the Selle, October 12, to the end

The battle of the Selle River—Reversion to open warfare—The valour of Lancashire—Haig's incessant blows—Weakening of the German morale—The battle of Mormal Forest—New Zealanders and the mediaeval fortress—Capture of the great forest—The Sambre bridged—A grand Division—Advance of Fergusson's Seventeenth Corps—The last phase 229

CHAPTER X
THE ADVANCE OF HORNE'S FIRST ARMY
From September 27 to the end

The Canadians at the Canal du Nord—Hard fighting at Bourlon—Strong counter-attack at Abancourt—Canadian valour—Godley's Twenty-second Corps—The Ecaillon valley—Forcing of the Rhonelle—General Heneker's attack—Capture of Douai . . 256

CHAPTER XI
OPERATIONS OF THE SECOND AND FIFTH ARMIES
September 28–November 11

King Albert in the field—Great Belgo-Franco-British advance—The last act on the old stage—The prophet of 1915—Renewed advance—Germans desert the coast—Relief of Douai and Lille—The final stage in the subsidiary theatres of war 281

CHAPTER XII
THE END 299

APPENDIX 307

INDEX 315

MAPS AND PLANS

	FACE PAGE
Map to illustrate the British Campaign in France and Flanders	1
Advance of Fourth Army, August 8, showing Gains up to August 12, and Final Position after the Fall of Peronne	24
Position of British Corps, end of September 1918 . .	79
Advance of First, Third, and Fourth British Armies from August 21, 1918, to September 2, 1918. Arrows point to the Rupture of the Quéant-Drocourt Line . .	80
General Position of the Allies immediately before the Armistice of November 11, 1918	256
Allied Advance in the North	281

IN TEXT

	PAGE
The Attack on the Selle	206

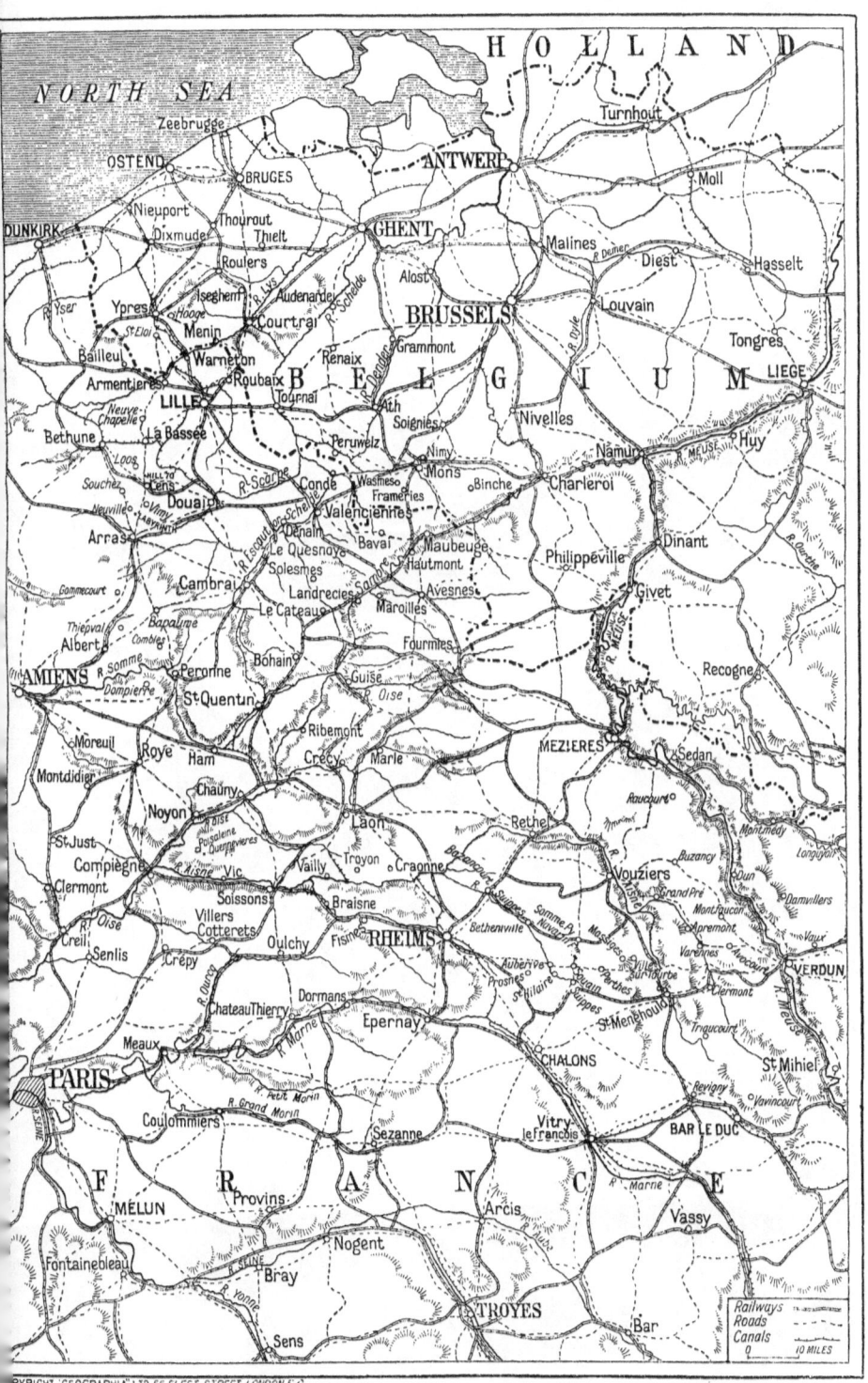

CHAPTER I

THE OPENING OPERATIONS

From July 1 to August 8, 1918

The general position—German attack of July 16—French counter-attack of July 18—Turn of the tide—Fifty-first and Sixty-second Divisions on the Ardres—Desperate fighting—The Fifteenth Scots Division at Buzancy—Le Glorieux Chardon d'Écosse—Nicholson's Thirty-fourth Division at Oulchy-le-Château—The campaigns on the periphery.

WHEN the year 1918 had run half its course the Germans appeared to be triumphantly in the ascendant. In Flanders they had pushed back the British to positions which were, on an average, to the rear of those occupied in 1914. On the Somme they had more than neutralised all the Allied gains of 1916, and were stretched now from Arras to Montdidier, covering ground which they had not touched since the early days of the war. On the Aisne they had reconquered all that the French had so laboriously won in three campaigns, and were back along the Marne and within gun-shot of Paris. These results had been achieved in three great battles which had cost the Allies some 200,000 prisoners and nearly 2000 guns. In July it would have seemed that the German Empire was victorious, and yet ere the year had ended the very name had changed its meaning in the map of Europe, and was known only in the list of

CHAPTER I.

The Opening Operations.

evil things which have had their day and then have passed. How this extraordinary change—the most sudden and dramatic in all history—came to pass is the theme of this final volume.

There were certain factors which even at the zenith of Germany's fortunes may have prepared a cool-headed critic for a swing of the scales, though the wisest and best informed could not have conceived how violent the oscillation would be. In the first place, the ever-pressing strangle-hold of the Navy, combined with an indifferent harvest and the exhaustion of certain stocks within the Empire, notably of copper, rubber, wool, and lubricants, produced great internal difficulties which grew worse with every month. Then again German successes had been bought in reckless fashion at a very heavy price, and if they brought a million men across from the Russian frontier it is probable that they had squandered nearly as many in the three great battles. Finally, there was the all-important factor of the American reinforcements which had been speeded up to meet the pressing emergency. By splendid international co-operation the Americans put all their proverbial energy into marshalling and equipping the men, while Great Britain threw every available unit of her sea power, mercantile or naval, into the task of getting them across. The long-suffering people of this island gladly cut down their requirements in every possible direction so as to secure the tonnage for this marvellous transfer. At a steady rate of a quarter of a million every month the Americans flowed into France—magnificent raw material which was soon to show how quickly it could develop into the most highly finished article.

This constant addition to the Allied forces, with the moral confidence which they brought with them, was the third contributory cause to the sudden change of fortune. It would be ungenerous, however, not to add that a fourth, without which all others might have been vain, lay in the commanding personality and extraordinary genius of the great Frenchman who now controlled the whole Allied battle front from the sea to the Alps, while two great civilians, Lloyd George and Clemenceau, rallied the home fronts of the two weary nations which had borne the brunt of the war.

It will be remembered from the last volume that in the first half of 1918 the sun of victory had never once in Western Europe rested upon the standards of the Allies save in Italy, where the Austrians had been defeated upon the Piave. June 17 was in truth the turning-point of the war, for from that date everything went well with the forces of freedom. The change in the West came later, however, than in Italy, and on July 16 the Germans attempted a new advance upon the largest scale, which seemed to have some small success at first though it was in truth the starting-point of all their misfortunes. Their previous advances had brought them forward on the line from Montdidier to Rheims, and now they enlarged their front by 25 miles on the eastern side of Rheims, while their attack also covered about the same distance to the west of that city, making some progress in this latter sector, which led them down the valley of the Oise, towards Villers-Cotterets, Compiègne, and finally Paris. The whole world held its breath in a hush of horror as it saw Foch's soldiers desperately struggling and yet losing mile after mile

CHAPTER I.

The Opening Operations. July 18.

of the short stretch which separated the Teutonic barbarians from the centre of the world's civilisation and culture. They had crossed the Marne that evening and had pushed the French and American line back for some miles, but the latter rallied and regained some of the ground. The most important point of the struggle, however, was to the east of Rheims, where that splendid soldier, General Gouraud, a one-armed bearded veteran of Gallipoli, created a false front which the enemy captured, and then whilst they were still in disorder attacked them from the real front, pushing them back with great loss. This development on the east of the line fully compensated for the German advance on the west, which was brought to a final halt within two days. Foch had now bled the Germans until they had lost some of their power of resistance. The moment for his great counter-attack was at hand, and the carefully husbanded reserves were ready for the crisis—those reserves which it was his supreme merit to have hoarded up when the temptation to spend them was more than the firmest will could have been expected to resist.

On July 18 the blow fell, and the Germans recoiled in a movement which was destined never to stop until they had crossed the Rhine. All important as the operations were they are only indicated here since this chronicle is necessarily confined to the British action, and no British troops were as yet engaged. Issuing under the cover of a storm from the great forest of Villers-Cotterets which had screened his preparations, the French Marshal hurled his line of tanks upon the enemy, clearing a path for his infantry. At the same moment the French-American line went forward over a front of 27 miles from the Oise to the Marne, striking the whole flank of the German advance. The attack extended from Vingre in the north to Château-Thierry. Everywhere the German flank fell back, their front had to withdraw across the Marne, Château-Thierry was reoccupied and 20,000 prisoners with 400 guns were left in the hands of the victors. Gradually, as the attack developed from day to day, a huge pocket was formed, bulging southwards from the Aisne, with its lower edge upon the Marne, the whole assuming much the shape which Spain does upon the map of Europe. This protrusion, instead of being a menacing point directed towards Paris, was now a much battered salient attacked simultaneously upon all sides, by Mangin in the west and by Gouraud in the south and east. Americans and French were on the Marne, French alone to the west of it, and British with French on the east of it. All were fighting with the cold fury of men who have reached a crisis where death is nothing and victory all. Nurses at the forward hospitals have testified how the French wounded were brought in mutilated and dying, but delirious with joy because they knew that the tide had turned. What matter anything else ? What matter life or limb ? The grey cloud was slowly, slowly drifting back whence it came.

But it was very slow, for the German soldier had never fought better, nor had his leaders ever shown greater skill in drawing him out from danger and yet selling every rearward position at the highest price of Allied blood. All three Allies were tried to their utmost, for the enemy had not yet learned that he was fated to retreat. The British, who had their

CHAPTER I.

Twenty-Second Corps on the Ardres. July 20–21.

own great task already planned, were in weak force, though that force was of the highest quality, for two better divisions than Campbell's Fifty-first Highlanders and Braithwaite's Sixty-second Yorkshiremen did not exist in the Army. It is their operations which we have now to examine, since the grand work of their American comrades-in-arms can only be included in the scope of this work where they actually fought in the British formations.

They occupied a point on the eastern face of the attack, nearly midway between the Marne and Rheims, and it was their task to force their way up that valley of the Ardres down which the remains of the British Ninth Corps had retreated from the disaster of the Aisne, and across which the Nineteenth Division had been drawn when it stopped the German advance near Bligny, as described in the last volume. Some memory of island valour should linger in that valley, for much good British blood has been shed there. The two divisions which were now hurried up to take their place in the French line formed the Twenty-second Corps under Sir John Godley, and were accompanied by some New Zealand and Australian Cavalry. They relieved a mauled Italian Corps, while they had Frenchmen on their left and Algerians on their right, so that it would be difficult to imagine a more cosmopolitan line of defence. The country in front was hilly and very difficult, and the line was bisected by the River Ardres, the Sixty-second advancing on the right of the stream and the Fifty-first on the left.

It was a very desperate and difficult business, which lasted for ten days, during which each division showed the most splendid courage and endurance,

THE OPENING OPERATIONS

as can be proved by the fact that their united losses came to 8000 men out of about 16,000 engaged, and that they met and defeated four German divisions, capturing 1500 prisoners, 140 machine-guns, and 40 cannon. The opening attack, during which the advancing lines passed through the ranks of the Second Italian Corps, was greatly stimulated by the news of the splendid Allied advance of the two previous days, July 18 and 19.

Twenty-Second Corps on the Ardres. July 20–21.

The fighting of both divisions was made very difficult by the underwood and the standing corn which lay before them, thickly sown with German machine-guns. On July 20 the 2/4th York and Lancasters, on the extreme right of the British line, captured Bouilly, but were driven out again. At the same time the 5th Yorkshire Light Infantry was held up and lost heavily in front of the Château of Commetreuil. It was a long, difficult, and expensive day for the 187th Brigade, and its only remaining battalion, the 2/4th Yorkshire Light Infantry, lost heavily as well.

The 185th Brigade on July 20 occupied the left of the divisional line, with the Highlanders on the other side of the Ardres. Marfaux and Cuitron lay before them, but neither could be quite reached, though again and again the assailants were on the very edge of the villages. Once some of the men of the 2/4th Hampshires from the supporting brigade actually penetrated the village, but they were seen no more. The 2/4th West Ridings, south of the village, were also held up. Meanwhile the 5th West Ridings attempted to work around Marfaux from the north, through the wood of Petit Camp. All attempts to debouch from the wood were vain, however, and again the attack was brought to nought. Some ground had been gained during the day, but both main efforts had failed, and all three brigades of the Sixty-second Division had been badly mauled. With no British reserves behind, General Braithwaite must have been sorely exercised in his mind that night.

On July 21 the attack eased down on the left, but on the right the 187th Brigade deployed and attacked the Bouilly Ridge. The 9th Durham Pioneers made a very fine advance, as did the 2/4th York and Lancasters, and some valuable ground was taken, but none of the villages. The attackers were encouraged, however, by learning from prisoners that the Germans had endured heavy losses, and had been compelled to demand reinforcements.

On July 22 the situation began to clear a little as Burnett's 106th Brigade, represented mainly by the 5th West Ridings, attacked the wood of Petit Camp, an ominous grove, already littered with British dead. So deliberate was their advance, in consequence of the difficult ground to be searched, that the barrage was at the rate of 100 yards in ten minutes. The place was one long succession of gun posts "en echelon," which were so concealed that they had no field of fire, and were the more deadly on that account as they fired by sound out of the bushes, and could not possibly be seen until one walked up to them. None the less the Yorkshiremen, helped by a wing of the 5th Devons, fought their way through this dreadful wood, dropping small posts as they went. Two hundred prisoners and 41 machine-guns remained in their hands, with 700 yards of new ground. The German losses were heavy, but so were

THE OPENING OPERATIONS

the British, Captain Cockhill's company of the West Ridings emerging with two officers and six men able to report for duty. It was a fine operation, well conceived and well carried through. The Germans fought with great tenacity all day.

On July 23 the south-western corner of the Petit Camp Wood, which was still in German hands, was cleared by the 6th West Ridings. The main attack, however, on Marfaux and Cuitron was carried out by the Durhams and the New Zealand Cyclist Battalion with magnificent success. Marfaux fell to the New Zealanders. The stormers broke through both villages and made their line 400 yards beyond. Two French tanks did good service in this assault. Two hundred prisoners and eight French 75's, taken previously by the Germans, were among the trophies of this fine advance. The Seventy-seventh French Division had attacked upon the right with equal success.

Up to this period the Highlanders of the Fifty-first Division had been striving hard on the southern side of the Ardres, with a task which was not less difficult than that of their English comrades on the north.

On July 20 they found the enemy opposite to them in great strength, as was shown by the fact that prisoners from three divisions, the Twenty-second (Saxe-Meiningen), the Hundred and third (Hessian), and the Hundred and twenty-third (Saxon) were taken that day. The great straggling wood of Courton, with a fringe of farms, mills, and other buildings, formed a strong advanced position. The Fifty-first Division has gained so splendid a record in the war that advantage may be taken of

Chapter I.

Twenty-Second Corps on the Ardres.

July 20-21.

this action to give in fuller detail its glorious units. The attack that morning was carried out by the 154th Brigade, consisting of the 4th Seaforths, 4th Gordons, and 7th Argyll and Sutherlands, on the right flank. On the left was the 153rd Brigade, consisting of the 6th and 7th Black Watch and 7th Gordons. In reserve was the 152nd Brigade, 5th and 6th Seaforths and 6th Gordons, with the 8th Royal Scots as pioneer battalion. The attack was supported by French artillery and also by the guns of the 255th and 256th Brigades R.F.A.

The advance was a most arduous one, especially after the first victorious rush when the troops found themselves involved in the thick brushwood which prevented co-operation to such an extent that the two brigades were entirely separated, but each struggled on independently, small knots of determined men fighting their way forward as best they might. The progress was better upon the left than on the right, but the casualties were heavy, for the German machine-guns had survived the barrage and were very deadly. Colonel Bickmore of the 4th Gordons led a company of his battalion against a German post but was brought down by a bomb, and his men driven back. When the ground was recovered the Colonel had been carried off as a prisoner. The German infantry seem to have taken hardly any part in the battle, which was fought between the splendid Scottish infantry on one side, and the determined German machine-gunners on the other. The Black Watch of the 153rd Brigade found an even blacker watch fighting on their flank, for the Senegalese infantry of the French Ninth Division went forward with them and did good work during the

THE OPENING OPERATIONS 11

whole arduous day. So sweeping was the machine-gun fire that at many points it was found to be impossible even to creep forward through the two-foot corn.

By evening the attack had been definitely held, and the Highlanders were forced to be content with their initial gains, while the French on the left, who had been assaulting the hamlet of Paradis all day, were also stationary. At 6.30 a company of German infantry attacked the Argylls, but were driven back with heavy loss. So the long day ended, the troops being much exhausted. The capture of 8 officers and 360 men, with many machine-guns, was an inadequate return for such heroic exertions. All day the enemy had been withdrawing upon the Marne front, and the holding of his flanks was so vitally essential that he was prepared to make any sacrifice for the purpose.

The attack was continued next morning, the 152nd Brigade pushing forward into the front line, while the other depleted units supported it and guarded its flanks. Things went badly at the outset, for the line had been altered during the night and the barrage was miscalculated in consequence, so that it was no great help to the 6th Gordons in their advance. All day mixed fighting went on in the wood, and it was most difficult to determine the exact position of the various units, groups of men stalking the machine-guns as hunters might stalk tigers, the fight ending as often in the death of the hunter as of the tiger. Once again the evening of a bloody day found things very much as they had been in the morning. It cannot be denied that the German resistance was a very stern one.

CHAPTER I.

Twenty-Second Corps on the Ardres. July 20–21.

CHAPTER I.

Twenty-Second Corps on the Ardres.

July 27.

After a pause of a day the Highland Division renewed its attack along a portion of its front, the main advance being carried out by the 152nd Brigade. Once more the deadly woods were penetrated, and once more there was a limited advance and considerable losses. On this occasion the barrage was more useful, though some French batteries on the left fell short and caused heavy casualties to a company of the 6th Gordons in their point of assembly. Such are the unavoidable chances of modern warfare. The 8th Royal Scots were thrown into the fight, and made a fine advance. Altogether there were signs this day of a weakening on the German front, which was confirmed in the patrol fighting of the next few days. There were many casualties in the 152nd Brigade, including Major Moir, C.O. of the 5th Seaforths, who was badly wounded.

Major operations were in abeyance until July 27, when severe fighting broke out once again upon the south side of the Ardres. The 187th Brigade had been sent across by General Braithwaite, and it now took its place in General Carter-Campbell's sector, with the 152nd on its right and the 153rd on its left, with the intention of making a vigorous attack upon the German line on this front. Tanks had been allotted, but rain had set in, the ground was marshy, and the monsters immovable. All immediate objectives were easily taken. The villages of Espilly and Nappes had both been occupied. So soft did the front appear that the Australian horsemen were pushed forward, while the troops north of the river moved on in sympathy. The final line was north-west of Chaumuzy. Here, on July 28, a very stiff German resistance was encountered, and Chambrecy

THE OPENING OPERATIONS

on the left flank represented the No Man's Land between the armies.

The Montagne de Bligny position, where the Nineteenth Division had distinguished itself in June, now lay immediately ahead, and the 8th West Yorkshires (Leeds Rifles) were ordered to attack it. They went forward so swiftly and with such spirit that they were into and over the position before the Germans realised what had happened. It was a notable performance, for the place was of great strength and strategic significance. The French Government bestowed a special mark of honour upon the 8th West Yorks for this deed, and it is certainly a singular coincidence that, of the few British battalions thus honoured, two should have won it at the same spot. There was no artillery support, and the casualties were heavy, but Yorkshire won home in spite of it. The enemy tried to regain it until the high corn was full of his dead, but it was all in vain. This day, with the co-operation of the French, Bligny village was also taken. No further ground was gained on July 29, as a new German division, the Two hundred and fortieth, had come into line with orders to hold on at all costs. The fighting was very severe at the junction between the French and British, where the liaison was so close between the two nations that it is on record that, when at a critical moment the French ran out of cartridges, the rifles and ammunition of the British casualties were handed over to them and saved the situation. Shortly afterwards the two British divisions were drawn from the line and returned to their own army. In a generous appreciation of their services General Berthelot, after enumerating their captures, said:

CHAPTER I.

Twenty-Second Corps on the Ardres.

July 28-30.

14   THE BRITISH CAMPAIGN, 1918

CHAPTER I.

Twenty-Second Corps on the Ardres.
July 30–31.

"Thanks to the heroic courage and proverbial tenacity of the British, the continued efforts of this brave Army Corps have not been in vain. . . . You have added a glorious page to your history. Marfaux, Chaumuzy, Montagne de Bligny—all those famous names will be written in letters of gold in the annals of your regiments." The French official bulletins offered also a very special tribute of praise to the 6th Black Watch, a Perthshire battalion, which, under Colonel Tarleton, had done particularly fine work during the long and arduous service of the Fifty-first Division.

Fifteenth Division at Buzancy.
July 28–August 1.

Whilst the Twenty-second British Corps had, as described, distinguished itself greatly in the valley of the Ardres on the east of the German salient, the Fifteenth Scottish Division under General H. L. Reed, V.C., had been detailed to aid the French line in its advance on Buzancy on the western German flank. This veteran division was thrown into the fight on July 28, and made its mark at once upon the formidable German position which faced it. It had relieved the First American Division which was much worn by its long and splendid service in General Mangin's Tenth Army. The Americans left their guns in the line to cover the advance, so that, for the first time in history, British, Americans, and French were all engaged as allies upon the same battle-ground. The village was very strongly held, and the high ground to the east of it was bristling with machine-guns, but the Scots infantry would take no denial. The 44th Brigade (Thomson) had attacked the village itself, the 5th Gordons and 8th Seaforths leading the assault. The latter battalion lost its commander, Colonel Smith, but was the first into the

THE OPENING OPERATIONS

objective, while the Gordons held and consolidated the ground to the north of it. Farther north still the 45th Brigade had advanced its whole line, while at the south flank of the attack the 91st French Infantry was clearing the woods in front of it. The machine-gun fire at this point was very heavy, however, and the French, after a gallant struggle, were forced back to their original line, with the result that the right of the attack was in the air. The Seaforths had carried the Château of Buzancy as well as the village, and the orders were at all costs to hold on to these important points; so part of the 4/5th Black Watch was pushed forward to strengthen the defenders, who were hard pressed and heavily gassed. There was desperate fighting all round the village, which was declared by a veteran French flammenwerfer section attached to the Highlanders to be the most bloody work seen by them in the war. With their flank naked the remains of the brave battalions were exposed about six o'clock in the evening to an overpowering German counter-attack which rolled up from the south-east and drove them, still fighting tooth and claw, through the village, from which six German officers and 200 men were brought as prisoners. Thus by seven in the evening the 44th Brigade, after their day of most heroic effort, were back on their original line. It was a sad end to a splendid deed of arms, but there was no disposition to blame the Eighty-seventh French Division on the right, who were already worn with much fighting, and who were faced with very difficult country. Many of the Highlanders wept bitter tears of rage and mortification when they found that the deaths of so many of their comrades had not bought the

CHAPTER I.

Fifteenth Division at Buzancy.

July 28–August 1.

village for which they gave their blood so willingly.

<small>Fifteenth Division at Buzancy. July 28–August 1.</small>

Orders were now received from the French Corps that the Scots Fifteenth Division should change place with its neighbour, the Eighty-seventh French Division, a difficult operation which was successfully accomplished, the artillery in each case being left in position. The new operation was to consist of an attack upon Hartennes Forest, the Twelfth French Division working round the south and the Fifteenth Scots Division round the north end of it, both meeting to the east, with Droisy as an ultimate objective. The attacking troops were concealed so far as possible in the cornfields on July 31, and went forward about eight o'clock in the morning of August 1, after the completion of a successful French advance further down the line. The brunt of this new advance was borne by the 6th Camerons and 13th Royal Scots of the 45th Brigade (Orr-Ewing), together with the 10th Scots Rifles and 7/8th Scottish Borderers of the 46th Brigade (Fortune). The left of the line made fine progress and reached the east side of the Soissons Road, but the 45th Brigade on the right was held up by terrible machine-gun fire, part of which came from several derelict French tanks. These were dealt with and blown to pieces by trench mortars. The advance was then resumed, the French Twelfth Division coming forward also in the south. About midday the Camerons had reached their mark, but were out of touch with the Borderers on their right, so that they were compelled to form a defensive flank from the cemetery to the road. The Germans lay in a series of wooded hills upon the right, and though these were smothered with shells the brave machine-

THE OPENING OPERATIONS 17

gunners still clung to their position. So heavy was their fire that the right flank could get no farther, and it was determined to hold on to the ground gained. During the night the 44th Brigade, in spite of its heavy losses three days before, took the place of the 46th.

Chapter I.
Fifteenth Division at Buzancy.
July 28–August 2.

It was evident on the morning of August 2 that the stern combat of the previous day had not been without its effect. The enemy was retreating all along the line, and his positions were being rapidly evacuated. The Twelfth French Division on the right was able to advance almost without opposition past the Hartennes Wood. There followed an exhilarating pursuit up to the banks of the Crise River. The 9th Gordon Pioneer Battalion pushed in with great dash, and was in Villeblain before evening, while the French Eighty-seventh Division reached the river east of Buzancy. The Fifteenth Division was then relieved by the Seventeenth French Division, and was restored to the First British Army amid a shower of congratulatory messages from French Generals and comrades. So deep was the feeling among the French over the magnificent fighting and heavy losses of the Scots Division that a monument was at once raised in their honour in front of the old German position with the inscription: "Ici fleurira toujours le glorieux Chardon d'Écosse parmi les Roses de France." Many brave Scots will lie for ever round this monument. Three splendid battalion commanders, Smith of the Gordons, Turner of the Royal Scots, and Kennedy of the Seaforths, were slain, while Hart of the Scots Borderers and Macleod of the Camerons were incapacitated—five Colonels out of ten battalions. The sufferings from gas were very

C

CHAPTER I.

Thirty-Fourth Division with the French.

July 25–August 1.

severe, and all the Brigade Headquarters were severely affected, General Thomson and his staff holding on for the duration of the battle, but collapsing on the evening of August 2.

Whilst the Fifteenth Division had been performing this notable service the Thirty-fourth British Division (Nicholson) had also been incorporated for the moment into Mangin's Fifteenth Army, and was heavily engaged in the battle line opposite Grand Rozoy, rather south of the point where the Scots were fighting.

So great had been the losses of this splendid Tyneside division in the terrible contests of the Somme and of Flanders that it was now entirely reconstituted with nothing of its previous personnel save its veteran commander and a handful of war-worn officers. The infantry were mostly Territorials from the Palestine campaign. On July 18 the Thirty-fourth became part of the Tenth French Army near Senlis. On the 22nd it was incorporated into General Penet's Thirtieth Corps, and relieved the French Thirty-eighth Division in the battle zone, on a line parallel to the Château-Thierry—Soissons Road, having its right just west of Coutremain and its left in Parcy Tigny. Woodcock's 101st Brigade was on the right, Williams' 102nd on the left, while Chaplin's 103rd Brigade was in support. French divisions, the Nineteenth and the Fifty-eighth, were on either side, so that Nicholson's men formed a curious isolated little bit of fighting England.

At 6 A.M. on the morning of July 25 the whole line in this section attacked with the intention of carrying the important road already mentioned from Château-Thierry to Soissons. It was a hard and disappointing day, for the French divisions on either side were held by the heavy fire from the Bois de Plessier and Tigny. The 101st Brigade was not more successful, but the 102nd on the left got forward nearly a mile, and then lay with its left flank thrown back to connect up with its French neighbours. Considering that it was the first experience which these men had had of German artillery and machine-guns, General Nicholson was well satisfied with his new material.

On July 27 the division was relieved by the extension of the flanks of its two neighbours, but it was at once fitted into the line again, filling a battle-front of 1500 yards, with its right east of Oulchy-le-Château. It was just in time for an attack which opened at 5 A.M. on July 29, and it was only by great exertions that the guns were registered and the infantry in their places. The objective was a horse-shoe ridge from Beugneux in the east to Grand Rozoy in the west. The 103rd Brigade was on the right, the 101st upon the left.

The barrage was not as deadly as usual on account of the pressure of time which had hampered the preparation and registration. The slopes were long and open, swept by the deadly machine-guns. It was all odds against the attack. The 103rd Brigade got to the outskirts of Beugneux, but was held up by the murderous fire from an adjacent mill. The 101st surmounted the ridge between Grand Rozoy and Beugneux, but could get no farther, for it was all open ground to the north.

In the early afternoon the 102nd Brigade advanced from the wood in which it lay with the intention of helping the 101st to storm Beugneux, but as it came forward it met the 101st falling back before a strong counter-attack. This movement was checked by the new-comers and the line was sustained upon the ridge.

The net result of an arduous day was that the division was still short of the coveted road, but that it had won about 2000 yards of ground, including a good position for future operations. Casualties were heavy, and included Colonel Jourdain of the 2nd North Lancashires as well as Captain Weeks, C.O. of the 4th Royal Sussex. The French had got Grand Rozoy upon the left flank, and though they were driven out of it again they won their way back in the early morning of July 30. All this day and the next the troops prepared for a new effort, lying under heavy shell-fire which, among other casualties, killed Colonel Dooner, the chief staff officer of the division.

On August 1 the attack was renewed under a very heavy and efficient barrage, which helped the infantry so much that within two hours all objectives had been won. Beugneux fell after the hill which commanded it had been stormed by the 8th Argyll and Sutherland Highlanders in a very gallant advance. Colonel Barbow fell while leading his men to victory. On the left the French Twenty-fifth Division had been held up by the deadly fire from a knoll, but Major Atkinson of the 2nd North Lancashires realised the situation and diverted his reserve company to storm the obstacle, enabling the French right to get forward. It was planned that two British battalions should push on beyond their objectives in order to cover the flanks of a further French advance. One of these, the 4th Cheshires, carried out its part to perfection in spite of heavy losses, which included Colonel Swindells, its commander. The 1st Here-

THE OPENING OPERATIONS 21

fords, however, whose rôle was to cover the left of the Sixty-eighth French Division, was unable to do so, as that division was itself held up. That night the enemy was in full retreat all along this line, and falling back upon the River Vesle. On August 3 the Thirty-fourth Division was returned to the area of the Second British Army, having done a fine spell of service which brought the warmest compliments from the French commanders, not only to the infantry, but to General Walthall's guns (152nd and 160th Brigades) as well as Colonel Dobson's 207th, 208th, and 209th Field Companies.

<small>Chapter I.</small>

<small>Thirty-Fourth Division with the French. July 25–August 1.</small>

The northward advance of the French, Americans, and British was slow up to the end of July, but became accelerated in the first week of August, Soissons falling to the French on August 2, and the Germans being driven to the line of the Vesle, when they held on very tenaciously for a time, their rearguards showing their usual high soldierly qualities. The Americans had a particularly hard struggle, being faced by some of the élite of the German Army, including the 4th Prussian Guards, but winning their way steadily forward in spite of many strong counter-attacks. The situation upon the Vesle and the Aisne seemed for the moment to have reached an equilibrium, when Marshal Foch called Marshal Haig to his assistance and a new attack was launched in which British troops were once more employed on the grand scale. Their great march had started which was to end only at the bank of the Rhine.

Before embarking upon this narrative, it would be well to prevent the necessity of interrupting it by casting a glance at those general events connected with the world war which occurred during this period,

<small>General Survey.</small>

Chapter I.
General Survey.

which reacted upon the Western front. It has already been shortly stated that the Austrian Army had been held in their attempt to cross the Piave in mid June, and by the end of the month had been driven over the river by the Italians, aided by a strong British and French contingent. The final losses of the Austrians in this heavy defeat were not less than 20,000 prisoners with many guns. From this time until the final Austrian debacle there was no severe fighting upon this front. In the Salonican campaign the Greek Army was becoming more and more a factor to be reckoned with, and the deposition of the treacherous Constantine, with the return to power of Venizelos, consolidated the position of the Allies. There was no decided movement, however, upon this front until later in the year. In Palestine and in Mesopotamia the British forces were also quiescent, Allenby covering the northern approaches of Jerusalem, and preparing for his last splendid and annihilating advance, while Marshall remained in a similar position to the north of Bagdad. A small and very spirited expedition sent out by the latter will no doubt have a history of its own, for it was adventurous to a degree which was almost quixotic, and yet justified itself by its results. This was the advance of a handful of men over 700 miles of desert separating the Bagdad front from the Caspian. Arriving at the town of Baku they kept the German-Turks out of that town for six weeks at a time when oil supplies were a most pressing problem for them, and so influenced the course of the war. Finally they withdrew in safety after a most remarkable exploit, hardly realised amid the clash of greater forces. Russia still remained in its distracted condition, hag-ridden by forces which at their worst surpassed all the classical excesses of the French Revolution. Regeneration began to appear out of chaos, however, though the end was still afar. Allied forces in Siberia and on the Murman Coast formed nuclei upon which the supporters of civilisation could rally. On the water the atrocities of the German submarines and their sinking of hospital ships, accompanied in several cases by the drowning of the sick and wounded men, were the outstanding feature. In the main, therefore, it can be said that there was a hush upon the periphery, while in the centre the Allies with concentrated energy hurled themselves upon their enemy with the fixed determination to have done with the thing for ever, fighting without a break until either they could fight no more or the German menace had passed from the world which it had overshadowed so long. Nowhere was there a thought of compromise. There could be no justice unless it were thorough justice. The criminal methods by which the war had been waged forbade every thought of an incomplete settlement. With stern and deliberate determination the French and British turned to their task, strengthened by the knowledge that the vanguard of America was already in the field, weak as yet in numbers, but the head of that long column which extended across the Atlantic and was based upon the virile nation of a hundred million souls beyond.

CHAPTER II

ATTACK OF RAWLINSON'S FOURTH ARMY

The Battle of Amiens, August 8-22

Great British victory—Advance of the Canadians—Of the Australians—Of the Third Corps—Hard struggle at Chipilly—American assistance—Continuance of the operations—Great importance of the battle.

<small>Chapter II.
Attack of Rawlinson's Fourth Army.
August 8.</small>

In the tremendous and decisive operations which we are now about to examine, it is very necessary to have some fixed scheme in the method of description lest the reader be inextricably lost in the long line of advancing corps and armies. A chapter will be devoted, therefore, to the attack made by Rawlinson's Fourth Army whilst it was operating alone from August 8 to August 22. At that date Byng's Third Army joined in the fray, and subsequently, on August 28, Horne's First Army came into action. For the present, however, we can devote ourselves whole-heartedly to the record of Rawlinson's Army, all the rest being inactive. When the others come in, that is, after August 22, a definite system of narrative will be adopted.

Before describing the great battle some reference should be made to the action of Le Hamel fought on July 4, noticeable as having been the first Allied offensive since the early spring. Its complete success,

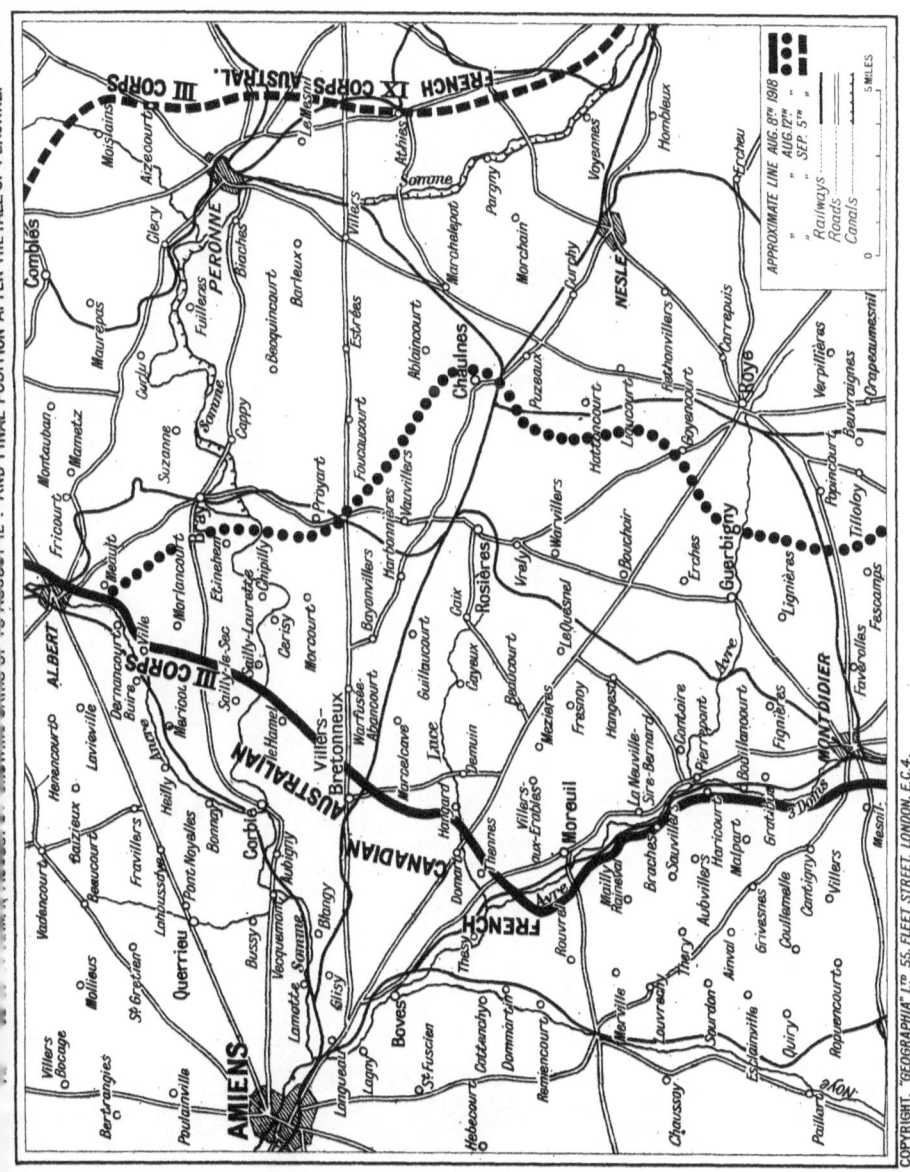

after the long series of troubles which had plunged all friends of freedom into gloom, made it more important than the numbers engaged or the gain of ground would indicate. It was carried out by the Australian Corps, acting as part of the Fourth Army, and is noticeable because a unit from the Thirty-third American Division took part in the operations. Le Hamel was taken and the Vaire Wood to the immediate south of the Somme. The gain of ground was about a mile in depth on a front of several miles, and the advance was so swift that a considerable number of prisoners, 1500 in all, were taken, many of them still encumbered by their gas-masks. Some sixty tanks took part in the advance, and did splendid work in rolling out the machine-gun nests of the Germans. Sir John Monash has attributed some of the splendid efficiency of the Australian arrangements and their cunning in the mutual support of guns, tanks, and infantry, so often to be shown in the next four months, to the experience gained in this small battle.

CHAPTER II.

Attack of Rawlinson's Fourth Army. August 8.

The front of the new and most important attack, which began in the early morning of August 8, was fifteen miles in length, and extended from near Morlancourt in the north to Braches upon the Avre River to the south. The right of the attack from Hangard onwards was formed by General Debeney's First French Army, while General Rawlinson's Fourth Army formed the left, the British portion being roughly three-fourths of the whole. The entire battle was under the command of Marshal Haig.

The preparations had been made with the skill which the British Command has so often shown in such operations, so that the Germans were swept off their feet by an attack which came upon them as a complete surprise. It was half-past four on a misty morning when the enemy's advanced line heard the sudden crash of the gun-fire, and a moment later saw the monstrous forms of the tanks looming up through the grey light of dawn. Behind the tanks and almost in touch of them came the grim war-worn infantry. Everything went down before that united rush. The battle was won as soon as begun. The only question was how great the success would be.

<small>CHAPTER II.

Attack of Rawlinson's Fourth Army. August 8.</small>

Taking a bird's-eye view of the advance, before examining the operations more closely, one may say that the Canadian Corps, now under a Canadian commander, General Currie, was on the extreme right of the British line, in touch with the French. Next to them, in the Morlancourt district, where they had never ceased for the last four months to improve their position and to elbow the invaders away from Amiens, were the indomitable and tireless Australians under General Monash. On their left, just south of Albert, was Butler's Third Corps, burning to avenge itself for the hustling which it had endured during that perilous and heroic week in March. These were the three units concerned in the new advance.

The opening barrage, though only a few minutes in length, was of a shattering severity, and was directed against very different defences from those which had defied the Army two years before upon the Somme. Everything flattened out before it, and even the German guns seemed to have been overwhelmed, for their reply was slow and ineffective. Only the machine-guns remained noxious, but the tanks rolled them down. Nowhere at first was there any check or delay. The French on the right of the line had done equally well, and by midday were storming forward upon the north bank of the Avre, their victory being the more difficult and honourable because the river prevented the use of tanks at the first attack.

CHAPTER II.

Attack of Rawlinson's Fourth Army. August 8.

The Canadians were on the top of their form that day, and their magnificent condition gave promise of the splendid work which they were to do from that hour until almost the last day of the war. They were probably the most powerful and efficient corps at that moment in the whole Army, for they had lain in front of Lens with few losses, while nearly every other corps had been desperately engaged and sustained heavy casualties, hastily made good by recruits. They had also kept their brigades up to a four battalion standard, and their divisions had that advantage of permanence denied to all British corps. When to these favouring points are added the great hardihood and valour of the men, proved in so many battles, it is probable that in the whole world no finer body could on that day have been let loose behind a barrage. They were weary from long marches before the battle began, but none the less their great spirit rose high above all physical weakness as they pushed forward against the German line.

They were faced at the outset by a problem which might well have taxed the brains of any staff and the valour of any soldiers. This was the crossing of the River Luce, which was covered upon the farther bank by several scattered woods, ideal haunts of machine-guns. So difficult was this operation that the French to the south had to pause for an hour after the capture of the front German line, to give time for it to be carried out. At the end of that period the

CHAPTER II.

Attack of Rawlinson's Fourth Army. August 8.

very complex operation had been carried through, and the whole Allied front was ready to advance. The Canadians had three divisions in the line, the Third (Lipsett) next to the French, the First (Macdonell) in the middle, and the Second (Benstall) on the left. The 2nd and 3rd British Cavalry Brigades with the Fourth Canadian Infantry Division (Watson) were in reserve. There was also a mobile force, called the Canadian Independent Force, which was kept ready to take advantage of any opening. This consisted of the 1st and 2nd Canadian Motor Machine-gun Brigades, with the Corps Cyclists, and some movable trench mortars on lorries.

The width of the Canadian attack was some 5000 yards from the Amiens—Roye Road to the Villers-Bretonneux Railway. Once across the river the whole line came away with a grand rush and every objective was soon attained, each division sweeping forward without a check. The prisoners reported that an attack had indeed been expected, but not so soon, and we can readily believe that the German Army, which had been so repeatedly assured that the British were finally dead and out of the war, must have been greatly amazed by this vigorous resurrection. By 10.40, Caix, which is a good five miles to the eastward, was reported by contact aeroplanes to be surrounded by tanks. The Cavalry and the Independent Force were both pushing to the front, and the latter deviated to the right in order to help the French, who were temporarily in difficulties near Mezières. In the afternoon the Cavalry Division had passed through the victorious and cheering lines of the Second Canadians, and were carrying out a number of spirited enterprises upon the

RAWLINSON'S FOURTH ARMY 29

German supporting lines. About the same time the Fourth Canadian Infantry Division pushed forward and was reported to the east of Beaufort and Cayeux. By evening all along the line the full objectives had been reached save at one point near Le Quesnel. In their splendid day's work men of the Dominion had taken some 5000 prisoners and great quantities of booty. Many of the prisoners and guns were taken by the cavalry, who had their best day in the war. "The best hunt we ever had, forty minutes and a kill in the open," was the characteristic description of one hard-riding dragoon.

CHAPTER II.

Attack of Rawlinson's Fourth Army. August 8.

We shall now turn to the advance of Monash's Australians in the centre of the British line. Fate owed Monash a great victory in this sector, for, during months of quiet but ceaseless work, he had been improving his position as the keen runner ensures his foothold and crouches his body while he awaits the crack of the pistol. For once Fate paid its debts, and with such a corps under his hand it would have been strange had it not been so. All those advantages already described in the case of the Canadians applied equally to the Australians, and if the former outlasted the others, it must be remembered that the Australians had been in the line for four months before the fighting began—months which included the severe action of Villers-Bretonneux. They were a grand corps, and they did grand work for the Empire—work which we can never forget so long as our common history endures.

The order of battle of the Australian Corps on August 8 was that the Second Division (Smyth) was on the right in touch with the Canadians, while the Third Division (Gillibrand) was on the left in touch with the Fifty-eighth British Division, the Somme being the dividing line between them. Behind the Second Australians was the Fifth (Hobbs), and behind the Third the Fourth (Maclagan), with orders in each case to leapfrog over their leaders when the first objectives were carried. The First Division (Glasgow) was in the immediate rear. Thus at least 50,000 glorious infantry marched to battle under the Southern Cross Union Jack upon this most historic day—a day which, as Ludendorff has since confessed, gave the first fatal shock to the military power of Germany.

All depended upon surprise, and the crouching troops waited most impatiently for the zero hour, expecting every instant to hear the crash of the enemy's guns and the whine of the shrapnel above the assembly trenches. Every precaution had been taken the day before, the roads had been deserted by all traffic, and aeroplanes had flown low during the night, so that their droning might cover the noise of the assembling tanks. Some misgiving was caused by the fact that a sergeant who knew all about it had been captured several days before. By a curious chance the minutes of his cross-examination by the German intelligence officer were captured during the battle. He had faced his ordeal like a Spartan, and had said no word. It is not often that the success of a world-shaking battle depends upon the nerve and the tongue of a single soldier.

Zero hour arrived without a sign, and in an instant barrage, tanks, and infantry all burst forth together, though the morning mist was so thick that one could only see twenty or thirty yards. Everywhere the enemy front posts went down with hardly a struggle. It was an absolute surprise. Now and then, as the long, loose lines of men pushed through the mist, there would come the flash of a field-piece, or the sudden burst of a machine-gun from their front; but in an instant, with the coolness born of long practice, the men would run crouching forward, and then quickly close in from every side, shooting or bayoneting the gun crew. Everything went splendidly from the first, and the tanks did excellent service, especially in the capture of Warfusée.

CHAPTER II.

Attack of Rawlinson's Fourth Army. August 8.

The task of the two relieving divisions, the Fourth on the left and the Fifth on the right, was rather more difficult, as the Germans had begun to rally and the fog to lift. The Fourth Australians on the south bank of the Somme were especially troubled, as it soon became evident that the British attack on the north bank had been held up, with the result that the German guns on Chipilly Spur were all free to fire across from their high position upon the Australians in the plain to the south. Tank after tank and gun after gun were knocked out by direct hits, but the infantry was not to be stopped and continued to skirmish forward as best they might under so deadly a fire, finishing by the capture of Cerisy and of Morcourt. The Fifth Division on the right, with the 8th and 15th Brigades in front, made an equally fine advance, covering a good stretch of ground.

Having considered the Canadians and the Australians, we turn now to the Third Corps on the north of the line. They were extended from Morlancourt to the north bank of the Somme, which is a broad canalised river over all this portion of its course. On the right was the Fifty-eighth London Division (Ramsay), with Lee's Eighteenth Division to the north of it, extending close to the Ancre, where Higginson's

CHAPTER II.
Attack of Rawlinson's Fourth Army.
August 8.

Twelfth Division lay astride of that marshy stream. North of this again was the Forty-seventh Division (Gorringe), together with a brigade of the Thirty-third American Division. Two days before the great advance, on August 6, the Twenty-seventh Wurtemburg Division had made a sudden strong local attack astride of the Bray—Corbie Road, and had driven in the Eighteenth Divisional front, taking some hundreds of prisoners, though the British counter-attack regained most of the lost ground on the same and the following days. This unexpected episode somewhat deranged the details of the great attack, but the Eighteenth played its part manfully none the less, substituting the 36th Brigade of the Twelfth Division for the 54th Brigade, which had been considerably knocked about. None of the British prisoners taken seem to have given away the news of the coming advance, but it is probable that the sudden attack of the Wurtemburgers showed that it was suspected, and was intended to anticipate and to derange it.

In the first phase of the attack the little village of Sailly-Laurette on the north bank of the Somme was carried by assault by the 2/10th Londons. At the same moment the 174th Brigade attacked Malard Wood to the left of the village. There was a difficulty in mopping up the wood, for small German posts held on with great tenacity, but by 9 o'clock the position was cleared. The 173rd Brigade now went forward upon the really terrible task of getting up the slopes of Chipilly Hill under the German fire. The present chronicler has looked down upon the line of advance from the position of the German machine-guns and can testify that the affair was indeed as

RAWLINSON'S FOURTH ARMY

arduous as could be imagined. The village of Chipilly was not cleared, and the attack, after several very gallant attempts, was at a stand. Meantime the 53rd Brigade on the left had got about half-way to its objective and held the ground gained, but could get no farther in face of the withering fire. Farther north, however, the Twelfth Division, moving forward upon the northern slopes of the Ancre, had gained its full objectives, the idea being that a similar advance to the south would pinch out the village of Morlancourt. There was a time in the attack when it appeared as if the hold-up of the Eighteenth Division would prevent Vincent's 35th Brigade, on the right of the Twelfth Division, from getting forward, but the situation was restored by a fine bit of work by the 1st Cambridgeshires, who, under Colonel Saint, renewed the attack in a most determined way and finally were left with only 200 men standing, but with 316 German prisoners as well as their objective. A wandering tank contributed greatly to this success.

The partial nature of the local victory was due not only to the excellent German dispositions and resistance, but to some want of liaison between tanks and infantry, as well as to the total disability of the flying service to furnish any reports before 12 o'clock. This want was partly made good by the excellent scouting of the Northumberland Hussars. The remainder of the day was spent in clearing the ground gained and holding a series of counter-attacks, one of which drove back an advanced line of the 53rd Brigade.

Summing up, then, the result of the first day's fighting, it may be briefly said that seven German Divisions had been cut to pieces, that 10,000 prisoners

Chapter II.

Attack of Rawlinson's Fourth Army. August 8.

CHAPTER II.
Attack of Rawlinson's Fourth Army.
August 9.

and 200 guns had been counted, and that an advance had been made which in the French sector reached Beaufort, and laid the British line well up to Caix, Framerville, and Chipilly. To those who associated those village names with the dark days when the Fifth Army, exhausted and decimated, was compelled to retreat through them, it was indeed an added joy that they should be the milestones of victory. The whole penetration, though not more than three miles north of the Somme, was seven or eight miles at the deepest point, which is the greatest ever yet attained on the first day of any Allied attack.

The battle was vigorously renewed on the morning of August 9, and once more the tide flowed eastwards, carrying the average depth of progress two or three miles farther. In the south the French directed their general advance rather to the right and reached Arvillers as their final point. Their take of prisoners had amounted altogether to 4000, and their depth of advance was over eight miles. To their north the Canadians had reached Rosières, and the Australians Rainecourt and Morcourt. To the north of the Somme the Third Corps had been temporarily hung up by the very vigorous German resistance in a strong position between Chipilly and Morlancourt. Before evening General Rawlinson was able to report the capture of a total for the two days of 17,000 prisoners and 250 guns.

To take the events of this second day of battle in closer detail, the Canadians resumed their attack at 10 A.M. with the same order of divisions in the line, but with their Fourth Division acting with the Independent Force upon the right, where in the early morning it captured Le Quesnel. There was heavy

RAWLINSON'S FOURTH ARMY

fighting all day along the Corps front, but the advance was pushed forward for another 2500 yards. Many villages were contained in this area, the Third Canadians on the right getting Folies and Bouchoir, the Second Canadians on the left Vrely, Rosières, and Mehari- court, while the First Canadians in the centre got Warvillers, Beaufort, and Rouvroy. The Germans had rushed up their anti-tank guns, and the casualties were heavy that day, especially near Le Quesnel, where many tanks were destroyed by direct hits from concealed batteries. To make a complete and connected narrative of the doings upon this front it may here be added that on August 10 the resistance thickened and the advance slowed. Le Quesnel [1] was taken early by the Third Canadians, upon which the Thirty-second British Division passed through their ranks and carried the advance on to the outskirts of Parvillers and Damery. The Fourth Canadian Division in turn had very stubborn fighting and considerable losses, but it ended the day in possession of Fouquescourt, Maucourt, Chilly, and Hallu. At night, great fires reddening the whole eastern sky gave promise of a further German retreat. On August 11 it was clear, however, that no further important advance could be made without fresh preparation, and orders were given for consolidation. A French attack on the right on Bois en Z had no success, nor was the Thirty-second Division able to take Damery. Instead of advance it was rather a day of strong counter-attacks, against which the attenuated lines, after three days of battle, were hard put to it to hold their own, a flank fire from Lihons helping the German attack at Hallu and Chilly. The line was in the main held, however, and

Chapter II.

Attack of Rawlinson's Fourth Army. August 9.

---

[1] There are two villages of that name.

CHAPTER II.
Attack of Rawlinson's Fourth Army.
August 9.

a total take of 8000 prisoners was in the Canadian cages that evening, while 167 guns had been taken by the one Corps. We shall now turn back and follow the fortunes of the Australians on the second and third days of the battle.

Upon August 9 General Monash's Corps still carried forward its victorious career, though a halt was called for the Fourth Division on the left which awaited developments upon the north bank of the river. On the right the Second Division passed through the Fifth in order to continue the advance, while the First Division thrust itself in upon the right flank, next to the Canadians. Progress was slower everywhere, but none the less it was substantial, Framerville being taken by the 7th Brigade. There was a misunderstanding about time, with the result that the First Division advanced some hours before their Canadian neighbours, with tragic consequences to their own right flank, formed by the 2nd Brigade. The advance was over open country, with the Lihons ridge and village in front, from which heavy gun-fire played upon the attack and caused considerable losses, while on the right a deadly fire was maintained from Rosières Station. So heavy were the casualties in the First and Second Divisions that reinforcements had to be sent up when the advance was resumed. In the evening some relief was obtained, for the region of the old French trenches was reached and the men were at last able to get some cover. Many of the Australians who fought through this long hot day had marched for five hours in order to reach the field of battle, so that it was a remarkable test of endurance. Finally Crepy and Crepy Wood were taken and held against three severe counter-attacks which broke upon them next day. On August 11 Lihons Ridge fell and the village was occupied by the 2nd Brigade, which again had to face determined attacks. The Germans fully appreciated the vital worth of this position, which commanded the plain both to west and east, so they strained every nerve first to hold and afterwards to recover it, but it was in stronger hands than theirs. The 3rd Brigade on the left of Lihons was particularly heavily attacked but threw back its assailants in confusion. Every yard gained was held. A final very serious German counter-attack in successive waves, with 400 in a wave, drove down from Lihu Wood in the north-east and actually penetrated the front Australian lines, but the 8th Battalion in support threw itself into the fight and soon the position had been completely restored.

In the meantime, the Fourth Australian Division had been released by the fact that the remains of the Fifty-eighth Division and the 131st American Infantry Regiment had, as will be told, cleared the Chipilly Ridge north of the river. Part of the Fourth Australians had crossed the river, fraternising greatly with the Americans, so that the officers on both sides had some trouble in sorting out their men—the more so as the comradeship had often taken the form of an exchange of hats and coats. On the night of August 10 the whole of the Fourth Australians had crossed to the north bank of the Somme near Sailly-le-Sec, and their commander, General Maclagan, had taken under him the Americans and also the 173rd and 174th Brigades of the British Fifty-eighth Division, much the worse for wear.

The Third Australian Division had taken the place south of the Somme vacated by their fellow-

CHAPTER II.

Attack of Rawlinson's Fourth Army. August 9.

countrymen, and on the morning of August 11 they continued the attack in the direction of Proyart, that village being eventually carried by the 10th Brigade. It is needless to say that books might, and probably will, be written as to individual adventures and deeds of heroism, which in their aggregate supplied the driving force which carried the line ever more and more to the eastward. In giving a condensed account of the effects one can hardly get down to the more human story of the causes. Yet few greater deeds of valour can have been anywhere done than that of Sergeant Statton of the 40th Battalion, who in this engagement of Proyart seeing a neighbouring battalion, the 37th, held up by a nest of machine-guns, ran across to their aid, shot all the gunners at one gun, captured three guns single-handed, and chased the crews from two others. Many a battalion has spent itself in doing less.

We shall now turn to the British Third Corps on the north of the Somme and so complete the account of the attack of the Fourth Army. It will be remembered that on the evening of August 8 they had made headway along the whole line but had been held up on the Chipilly Spur.

The attack upon Chipilly was renewed at 4.15 next afternoon, the delay being caused by the need of assembling the reserves, which consisted of the remainder of the Fifty-eighth Division and of the 131st Regiment of the Thirty-third Division (Bell) of the United States Army. The assault was made by the 6th and 2/10th London Battalions, but they were opportunely and very efficiently aided by two companies of the Americans, who had lost their direction for the main attack planned to the north, but who

RAWLINSON'S FOURTH ARMY

seemed indifferent which fight they were in so long as they were fighting. There was a check at the outset, but the attack, while demonstrating from the west, really materialised from the north, and both village and ridge were captured with a number of prisoners. This was a very important little victory from the point of view of the Australians to the south who had been commanded by the German guns from this elevated position.

Chapter II. Attack of Rawlinson's Fourth Army. August 9.

The main attack was north of the Chipilly Spur, and was planned to gain Cressaire Wood and a line across from the Somme to the Ancre corresponding with such an advance. The assault was made by two weak brigades of the Fifty-eighth Londoners upon the right, the 131st American Regiment in the centre, and the remains of the Fifty-eighth upon the left. Farther north the Twelfth Division, with the 37th Brigade in front, carried on the line. Both Londoners and Americans advanced with equal valour, and after a stiff fight the main portion of the objectives was won, though it took three hours of hard work to win them. Much credit was due to all, but most to the American infantry, who had their first experience of modern fighting and who were naturally embarrassed by the disappearance of two of their companies which had drifted into the Chipilly affair. For a time there was a gap between divisions, but before evening the Twelfth extended to the right and all was well. The correction was very necessary, for at 3 A.M. on August 10 a German counter-attack broke without effect upon this very point of junction. The Twelfth Division had had a very good day on August 9, Incledon-Webber's 37th Brigade especially distinguishing itself. The 6th Buffs and 6th West

CHAPTER II.

Attack of Rawlinson's Fourth Army. August 10.

Kents had heavy losses, but took 350 prisoners, two field-guns, and a number of machine-guns. Two of these were taken single-handed by Sergeant Harris of the West Kents, who met his death in attacking a third. The Victoria Cross was his posthumous reward.

On August 10 the Third Corps front was pushed forward in the morning by a system of infiltration, British and American patrols scouting and fighting through the eastern portion of Cressaire Wood. Before evening, without any serious fighting, they reached the old French Amiens defence line, which was the original full objective upon this front. Having entirely accomplished his arduous task General Butler, who had been handicapped by an illness which he disregarded while his work called for his presence, took a short spell of rest, his place being taken by General Godley. The Forty-seventh Division (Gorringe) came across to the right wing, relieving the Eighteenth Division, while shortly after the Thirty-third American Division, to the great regret of their British comrades, entrained for the south to join the main American army, but not before their 133rd Regiment, acting with the 13th Australian Brigade, had taken Etinehem Spur, to the north of the River Somme. The action now died down in this quarter. In the three days of fighting General Butler's Corps had taken 90 guns and 3000 prisoners, while, in the words of General Rawlinson, " in protecting the left flank of the Fourth Army they were given a difficult task which was carried out with a determination and gallantry beyond all praise." The losses had been 6500, 500 of which were from the American Regiment. The general result of the battle by the night of August 11 was that the French had taken 8000 and the British 21,000 prisoners with 400 guns, so that it was already clear that the greatest victory which the British Army had yet won was that which initiated the final advance. In spite of all this success it is to be borne in mind, however, that the Allies had only reached the old German front line trenches of 1916, which were now a valuable barrier for the rear of the retreating army. There was a pause now while the Fourth Army was waiting for their comrades of the Third Army on the left to develop their extension of the attack. Meanwhile many small actions and local advances on Rawlinson's front kept his opponents from having time to reorganise. On August 13, as already mentioned, Americans and Australians advanced the line to the north of the river along the strip which is bounded upon the left by the Bray—Corbie Road. On August 14 the Canadian 7th Brigade took Parvillers after some very stiff local fighting. They were driven out again that night by the heavy concentration of the German artillery, but next morning, with the cooperation upon their flank of their comrades of the 9th Brigade, they won it once more. In this operation the 52nd Battalion took Damery, while the French carried the wood to the south of the village. There was a strong counter-attack in the afternoon by the German One hundred and twenty-first Division, but it was beaten back, leaving a number of prisoners. About August 20 the Canadians began to slip quietly out of the line, and were conveyed, unknown to the Germans, to a new front where they came under the command of General Horne of the First Army. Their exploits upon this new stage will be described later.

CHAPTER II.

Attack of Rawlinson's Fourth Army. August 10.

CHAPTER II.

Attack of Rawlinson's Fourth Army.

The French were now on the immediate right of the Australians until the time came for the advent of the British Ninth Corps.

Amid the tremendous events which followed each other in a stupendous historical procession during the latter half of 1918 it is hard to select those which were decisive from those which were merely great. It may safely be said, however, that three dates stand out as great military crises — the turn of the tide on July 18, the British advance on August 8, and the breaking of the Hindenburg Line on September 29. It has been admitted by General Ludendorff that it was the second of these which broke the confidence of the German Staff and finally convinced them that the war must go against them. A very special honour rests, therefore, with the three corps, British, Australian, and Canadian, who brought about this victory, as well as to the tanks, the cavalry, and the airmen who led or followed the victorious infantry and the masterful guns during these days of doom.

CHAPTER III

CONTINUATION OF THE OPERATIONS OF RAWLINSON'S FOURTH ARMY

From August 22 to the Battle of the Hindenburg Line, September 29

Further advance of the Australians—Of the Third Corps—Capture of Albert—Advance across the old Somme battlefield—Capture of Mont St. Quentin—Splendid Australian exploit—Fall of Peronne—Debut of the Yeomanry (Seventy-fourth) Division—Attack on the outliers of the Hindenburg Line—Appearance of the Ninth Corps—Eve of the Judgment.

WE have now reached the date when Byng's Third Army joined in the fray, and it is necessary to find some means of co-ordinating the narrative and carrying it on in definite stages. The next well-marked crisis which affects each of the armies engaged is the great general attack on September 29, which broke the Hindenburg Line. Therefore, in separate chapters the operations of each army will be brought up to that date, and then further chapters will cover the doings of each up to the date of the Armistice. Since we have dealt with the Fourth Army, we may as well continue with it now until we are in close touch with the Hindenburg Line, premising only that instead of an inert neighbour upon the left we have a very active advancing British Army. We shall then go on to the

44   THE BRITISH CAMPAIGN, 1918

CHAPTER III.

Continuation of the Operations of Rawlinson's Fourth Army.

August 22.

Third and to the First Armies, and bring each of them in turn up to the same point.

On August 22 and the following days, the Fourth Army, with only two Corps—the Third and the Australians—in front, renewed its attack, greatly strengthened by the movement of the Third Army on its left, which ensured that at least five British corps were all moving forward together, distributing the advance over so wide an area that the Germans were less able to concentrate reserves of men or of guns at any one point—a result which was much aided by the fine work of General Mangin's Army on the right.

The main part of the fighting on the front of the Fourth Army on August 22 was north of the Somme, where the Third Australian Division covered the right flank of the Third Corps. On the south of the river the Australian Corps advanced on a front of $4\tfrac{1}{2}$ miles, and took all their limited objectives, which represented a depth of $1\tfrac{1}{2}$ miles. This was effected by the Fifth Australian Division on the right and the Fourth on the left, supported and finally supplanted by the First Australian and Lambert's Thirty-Second British Divisions, the latter on the right. The advance, which began at dawn, was no easy one, as the country was much cut about with many obstacles, seamed with trenches, and dotted with scattered woods. The determined infantry would take no denial, however, and Herleville, Chuignies, and several other small village sites were captured. The heaviest fighting was in the woods, but a skilful system of encircling points of danger had been carefully worked out, and the losses were less than might have been anticipated.

RAWLINSON'S FOURTH ARMY

Sixteen guns, 80 officers, and 2463 men were the trophies of the day. Early in the morning of August 24 the Third Australian Division moved suddenly forward north of the river, captured the town of Bray, and formed a permanent line upon the further side. On August 25 this same unit advanced 3000 yards on a 4000-yard front with very little resistance, always covering the right of the Third Corps.

Chapter III.

Continuation of the Operations of Rawlinson's Fourth Army. August 22.

Let us now follow the work of this Corps from August 22 onwards.

It covered the ground from Albert in the north, where it was working in close liaison with the Welsh Division on the right of the Fifth Corps, down to a point near the Somme where it was in touch with the Australians. The immediate object of the operations was to eject the enemy from the positions in and around Albert which he had held for four months, and also from his whole defensive system opposite to the Amiens defence line, which latter had been regained in the previous fighting. On the day of battle the Forty-seventh London Division was on the right of the Corps line, the Twelfth Division in the centre, and the Eighteenth Division on the left. To this last was confided the difficult and important operation of clearing Albert, and of establishing light bridges over the Ancre so as to cross that stream and attack the high ground east of the town on the Becourt Road. There was to be no preliminary bombardment, but machine-gun and artillery barrages were to cover the infantry.

The zero hour was 4.45, and at the signal the Forty-seventh and Twelfth Divisions advanced behind a creeping barrage, moving at the rate of 100 yards in four minutes, and as thick as 250 field-guns could make it. With such a van of destruction in front the infantry came forward without undue losses, though a particular strong point named the Pear Tree just on the interdivisional boundary held fast and was destined to give trouble for several days to come. As an observer remarked, "Anything British, from a helmet to a tank, which showed over the crest was met by the sweeping fire of many machine-guns, while shells from trench mortars fell in the ranks of men following up. It was only when the general attack was continued that this hornet's nest could be cleared." Save for this point the general objectives marked out for these divisions, which meant an advance of between two and three miles, were successfully made good, but an attempt to follow up with cavalry and whippet tanks could not be persevered in, so stiff was the opposition. It was soon found that the enemy in the Forty-seventh Division sector was not only capable of defence, but of aggression, for about 4 in the afternoon his infantry advanced in a strong attack with a powerful artillery backing, and drove with such violence into the 22nd, 23rd, and 24th Londons, forming the 142nd Brigade, that they were temporarily thrown back. Their right held firm, however, as did the Third Australian Division to the south, so that no gap was formed. Being reinforced by the 175th Brigade from the Fifty-eighth Division in reserve, the Londoners soon reformed their ranks, greatly thinned both by their advance in the morning and by the German onslaught in the afternoon. The enemy's front was so menacing that the rest of the day and part of August 23 were spent in reorganisation and consolidation.

Meanwhile on the left, Lee's Eighteenth Division,

RAWLINSON'S FOURTH ARMY 47

a famous all-English unit of the type which, however brilliant its comrades, has always formed the solid core of the magnificent tireless Imperial Army, was carrying out its difficult task at Albert. It had two brigades in the line, the 54th to the south and the 55th to the north of the town. The Germans in front held the line of the Ancre, with Albert as a bridgehead, the ruins and cellars of the town being sown with snipers and machine-guns. To clear the town, to occupy the high ground to the east, and by these operations to cover the flanks of two armies was the function of this Division, and also to secure crossings at Albert by which the Welsh on their left could get across.

<small>CHAPTER III.

Continuation of the Operations of Rawlinson's Fourth Army.

August 22.</small>

The stream in this part was 6 feet deep and 14 wide, with swampy banks strongly held by the enemy. There were unguarded bits, however, and patrols got across on the 21st, which simplified the task, though it deranged at the last moment all the preparations for barrage. Part of the 6th Northamptons and the 11th Royal Fusiliers crossed early on the 22nd and formed up along the edge of the Albert—Meaulte Road, while the rest of the 6th Northamptons fought hard for elbow-room on the right flank, working in close liaison with the 36th Brigade on the left of the Twelfth Division who were attacking Meaulte. About 6 the whole front line advanced in this quarter, flooding over the scattered German posts, and capturing eighty machine-guns with their crews. At the same time the 8th East Surreys on the left had rushed Albert, and after some fine confused fighting had cleared the ruins and taken the whole town, with the river crossings. The 7th Buffs at once pushed out on the Albert—Pozières

CHAPTER III.

Continuation of the Operations of Rawlinson's Fourth Army.

August 22.

road, but were held up by very heavy fire. The 11th Royal Fusiliers further south had also been held up by the guns on the summit of Shamrock Hill, east of the town, but a company of the 2nd Bedfords, led by Captain Doake, captured this strong point and the line went forward. Altogether it was a good day's work, and save on the extreme left most of the objects were attained at the cost of reasonable casualties, which included General Sadleir-Jackson of the 54th Brigade, who was badly wounded in the leg. The 53rd Brigade continued their advance up to 10 P.M., so as to gain the high ground on the Becourt Road, and thus prepare for the next day's operations.

The 113th Brigade of the Welsh Division on the left had been passed over by the Albert bridges, and the 53rd had also passed in the night. The plan of August 23 was that these two brigades should attack Usna and Tara Hills respectively, on the high ground to the west of Becourt Wood. The Usna attack is described under the operations of the Fifth Corps. The Tara attack was completely successful, and four tanks rendered conspicuous service. The work was carried out by the 10th Essex, 7th West Kents, and the 7th Queen's from the 55th Brigade. It was a fine military feat, far more important than 350 prisoners would imply, for it broke the girdle round Albert and cleared the road for the advance. No progress was made at the other portions of the corps front on this date, save for some advance on the left of the Twelfth Division near Meaulte.

August 24.

It had been determined to keep up incessant pressure, and to test Hindenburg's incautious maxim that the side with the best nerves would wear down the other. At 1 A.M. on August 24 the whole line burst into flame once more, and under a clear moon the Army rolled forward. On the right the Forty-seventh Division had ample revenge for its temporary check, as its 140th, together with the 175th Brigade of the Fifty-eighth Division, Londoners all, swept across the debated land of the Happy Valley and secured it. The Eighteenth Division also made good its objectives, the chief impediment being the historical mine craters of 1916 at La Boiselle ; 250 prisoners were taken out of these by the 8th Royal Berks, a party of whom under Captain Nicholson, covered by Captain Sutherst's 53rd Trench Mortar Battery, cleared up this difficult point. In the morning the Eighteenth Division was well to the east of Becourt. The only check was in the centre, where the general advance of the Twelfth Division was still held up by that Pear Tree strong point which had already caused so much trouble. Before evening, however, it was clear that the enemy was effecting a general retreat, and the 37th Brigade was able to take possession of this very well defended portion of the ridge.

Chapter III. Continuation of the Operations of Rawlinson's Fourth Army. August 24.

It was clear now that the German front was crumbling, and the whole British line was pushing ahead. The chief obstacle on the morning of August 25 came from an all-pervading mist. There was no check, however, anywhere in the advance up to 2 P.M., when the general line of the front was up to Mametz. The hardest fighting of the day was done at Billon Wood by the 173rd Brigade, all three battalions, the 2/2nd, 3rd, and 2/4th London, having real hard work, and standing to it like men. The place was strongly held with powerful artillery support, but it had been cleared before nightfall. By the same hour the Twelfth Division was east of Mametz, and the 8th

August 25.

CHAPTER III.

Continuation of the Operations of Rawlinson's Fourth Army.

August 26–28.

East Surreys were on the far side of Mametz Wood. As these familiar places came once more into their possession the troops felt that the tide had indeed turned. On August 26 the Eighteenth Division had cleared the ruins of Montauban, and the Twelfth, Carnoy, while the Fifty-eighth pushed on from Billon Wood, and wound up within a few hundred yards of Maricourt. This village was passed the next day, and altogether, on August 27 and 28, another three miles were added to the advance of the Twelfth and Fifty-eighth Divisions, the progress never ceasing, but being continually accompanied by fighting and maintained always against severe artillery fire. The Germans had thrown in three fresh divisions upon this front and the resistance was still very stiff.

This was especially evident at Trones Wood, which was carried for the second time in this way by the Eighteenth Division on August 27. This fine assault was made by the 8th Berks and 7th West Kents, who carried it out with both flanks open to the enemy since the Welsh had been held in front of Delville. So heavy were the losses that the Berkshires were in danger of not being strong enough to hold what they had gained, so the 10th Essex were pushed into the fight. At 8 A.M. on August 27 a German Guards battalion drove through Trones Wood and pushed out the British stormers, but they held on by their teeth to the eastern edge of Bernafoy Wood. Here General Barker of the 53rd Brigade reorganised his very weary ranks, which had been greatly mixed in the advance and retreat. Just as evening was falling the remains of the gallant brigade darted forward once more and came to grips with the Francis Joseph Prussian Guards, who lay with many a machine-gun among the brushwood. Led by Colonel Banks of the 8th Berkshires, the English infantry rushed into the wood and poured over the German position, taking forty machine-guns and completely overcoming the resistance. It was a fine exploit, and when the 53rd Brigade gave place to the 54th on the morning of August 28 they handed over to them the whole of this terrible grove, which has been so drenched by the bravest blood of two great nations. There was no further action in this quarter on August 28, but on the 29th the 54th Brigade, now under Colonel Perceval, was heavily engaged. Guillemont was passed, though no trace of this large village could be distinguished, and all day the 2nd Bedfords on the left and the 6th Northants on the right were working forward across the grim old battlefield. On August 28 the Twelfth Division took Hardecourt, and General Higginson, who may well have been disturbed by the constant flow of youngsters into his ranks to take the place of his disabled veterans, must have had his fears removed and his heart gladdened by the splendid conduct that day of 250 men of the 9th Royal Fusiliers under Colonel Van Someren, none of whom had been in France more than three weeks. On August 30 a great centre of German resistance was Priez Farm, which held up the 11th Royal Fusiliers, and also the Forty-seventh Division which had taken the place of the Twelfth in the centre of the corps. The enemy was clinging hard to Morval, also in the Welsh area, and this made any advance on the front of the Eighteenth Division impossible. It was clear that a regular battle with artillery preparation was needed, and this was arranged for September 1. The right wing of the corps had in the meantime got to

CHAPTER III.

Continuation of the Operations of Rawlinson's Fourth Army. August 26–28.

the line of Maurepas, and on August 31 the Forty-seventh Division in the centre made a good advance up to Long Wood with a number of prisoners to show for it. The Fifty-eighth Division closed in upon Marrières Wood, which they took after some heavy fighting, avenging the brave South Africans who had died so gallantly there five months before. It was clear that the enemy were now standing in a strong line, and were by no means beaten, which was shown also by the bearing of the prisoners, whose morale was high, and who spoke with as much pride and assurance as ever of the ultimate military success of their country. Yet during the last week they had been steadily driven back some 3000 yards every day by the remorseless barrage of the British guns followed by the disciplined rush of the British infantry.

We shall now leave the Third Corps for a time at this line of fixed resistance and return to consider the advance of the Australians to the south. This had been victorious and unbroken, though no very serious resistance had to be overcome. Smoke by day and fire by night, with explosions at all hours, heralded the German retreat. On August 26 Cappy was occupied. On the 27th Vaux Wood was occupied north of the river, while Foucaucourt and Vermandovillers were submerged to the south, villages no longer, but at least marks of progress upon the map. On the 28th the Germans were still retreating with the toes of the Australians upon their very heels, but the heavier shelling warned General Monash that there was a fixed line ahead, as might well be expected, since his men were now nearing the point where the bend of the Somme brought the river right across their front. Dompierre, Fay, Estrées, and other old centres of

RAWLINSON'S FOURTH ARMY 53

contention were taken that day. On the 29th the 3rd Australians got Hem, while on the south the rest of the corps advanced 2000 yards to the bank of the river, taking the whole line of villages from Biaches to Villers-Carbonnel. The task of capturing such places was much complicated by the difficulty of knowing where they were after you had got them. The present writer was in Carbonnel, which was a considerable place, some weeks later, and was unable to find any trace of habitation save a signboard upon which was printed the words : " Here was the village of Villers-Carbonnel."

At the end of August the resistance had stiffened, and it was clear that the Germans meant to take advantage of the unique situation of Peronne in order to make it a strong centre of resistance. To the civilian observer it would have seemed that such a place was impregnable against assault, for it is girt in with reedy marshes on the west, and with a moat on the north, while the south is defended by the broad river, even as in the days when Quentin Durward formed part of the garrison. Yet the Australians took it in their stride by a mixture of cleverness and valour which must have greatly rejoiced General Rawlinson, who saw so formidable an obstacle removed from his path. As a preliminary operation the Third Australian Division had taken Clery in the north, which they held against a vigorous counter-attack on September 30. Halles was afterwards captured. The question now was how to approach the town. Immediately to the north of it there lies a formidable hill, well marked, though of no great height. This place, which is called Mont St. Quentin, commanded all approaches to the town as well as

CHAPTER III.

Continuation of the Operations of Rawlinson's Fourth Army. August 26–31.

CHAPTER III.

Continuation of the Operations of Rawlinson's Fourth Army.

August 31.

the town itself. The Germans had recognised the importance of the position and had garrisoned it with picked troops with many machine-guns. Standing upon its pitted crest, where one is often ankle-deep in empty cartridges, one cannot imagine as one looks west how a rabbit could get across unscathed. This was the formidable obstacle which now faced the Australians.

They went at it without a pause and with characteristic earnestness and directness, controlled by very skilful leadership. Two brigades, the 5th and 6th of Rosenthal's Second Australian Division, had been assembled on the north of the Somme bend, the men passing in single file over hastily constructed foot-bridges. By this means they had turned the impassable water defences which lie on the westward side of Peronne, but they were faced by a terrible bit of country, seamed with trenches, jagged with wire, and rising to the village of St. Quentin, which is a little place on the flank of the hill. The hill itself is crowned by a ragged wood some acres in extent. Mont St. Quentin lies about equidistant, a mile or so, from Peronne in the south, and from the hamlet of Feuillaucourt in the north. On this front of two miles the action was fought.

Early in the morning of August 31 the 5th Brigade, under General Martin, advanced upon the German position. The 17th Battalion was in the centre opposite to Mont St. Quentin. The 19th was on the right covering the ground between that stronghold and Peronne, the 20th on the left, extending up to Feuillaucourt, with that village as one of its objectives. The 18th was in close support. A very heavy and efficient artillery bombardment had prepared the way for the infantry assault, but the defending troops were as good as any which Germany possessed, and had endured the heavy fire with unshaken fortitude, knowing that their turn would come.

From the moment that the infantry began to close in on the German positions the battle became very bitter and the losses very serious. The 19th Battalion on the right were scourged with fire from the old fortified walls of Peronne, from St. Denis, a hamlet north of the town, and from scattered woods which faced them. Every kind of missile, including pine-apple-bombs and rifle-grenades, poured down upon them. The long thin line carried on bravely, halted, carried on once more, and finally sank down under such poor cover as could be found, sending back a message that further artillery bombardment was a necessity. On the left of the attack the 20th Battalion seems to have had a less formidable line before it, and advancing with great speed and resolution, it seized the village of Feuillaucourt. In the centre, however, a concentration of fire beat upon the 17th Battalion, which was right under the guns of Mont St. Quentin. Working on in little groups of men, waiting, watching, darting forward, crouching down, crawling, so the scattered line gradually closed with its enemy, pre-senting a supreme object lesson of that individual intelligence and character which have made the Australian soldier what he is. A little after 7 o'clock in the morning the survivors of two companies drew together for the final rush, and darted into the village of Mont St. Quentin, throwing out a line of riflemen upon the far side of it. On that far side lay the culminating slope of the hill crowned with the dark ragged trees, their trunks linked up with abattis,

Chapter III.

Continuation of the Operations of Rawlinson's Fourth Army. August 31.

laced with wire, and covering machine-guns. The place was still full of Germans and they had strong reserves on the further side of the hill.

The 17th had reached their goal, but their situation was very desperate. Their right was bent back and was in precarious contact with the 19th Battalion. Their left flank had lost all touch. They were a mere thin fringe of men with nothing immediately behind them. Two companies of the supporting battalion had already been sent up to stiffen the line of the 19th Battalion, and the remaining two companies were now ordered forward to fill the gap between the 17th and 20th. Not a rifle was left in reserve, and the whole strength of the Brigade was in the firing-line. It was no time for hedging, for everything was at stake.

But the pressure was too severe to last. The Australian line could not be broken, but there comes a point when it must bend or perish. The German pressure from the wood was ever heavier upon the thin ranks in front of it. A rush of grey infantry came down the hill, with showers of bombs in front of them. One of the companies in the village had lost every officer. The fire was murderous. Guns firing over open sights had been brought up on the north of the village, and were sending their shells through the ruined houses. Slowly the Australians loosened their clutch upon their prize and fell back to the west of the village, dropping down in the broken ground on the other side of the main Peronne Road, and beating back five bombing attacks which had followed them up. Still the fire was murderous, and the pressure very heavy, so that once more, by twos and threes, the survivors fell back 250 yards west of the road, where again they lay down, counting their dwindling cartridges, and dwelling upon their aim, as the grey crouching figures came stealthily forward. The attack was at an end. It had done splendidly, and it had failed. But the scattered survivors of the 5th Brigade still held on with grim tenacity, certain that their comrades behind would never let them down.

All night there was spasmodic fighting, the Germans pushing their counter-attack until the two lines were interlocked and the leading groups of the 5th Brigade were entirely cut off. In some places the more forward Germans finding a blank space—and there were many—had pushed on until they were 500 yards west of the general line of the 5th Brigade. Thus when Robertson's 6th Brigade attacked at an early hour of September 1, they came on German infantry posts before they connected up with the main line of their own comrades. Their advance had been preceded by a crashing bombardment from everything which would throw a projectile, so that the crest of the hill was fairly swept with bullets and shells. Then forward went the line, the 23rd Battalion on the right, the 24th on the left, 21st and 22nd in support. From the start the fire was heavy, but all opposition was trampled down, until the two leading battalions were abreast of the hill. Then once more that terrible fire brought them to a halt. The 23rd on the right was held by the same crossfire which had beaten upon the 19th the day before. Its losses were heavy. The 24th got forward to Feuillaucourt and then, having occupied it, turned to the right and endeavoured to work down to Mont St. Quentin from the north. But the fire was too murderous and the advance was stopped. Other

CHAPTER III.

Continuation of the Operations of Rawlinson's Fourth Army. Sept. 1.

elements were coming into action, however, which would prevent the whole German effort being concentrated upon the defence of the one position. In the north the 10th Brigade of the Third Australian Division, with the 229th British Yeomanry Brigade upon their left, were swinging round and threatening to cut in on the German flank and rear. In the south the 14th Australian Brigade of the Fifth Division was advancing straight upon the town of Peronne, attacking from the south and east simultaneously. But even now the nut was too hard for the crackers. The British and the 10th Australian Brigades were fighting their way round in the north and constant progress was being made in that indirect pressure. But the 6th Brigade after its splendid advance was held up, and old Peronne, spitting fire from its ancient walls, was still keeping the 14th Brigade at a distance. At 8 o'clock the attack had again failed. Orders were then given for the reorganisation of the troops and for a renewed effort at half-past one. The artillery had been brought up and reinforced, so that it now fairly scalped the hill. At the hour named the direct advance of the 6th Brigade was resumed, the fresh 21st Battalion being pushed into the centre, between the 23rd and 24th which had both suffered severely in the morning. This time General Rosenthal was justified of his perseverance. At the signal the troops poured forward and under a hail of bullets seized the ruins of the village once more, streaming out at the further side and falling into a long skirmish line on the western edge of the wood. The brave German defenders were still unabashed and the losses were so heavy that the wood could not instantly be carried, but the position was consolidated and held, with the absolute certainty that such close grips in front with the threatening movements upon his flank must drive him from the hill. So it proved, for when on the morning of September 2 the 7th Brigade passed over the fatal plain, which was sown with the bodies of their comrades, they went through the village and on past the wood with little opposition, forming up at last in a defensive line facing south-east, while the Fifth Division on the south drove home its attack upon Peronne, where the defence was already hopelessly compromised by the various movements to the north.

Chapter III. Continuation of the Operations of Rawlinson's Fourth Army. Sept. 1.

Thus fell Mont St. Quentin, and as a consequence Peronne. Sir Henry Rawlinson in his official dispatch remarked that he was " filled with admiration for the surpassing daring " of the troops who had taken a position of the greatest " natural strength and eminent tactical value." Men of the Second Guards Division and of four other German Divisions were found among the prisoners. The Australian exploit may be said to have been of a peculiarly national character, as there was not one of the Australian communities— Victoria, New South Wales, Queensland, West Australia, Tasmania—which did not play some honourable part in the battle.

Passing northward from the victorious Australians, September 1 saw the attack carried all along the line, the 3rd Corps advancing upon Rancourt, Priez Farm, and the line to Bouchavesnes. On the left the hardworked 54th and 55th Brigades did splendidly, especially the 8th East Surrey under Colonel Irwin. Surrey men and Germans lay thick round Priez Farm, but this key-position remained in the hands of the English, after a very bitter struggle. The 7th Queen's

CHAPTER III.

Continuation of the Operations of Rawlinson's Fourth Army.
Sept. 1, 2.

took Fregicourt, while the 7th West Kents helped the Welshmen at Sailly-Sallisel. The trench mortar batteries, pushing right up regardless of all risk and smothering the German strong points by their concentrated fire, did great work in these operations, especially the 142nd T. M. Battery near Priez Farm. All these various advances were as remarkable for their tactical skill as for the valour shown by all ranks. The latter had been a constant asset, but the former grew with time.

Meanwhile the Forty-seventh and Fifty-eighth Divisions had each done splendidly and secured their objectives, including Rancourt and Bouchavesnes. The main road from Bapaume to Peronne had been passed and the whole of the old Somme battlefield been cleared in this direction. Prisoners were taken from four different divisions in the course of the fight. It had taken four months' fighting in 1916 to conquer the ground which had been now cleared by the Fifth and Third Corps inside of ten days.

The advance was continued on September 2, as it was argued that however exhausted the victors might be the vanquished would surely be even more so. A new actor made a first appearance in the greatest of all dramas about this time, for the Seventy-fourth Division, which had done good service in Palestine under General Girdwood, made its first attack in a European line of battle. This unit was originally composed entirely of Yeomanry, and it had still retained a large proportion of this splendid material in the ranks, with a broken spur as their witty and picturesque divisional emblem. The tale of the British Yeomanry in the East is one which will be among the most romantic in the war; and the way in which farmers' sons from Dorset or Fife charged with cold steel and rode down the Eastern cavalry or broke the ranks of the Turkish infantry is as fantastic an incident as the mind of a prophetic novelist could have furnished. Indeed it may be said generally that none of the many imaginary forecasts of the coming war equalled the reality in the broad sweep of its incidents and the grotesque combinations which ensued.

CHAPTER III.
Continuation of the Operations of Rawlinson's Fourth Army.
Sept. 1, 2.

The Seventy-fourth had now taken over from the Fifty-eighth Division. They were pushed at once into heavy fighting, advancing rapidly down the western slope of the Tortille valley, through Moislains, and over the canal. In their eager zeal they had not mopped up sufficiently, and they soon found themselves under a fire from front and rear which no troops could endure. They were driven back to near the point from which they started and their losses were considerable. The Australians formed a defensive flank on the south, and the Forty-seventh on the north, and a line of resistance was built up between them from Haut Allaines on the right to the western bank of the Tortille. The Yeomanry had before evening endured a very terrible welcome to the Western front.

The Eighteenth Division on the left had also had some severe fighting which fell chiefly upon the depleted 53rd Brigade. It secured the high ground in the north of St. Pierre Vaast Wood, the whole of which was cleared by the 8th Berkshires. On September 3 and 4 the division continued to advance across the canal and the Tortille upon the line of Nurlu. On the evening of September 4 its long term of hard and glorious service was ended and the

CHAPTER III.

Continuation of the Operations of Rawlinson's Fourth Army.

ept. 2–10.

Twelfth Division took its place. Its losses had been 2700, while it had captured during the battle some 1800 prisoners and many guns.

From this date until September 10, which saw them in front of the outposts of the Hindenburg Line, the record of the Third Corps was one of steady and uninterrupted progress. The German machine-guns were now, as always, a cause of constant worry, loss, and delay, but the remorseless drive of the British infantry was for ever beating in the obstinate rearguards. September 6 marked an advance of nearly three miles along the whole Corps front, the Twelfth, Forty-seventh, and Seventy-fourth moving in line and flooding over the village sites of Nurlu, Templeux, Driencourt, and Longavesnes. The work of Owen's 35th Brigade at Nurlu was particularly trying, for it was held up by wire and machine-guns, the 7th Sussex, 7th Norfolks, and 9th Essex all losing heavily in some very desperate fighting which gave little result. Finally, on September 6, the 1st Cambridge and 5th Berkshires reinforced the troops already mentioned and, under a renewed barrage, they broke the line and carried the position. On this date the Forty-seventh Londoners, who had done such solid work, were ordered off to join another corps, the Fifty-eighth moving up once more to take their place.

On September 7 the weather, which had been excellent since August 22, broke badly, but the Corps improved its position in spite of wind and rain, closing up to what was known to be the German fixed position. On the 8th both Epéhy and Peizières were touched, but the Germans were fairly at bay now, and instant counter-attacks showed that their resistance would be serious. The final position was about 1000 yards

RAWLINSON'S FOURTH ARMY 63

west of these villages. The Fifty-eighth Division
on September 10 endeavoured to gain more ground
in this quarter, but neither they nor the Seventy-
fourth upon their right could make any impression
upon the strong German line. There was a definite
pause, therefore, while tanks, guns, and all other
appliances for a serious assault upon a fortified
position were hurried to the front. On this date,
September 12, General Butler was able to resume his
command of the Third Corps, while General Godley,
after his term of brilliant service, returned to his own
unit, the Twenty-second Corps.

We must now return to the Australian Corps on
the right, whom we left in the flush of victory after
their fine conquest of Peronne. Up to the end of
August, Monash and his men had accounted for
14,500 prisoners and 170 guns since the beginning of
the advance. On September 1, as already mentioned, Peronne had been penetrated by the Fifth
Australian Division, but after the fall of Mont St.
Quentin, and the failure of their efforts at recovery,
the Germans must have seen that it was hopeless to
hold the place, so that the stormers were eventually
only faced by a rearguard of stalwarts. Anvil Wood
to the north-east was taken on the same day. The
order of the Divisions upon the Australian front at
this time was that the Third was on the extreme left,
acting with the Third Corps, the Second was just
north of Peronne, the Fifth was opposite to Peronne,
and the Thirty-second British Division was on the
extreme right, near Brie and St. Christ, in touch with
the French.

Early in the morning of September 2 Rosenthal's
indefatigable Second Division continued to advance

CHAPTER III.

Continuation of the Operations of Rawlinson's Fourth Army. Sept. 2–10.

from Mont St. Quentin, attacking to the north-east so as to get possession of the high ground south-west of Aizecourt. They attained their objectives and formed a flank along the spur from Mont St. Quentin to Aizecourt in order to protect the Third Corps in the difficult operations already described. By this movement to the north the Second Australian got in front of the Third Australian Division, which was crowded out of the line, all but two battalions. The Fifth Australians spent the day in clearing up Peronne. Altogether some 500 additional prisoners fell into their hands during the day.

There was some readjustment and reorganisation necessary after this strenuous work, but by September 5 the advance was going forward again and Flamicourt was taken. It is an open rolling country of large horizons, and the Germans were slowly retreating with strong rearguards. Doingt, Le Mesnil, and the river crossings of Brie and St. Christ were all occupied, though the latter cost a severe fight, with 150 prisoners as trophies. On the 6th and 7th the Corps were sweeping on with their own 13th Australian Light Horse doing the cavalry work in front of them, fit representatives of those splendid horsemen who have left an enduring reputation in Egypt and Palestine. Late in the afternoon of September 7 the Corps front crossed the railway between Vermand and Vendelles, and began to approach the historic point which had marked the British line before March 21. On September 10 Strickland's First British Division arrived in this area, and with the Thirty-second Division and some other units began to form the nucleus of another Corps, the Ninth, which should operate under General Braithwaite to the right of the

Australians. On the 12th the Australians took Jeancourt, and were in touch with the outlying defences of the great Hindenburg Line, which they at once proceeded to attack. On September 13 there was a sharp fight round Le Verguier, and an advance all along the line in which the objectives were taken and the tanks did some particularly fine work. Tanks and barrages that day combined to keep the Australian losses at a very low figure, and yet some 40 guns and 4500 prisoners had been taken before next morning. The First Australian Division on the left secured all the front defences which guarded the main Hindenburg position, while the Fourth on the right worked its way well forward, though hardly level with its neighbours. The Ninth Corps on the right had also come on, though it was also rather behind the Australians. The average advance of the latter amounted to three miles in depth on a four-mile front.

Nothing could be more in-and-out than the German fighting during all this stage of the war. Sometimes their conduct was heroic in the extreme, sometimes it was exceedingly cowardly and slack. The observer could not but recall the famous description which an American General of old gave of his militia when he said with native raciness that " they either fought like the devil or ran like hell." The machine-gunners were usually, however, in the former category, and they, with the heavy guns, represented the real resistance, while the infantry only needed to be reached—in some cases not even that—to throw up their hands and come over as joyful captives. There were already two Germans in British hands for every Briton in Germany, in spite of the heavy losses in March and April.

CHAPTER III.

Continuation of the Operations of Rawlinson's Fourth Army. Sept. 5–12.

66   THE BRITISH CAMPAIGN, 1918

CHAPTER III.

Continuation of the Operations of Rawlinson's Fourth Army.
Sept. 18.

Returning to the Third Corps, which we left in front of the Hindenburg system in the second week of September in the Epéhy district. The obstacle in front of the British was very formidable, for it consisted of their own old trench lines of March, with the Hindenburg system behind them. They had now reached the former British reserve line which had Ronssoy, Lempire, Epéhy, and Peizières as *points d'appui*. It was a front so strong that in March it is doubtful if the Germans could have carried it had the line not given way elsewhere. It was particularly necessary that the enemy should hold on to this stretch, because it covered the point where the great Canal du Nord ran under a tunnel for six miles between Bellicourt and Vandhuile—the only place where tanks could be used for an advance. The Germans had therefore massed strong forces here, including their famous Alpine Corps.

The first task of the Third Corps was to get possession of the old British line in front of it, whence observation could be got of the Hindenburg position. This attack would form part of a general movement by the two southern Corps of the Third Army, the three Corps of the Fourth Army, and the northern portion of the First French Army. On that great day of battle, September 18, there was a universal advance along the line, which was carried out in the case of the Third Corps by the Seventy-fourth Division (Girdwood) on the right, the Eighteenth (Lee) right centre, the Twelfth (Higginson) left centre, and the Fifty-eighth Division left. Many of the characteristics of old trench warfare had come back into the battle, which was no longer open fighting, but is to be conceived as an attack upon innumerable scattered trenches and posts very strongly held by the Germans, and their ultimate reduction by independent platoons and companies acting under their own regimental officers.

Chapter III.

Continuation of the Operations of Rawlinson's Fourth Army. Sept. 18.

The advance was at 5.20 in the morning, with a thick mist and driving rain to cover, and also to confuse, the movement. The Yeomen of the Seventy-fourth upon the right came away in excellent style, keeping in close touch with the Australian left, and were soon in possession of the Templeux quarries, a very formidable position. At the other end of the line a brigade of the Fifty-eighth Londoners did excellently well, and by 10 o'clock had a good grip upon the village of Peizières. In the centre, however, the resistance was very stiff and the losses heavy. None the less the Eighteenth Division, which has always been a particularly difficult unit to stop, made their way through Ronssoy and Lempire. The Eighteenth Division did wonderful work that day, and though nominally only the 54th and 55th Brigades were engaged, they were each strengthened by a battalion from the spare brigade. There were particular difficulties in the path of the 55th Brigade, but General Wood personally accompanied the leading battalion and so kept in touch with the situation, varying his activities by throwing bricks and old boots down a German dug-out, and so bringing out 20 prisoners as his own personal take. He was wounded in the course of the day. Ronssoy, which fell to the 55th Brigade, was held by the Alexander Regiment of Prussian Guards, several hundred samples being taken for the British cages. The taking of Lempire, carried out mainly by the 11th Royal Fusiliers, was also a very gallant affair, though it was a day or two before it was completely in British possession. The Twelfth, which is also an all-English division with a splendid fighting record, was held for a time before Epéhy, but would take no denial, and after heavy losses and severe fighting was east of that village by 11 o'clock. Thus by midday the whole line of villages was in the hands of General Butler's Corps. The left was out of touch with the Fifth Corps, but all else was in perfect order. These positions were full of wire and concrete, and were defended by the hardy German Alpine Corps who fought to the death, so that the achievement was a great one.

All four divisions endeavoured to improve their positions in the afternoon, but they had no great success. The Seventy-fourth Division did the best, as on the right it was able to secure Benjamin's Post, but on the left it was held up by the general stagnation of the line. The centre divisions met a German counter-attack delivered by the Hundred and twenty-first Division, who had been rushed up in buses from Maretz, and this they entirely dispersed, but neither they nor the Fifty-eighth on the left were able to make any notable advance.

The troops were now faced by a perfect warren of trenches and posts which were held with great gallantry by the Alpine Corps. There was no rest for the British, and the night of the 18/19th was spent by the same men who had been fighting all day in bombing up the trenches and endeavouring to enlarge their gains. The same sort of fighting, carried on by small groups of determined men led by subalterns or non-commissioned officers, and faced by other small groups equally determined, went on along the whole line during September 19 and 20.

In those two days the advance went steadily on, in spite of many a local rebuff and many a temporary check. On September 21 the battle was renewed still in the same fashion with heavy losses upon both sides. At one time the steady flow of the British tide turned for a time to an ebb, as a very strong German counter-attack came rolling into it, and swept it back along the whole front from the positions which it had overflowed in the morning. The Seventy-fourth was forced out of Quinnemont Farm, the Eighteenth out of Doleful Post, the Twelfth were checked at Bird Trench, while the Fifty-eighth, intermingled with men from the right wing of the Fifth Corps, could not get past Kildare Avenue. These fanciful names, unseen on any save a large-scale trench map, bulked large in this bloody battle, for they were master points which controlled the ground around. The sun set with the Germans in the ascendant, and the British clawing desperately at a series of posts and farms which they could just hold against very heavy pressure. One of the most severe engagements was that of the 10th Essex of the 53rd Brigade when they attempted the Knoll, a position from which the whole Hindenburg Line would have been exposed. It was said by experienced soldiers that more severe machine-gun fire had seldom been seen than on this occasion, and the tanks engaged were unable to use their own guns, so thick were the driving storms of bullets which beat upon their iron sides and searched every aperture. The Essex men lost heavily, and the Knoll was not taken. This and the other posts mentioned above were the cause of much trouble to the Americans on September 27.

It was a disappointing day, but the British soldiers,

CHAPTER III.

Continuation of the Operations of Rawlinson's Fourth Army.
Sept. 22.

dog-weary as they were, were in no mood to leave matters undecided. The operations must be carried to a successful end. "Hard pounding, gentlemen," as the great Duke said, "but we shall see who can pound longest!" Just after midnight the tired ranks were stumbling forward once more, determined to have those posts back if human resolution could win them. They had their reward, and it was a conspicuous illustration of the maxim that, however weary you may be, the enemy may be even more so. Before the full light of morning half the line of posts was in the hands of the persevering British. The capture of Bracton Post by Colonel Dawson's 6th West Kents was a particularly brilliant bit of work. The success stretched along the whole Corps front, and though the afternoon of September 22 saw a whole series of counter-attacks, especially upon the Seventy-fourth and Eighteenth Divisions, there was no weakening of the new line. One German battalion engaged in these counter-attacks was literally annihilated as a barrage fell behind them through which they could not retire. It is on record that in spite of the very arduous service the spirits and morale of the men were never higher. Twice after a German repulse the men of the 6th Northants and 11th Royal Fusiliers could not be held back from jumping out of the trenches and tearing after them, while a stretcher-bearer was observed to run up and down the parados of the trench throwing cartridges down to the defenders and shouting, "Shoot, boys, shoot!"

By September 23 the Third Corps had gained most of those posts which had been its objectives on September 18, and if the battle took longer than had been anticipated it was all the greater drain upon the worn resources of the Germans. They were still intent upon making machines do the work of men, and it was no unusual thing to take about as many machine-guns as prisoners in some of their posts. The situation was still not quite clear on the left, where the right flank of the Fifth Corps was engaged in severe local fighting in the neighbourhood of Kildare and Limerick Post. The Egg Post on the front of the Eighteenth Division had also been able to maintain itself in the German line. These various isolated strong points were the same which had held out with such unavailing gallantry on March 21, when, instead of forming the German rear, they were the extreme outliers of Gough's Army.

Chapter III.

Continuation of the Operations of Rawlinson's Fourth Army. Sept. 22.

Whilst the Third Corps on the left of the Fourth Army had been gradually fighting its way forward from September 18 onwards, beating down one after the other the outposts and obstacles which, like the moraine before a glacier, formed a rugged line in front of the great main Hindenburg system, Sir John Monash and his men were keeping pace with them, step by step, on their right, the First Australian Division being in close liaison on September 18 with the Seventy-fourth Yeomanry. Many a separate volume will be written upon the exploits of our Australian brothers, and General Monash has himself written a record of their last glorious hundred days, so that the chronicler has the less compunction if he is not always able to give the amount of detail which he would desire.

At 5.20 on September 18 the Australians went forward with a rapidity which seems to have completely taken aback the German defenders, who in many cases ran from their guns, or threw up their hands in detachments, when they saw the active figures of the infantrymen springing eagerly forward behind the line of tanks. The weather was bad, the ground slippery with rain, and the attack expected, but none of these factors interfered with the result. The First Australians, as stated, were in the line on the left, the 1st and 3rd Brigades in the van, while on the right were the 4th and 12th Brigades of the Fourth Australian Division in close touch with the British First Division on their right. By midday everything had gone down before them, and the measure of their success was the 146 officers and 3900 men with 77 guns which formed their trophies before evening. On one side they had reached Le Verguier, and on the other they were past Templeux. A minefield containing thirty-five mines was found in front of the Fourth Australian Division, another instance of the fact that the tanks had brought a nautical element into warfare. The Australian casualties were surprisingly light considering their splendid results, for they did not amount to more than a thousand men.

Some description must now be given of the work of the Ninth Corps, which had assembled under General Braithwaite on the extreme right of the British Army and which first came into action on September 18 in this hard fight for the Hindenburg Outpost Line. The Corps consisted at this time of three divisions, the First, Sixth, and Thirty-second, under Strickland, Marden, and Lambert. On September 18 the Corps attacked with the Sixth Division in touch with the French on the right, and the First Division with the Fourth Australians on the left. The order of brigades from the right was 71, 16, 1, and 2. It was known that two German divisions, the Seventy-ninth and Twenty-fifth, with two others in reserve, were lying opposite behind strong defences, so that a hard battle might well be expected.

The Thirty-fourth French Division on the immediate right brought off a very useful and successful coup on September 17 by capturing Round Hill and part of Savy Wood, which reassured General Marden as to the safety of his right flank. This division appeared to have the more difficult task as Badger Copse, the village of Fresnoy, and part of the very strong system known as the Quadrilateral came within their area.

The attack went forward under pelting rain at 5.20 in the morning of September 18. Following the operations from the north we have to deal first with the 2nd Brigade on the flank. The left-hand battalion, the 2nd Sussex, kept up with the Australians, who had advanced without a check and carried every obstacle. The 2nd King's Royal Rifles, on the other hand, had lost direction and, wandering too far south across the face of their neighbours, found themselves mixed up with the Sixth Division in its fruitless attempt upon the powerfully defended village of Fresnoy. The 1st Brigade, to the south, was led by the 1st Camerons and the 1st Loyal North Lancashires. The former stormed on, breaking through all opposition and throwing out defensive flanks as their valour carried them ahead of the line. Meanwhile the failure of the Sixth Division to take Fresnoy made it impossible to pass along the valley which is overlooked by that village, so that the right of the First Division was entirely hung up. On the

CHAPTER III.

Continuation of the Operations of Rawlinson's Fourth Army. Sept. 18.

CHAPTER III.

Continuation of the Operations of Rawlinson's Fourth Army.
Sept. 18.

other hand, the 2nd King's Royal Rifles recovered their bearings as the day went on, and fought their way up the right side of the Omignon valley in splendid style until they were in touch with the 2nd Sussex on the northern slope. In the south, however, the task of the Sixth Division continued to be a very hard one, and the Seventy-ninth German Division resisted with great determination. The Quadrilateral consisted of a system of trenches sited on the highest part of the plateau between Holnon and Fayet, its northern face at this time forming part of the German front line. This proved to be an exceedingly difficult work to silence, as reinforcements could be dribbled up through cleverly concealed communication trenches. In spite of everything, however, the 71st Brigade and their French neighbours captured Holnon village and the western edge of the Quadrilateral by 8 A.M. The main body of the work was not yet taken, however, so the East Anglians of the 71st Brigade had to form a defensive line facing towards it and the village of Selency, to meet any counter-attack which might sweep up against the flank of the Corps. The left of the line then got forward in safety, and the 2nd Brigade was able to report at noon that both they and the Fourth Australians were on their extreme objective. Indeed the latter, having completely crumpled up the One hundred and nineteenth German Division, were now considerably ahead of the allotted line.

Berthaucourt had been captured by the First Division, but progress in the Fresnoy direction was still very slow. About 3.30 P.M. hostile counter-attacks were launched south of Berthaucourt and opposite Fresnoy. These were repulsed by steady rifle-fire, but the general situation was still obscure. All the afternoon there was very heavy fighting on the front of the Sixth Division, especially east of Holnon village, and on the west side of the Quadrilateral. The French had been held up on the right. So matters remained until evening. It had been a day of hard work and varying success on this portion of the line, but the capture of 18 officers and 541 men with 8 field-guns showed that some advance had been made. It was short, however, of what had been hoped.

Chapter III. Continuation of the Operations of Rawlinson's Fourth Army. Sept. 19.

The next morning saw the battle renewed. The neighbourhood of Fresnoy and of the Quadrilateral was now more strongly held than ever, the Germans being encouraged, no doubt, by their successful defence of the day before. The fighting during this day was desultory, and no particular advance was made by either division. In the south the French failed to capture Manchester Hill, which was an ugly menace to the right flank of the Ninth Corps.

The Forty-sixth Division (Boyd) had been added to the strength of the Ninth Corps, and when this welcome addition had been put in upon the left wing it enabled the others to contract their front and thicken their array. At 7 p.m. on September 22 the Germans attacked the Forty-sixth Division in its new position, just east of Berthaucourt, but they were driven back after a slight initial success.

There was a fresh attack on September 24 in which the Ninth Corps co-operated with the Thirty-sixth Corps on its right, in order to try and overcome the German strongholds on the right of their front which were holding them off from the Hindenburg Line. The order of the British line was that

> CHAPTER III.
>
> Continuation of the Operations of Rawlinson's Fourth Army.
> Sept. 24.

the Sixth Division was on the right, the First in the centre, and the Forty-sixth on the left.

Although this attack, which was launched at 5 A.M., was expected by the enemy, good progress was made along the whole front. The Quadrilateral again proved, however, that it was a very formidable obstacle, and there was stout resistance from Pontruet village, just east of Berthaucourt. The Sixth Division had closed in on the Quadrilateral from north, west, and south, and were at close grips with it at all three quarters. There was continuous bomb-fighting all day in this neighbourhood, but the situation was still obscure, and until it cleared no progress could be made towards Selency. The First Division in the centre had made splendid progress, but the Forty-sixth Division had been unable to take Pontruet, and the guns from this village struck full against the left flank of the 2nd Brigade in its advance, causing very heavy losses to the 1st Northamptons. So murderous were the casualties in this portion of the field that the position of the forward troops was untenable, and the remains of the Northamptons had to throw back a protective flank to the north to cover the approaches from Pontruet. The 2nd Sussex on their right managed to retain their advanced position, and one company, though very weak and short of cartridges, baffled a counterattack by a sudden bayonet charge in which they took 50 prisoners.

The attack upon Fresnoy village was made by the 3rd Brigade, the 1st Gloucesters being immediately opposite to it. Advancing under a strong barrage the West Country men went straight for their objective, taking both the village and the strongly organised cemetery to the south of it. On the left of the village the British were held up by strong wire and several vicious machine-guns, but the Germans made the gallant mistake of running out in front of the wire with bombs in their hands, upon which they were charged and many of them were taken by the Gloucesters. The German gunners in the rear then turned their pieces upon both captors and captives, so the company concerned was held down in shell holes all day and withdrew as best they could after dark. The 3rd Brigade then extended, getting into touch with the 2nd Brigade near Cornovillers Wood.

CHAPTER III.

Continuation of the Operations of Rawlinson's Fourth Army. Sept. 24.

On the left of the 3rd Brigade the strong position of Fresnoy Cemetery had been carried, and the tireless infantry swarmed on into Marronnières Wood, which was full of lurking machine-guns and needed careful handling. It was finally surrounded by the 3rd Brigade, who mopped it up at their leisure, taking out of it a large number of prisoners. The 2nd King's Royal Rifles of the 2nd Brigade kept parallel with their advance, and also cleared a considerable stretch of woodland, while the 3rd Brigade, seeing signs of weakening on the German front, pushed forward and seized Gricourt, a most important point, the 2nd Welsh gaining the village and driving back a subsequent counter-attack. Finally, the complete victory in this portion of the field was rounded off when, after dark, the 2nd King's Royal Rifles secured a dangerous sunken road across the front which had been a storm-centre all day.

Meanwhile the Forty-sixth Division had fought its way to the north of Pontruet, but as this unit was relied upon for the great pending operations on the Hindenburg Main Line, it was thought impolitic to involve it too deeply in local fighting. The line was drawn, therefore, to the west of the village. The total captures of the day had been 30 officers and 1300 men. The French to the south had also had a good day, capturing all their objectives except Manchester Hill.

The Sixth Division had not yet cleared the Quadrilateral, and the whole of September 25 was devoted to that desperate but necessary work. It was a case of bomb and bayonet, with slow laborious progress. Finally, about 6 P.M. General Marden was able to announce that the whole wide entanglement had been occupied, though not yet mopped up. The village of Selency had also fallen, while on the right the French had attacked and captured Manchester Hill. Strong resistance was encountered by the First Division near Gricourt. The German soldiers were again and again seen to hold up their hands, and then to be driven into the fight once more by their officers with their revolvers. Late on the 26th, after a short hurricane bombardment, the 3rd Brigade rushed forward again. The enemy had disappeared into their dug-outs under the stress of the shells, so that the British infantry were able to get on to them before they could emerge and to make many prisoners. Colonel Tweedie of the Gloucesters was in local command of this well-managed affair. Altogether it was a good day for the First Division, which had gained a line of positions, repelled heavy counters, and secured 800 prisoners, 600 falling to the 3rd Brigade, who had done the heavy end of the work.

All was now ready for the great move which should break the spine of the whole German resistance. There was still some preliminary struggling for posi-

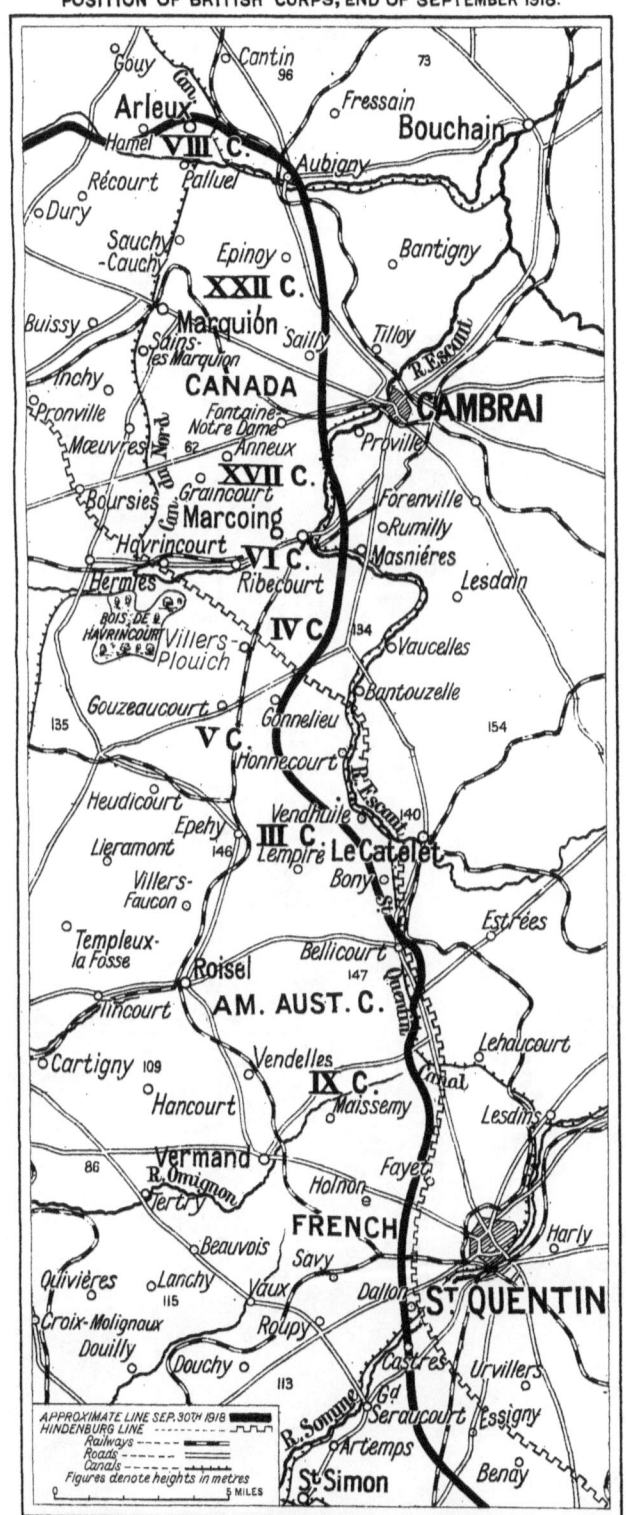

POSITION OF BRITISH CORPS, END OF SEPTEMBER 1918.

tions of departure and final readjustments of the line, but they were all part of the great decisive operation of September 29 and may best be included in that account. The chronicler can never forget how, late upon the eve of the battle, he drove in a darkened motor along pitch-black roads across the rear of the Army, and saw the whole eastern heaven flickering with war light as far as the eyes could see, as the aurora rises and falls in the northern sky. So terrific was the spectacle that the image of the Day of Judgment rose involuntarily to his mind. It was indeed the day of Judgment for Germany—the day when all those boastful words and wicked thoughts and arrogant actions were to meet their fit reward, and the wrong-doers to be humbled in the dust. On that day Germany's last faint hope was shattered, and every day after was but a nearer approach to that pit which had been dug for her by her diplomatists, her journalists, her professors, her junkers, and all the vile, noisy crew who had brought this supreme cataclysm upon the world.

CHAPTER III.

Continuation of the Operations of Rawlinson's Fourth Army.

The reader will note then that we leave the Fourth Army, consisting from the right of the Ninth Corps, the Australians, and the Third Corps, in front of the terrific barrier of the main Hindenburg Line. We shall now hark back and follow the advance of Byng's Third Army from its attack on August 21st until, five weeks later, it found itself in front of the same position, carrying on the line of its comrades in the south.

CHAPTER IV

THE ATTACK OF BYNG'S THIRD ARMY

August 21, 1918, to September 29, 1918

Advance of Shute's Fifth Corps—Great feat in crossing the Ancre—Across the old battlefield—Final position of Fifth Corps opposite Hindenburg's Main Line—Advance of Haldane's Sixth Corps—Severe fighting—Arrival of Fifty-second Division—Formation of Fergusson's Seventeenth Corps—Recapture of Havrincourt—Advance of Harper's Fourth Corps—Great tenacity of the troops—The New Zealanders and the Jaeger—Final position before the decisive battle.

ON August 20 General Mangin had pushed forward the Tenth French Army, which formed the left of his force, and attacked along a sixteen-mile front from the Oise to the Aisne, thus connecting up the original operations with those initiated by Marshal Haig. The movement was very successful, taking some 10,000 prisoners and gaining several miles of ground. We have now to turn to the left of Rawlinson's advance, and to consider the new movement which brought Byng's Third British Army into the fray.

Upon the left of the Third Corps, which was, as already described, fighting its way along the north bank of the Somme, there lay the Fifth Corps (Shute). On its left was the Fourth Corps (Harper), and north of that the Sixth Corps (Haldane). It was to these

ADVANCE OF 1ST, 3RD AND 4TH BRITISH ARMIES FROM AUGUST 21ST 1918 TO SEPTEMBER 2ND 1918.

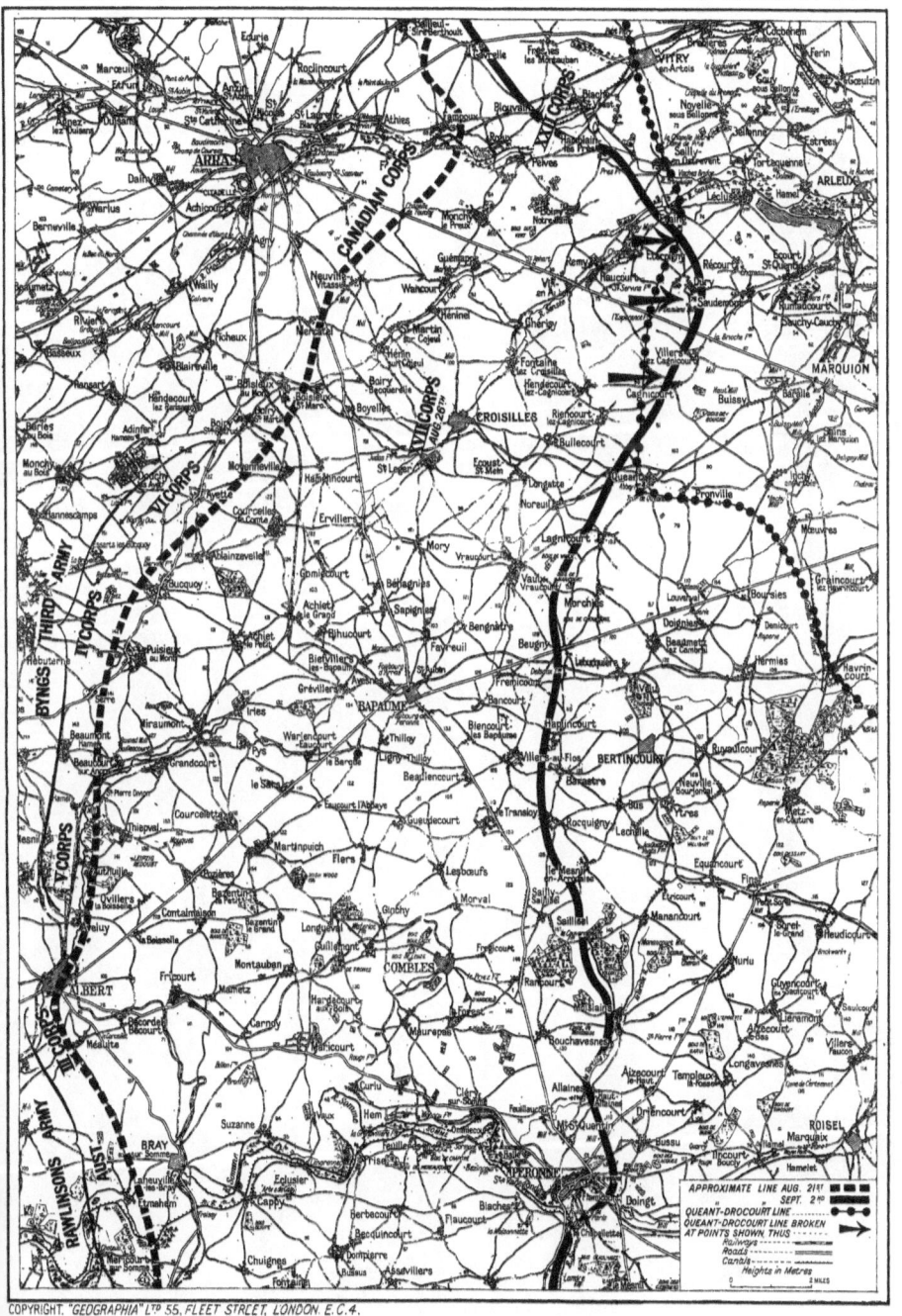

three units that the opening of the attack was entrusted. The frontage was about ten miles, extending from Moyenneville in the north to the Ancre in the south, so that it just cleared the impossible country of the first Somme battlefield — which even now a spectator cannot survey without a feeling of wondering horror, so churned up is it from end to end by the constant thresh of shells, burst of mines, and the spade-work of three great armies. The result of the first day's fighting was an advance of several miles along the whole front, with the capture of Beaucourt, Bucquoy, Moyenneville, and other villages, the farthest advance coming close to the Arras—Albert Railway, and to the village of Achiet-le-Grand.

CHAPTER IV.

The Attack of Byng's Third Army. August 21.

There had been some recent retirement of the German line at Serre, which gave the clue to the British Commanders that a general retreat might take place on this particular portion of the front. It was very necessary, therefore, to strike at once while there was certainly something solid to strike against—and all the more necessary if there was a chance of catching the enemy in the act of an uncompleted withdrawal.

It was nearly five o'clock when the battle began, and it was the turn of the Germans to find how fog may disarrange the most elaborate preparations for defence. The mist was so thick that it could only be compared to that which had shrouded the German advance on March 21. Several miles of undulating country lay immediately in front of the attackers, leading up to a formidable line of defence, the old Albert—Arras Railway lying with its fortified embankments right across the path of the British Army.

G

Bucquoy in the centre of the line, with the Logeast Wood to the east of it, and the muddy, sluggish Ancre with its marshy banks on the extreme right, were notable features in the ground to be assaulted.

The Fifth Corps, under General Shute, followed the curve of the River Ancre on a front of 9000 yards. It was poorly provided with guns as the Corps to the left required a concentration of artillery, and it had no tanks since the marshy valley and sluggish stream lay before it. The Thirty-eighth Welsh Division (Cubitt) lay on the right and Campbell's Twenty-first on the left, each of them with two brigades in front and one in reserve. The Seventeenth Division (Robertson) was in support. The problem in front of General Shute's Corps was a most difficult one. Before it lay this evil watercourse which had been flooded by the Germans and was 300 yards wide at one part. All bridges were gone, and the banks were low and boggy. The main stream was over six feet deep, and its channel could not be distinguished from the general flood. The whole morass was covered by a tangle of fallen trees, reeds, and artificial obstructions. To the east of the river ran high ground, strongly held and fortified, from Tara Hill above Albert to the Thiepval Height, south of Grandcourt. The west bank was so overlooked that no one could move unscathed. And yet it was clear that until this formidable obstacle was surmounted it was neither possible for Rawlinson to advance from Albert, nor for the Fourth Corps on the left to assault Miraumont.

The movements of Shute's Corps on August 21 were preliminary to their real attack. On that date the Twenty-first Division advanced on the left flank, in close touch with the Forty-second Division of the Fourth Corps. Beaucourt was taken in the movement. By this operation the Twenty-first Division reached a point where the flood was narrower at St. Pierre Divion, and here some bridges could be constructed and preparations made for the passage.

CHAPTER IV.

The Attack of Byng's Third Army. August 21.

In the case of Harper's Fourth Corps on the left the advance on August 21 was limited, since no serious attack could be made upon Miraumont while the high ground to the south was untaken. At this date Harper's Corps consisted of five divisions, the Fifth, Thirty-seventh, Forty-second, Sixty-third, and the New Zealanders. Of these the Thirty-seventh Division (Williams) was on the left, covering the flank of the Sixth Corps, while the Forty-second (Solly-Flood) was on the right. We shall now follow in the first instance the work of the Fifth Corps on the extreme right from the beginning of the battle until the pause preceding the attack of September 18. There are, it is true, objections to continuous narrative, since it stands in the way of a bird's-eye view of the whole operation; but on the other hand the object and scope of any series of advances become unintelligible unless they are linked up from day to day. We shall therefore take the Fifth Corps as one story until it reaches the Hindenburg Line. We shall then follow the work of the other flank corps of Byng's Third Army, which was Haldane's Sixth Corps, bringing it up to the same point. It will finally, after we have established two solid bastions, be easy to deal with the central unit, Harper's Fourth Corps, which filled up the space between. We shall

CHAPTER IV.

The Attack of Byng's Third Army. August 22.

then have a narrative which will cover four strenuous weeks in which the Third Army carried out a notable advance.

It has been explained that Shute's Fifth Corps found itself with 9000 yards of river in front of it, and that on August 21 the Twenty-first Division had seized a favourable point for crossing near St. Pierre Divion. There was no further advance on the morning of the 22nd, but to the south Rawlinson's left was fighting its way to the eastern exits of Albert, and the bridges in the town were being got ready for use. All day a heavy fire was kept up on the German lines east of the river, and especially upon the rising ground called Usna Hill. As the day passed small bodies of troops began to cross the Ancre from the Fifth Corps front and to make a lodgement at the farther side. South-west of Thiepval part of the 14th Welsh from the 114th Brigade, wading over breast deep with their rifles and pouches held high, got into a trench on the farther bank and held their own. The Twenty-first Division also got some companies across at St. Pierre, while it beat off several attacks upon the north side of the river. During the night the 50th Brigade of the Seventeenth Division was slipped into the line, between Campbell's North Countrymen on the left and Cubitt's Welshmen on the right. General Shute was now ready for his great effort in crossing the river.

The first stage in this difficult operation was carried out early on August 23, when the 113th Welsh Brigade, which had quickly passed over the Albert bridges, made a sudden attack about dawn on Usna Hill, at the same time as the Eighteenth Division to the south attacked Tara Hill. The position was

BYNG'S THIRD ARMY

taken with 200 prisoners, while the 115th Welsh Brigade got up to the chalk-pit, east of Aveluy, where they joined hands with their comrades on the Usna line. Thus, before evening of August 23 the Thirty-eighth Division was east of the river from Albert to Aveluy, while the Twenty-first still held its bridgeheads at St. Pierre Divion. The slope of the Thiepval Ridge with all its fortifications still lay in front, and this was the next objective of the Fifth Corps. It was carried by a night attack on August 23–24.

CHAPTER IV.

The Attack of Byng's Third Army. August 23.

A large portion of the central line was so flooded that no advance was possible. It was planned, therefore, that the assault should be on both wings, the area around Authuille being nipped out and cleared at a later stage. The operation began on the evening of August 23 by a movement along the northern bank of the river to the south-east of Miraumont, so as to partly encircle that village and help forward the Fourth Corps on the left, who were still held up in front of it. The main Ancre attack was carried out by the 113th Brigade on the right, who came away with a fine impetus on the eastern slopes of Usna Hill, capturing La Boiselle and reaching a point 1100 yards west of Ovillers. The 114th Brigade on the left had with great difficulty and corresponding valour crossed the Ancre under machine-gun fire and had established themselves on the slopes, fighting their way forward all day until they reached a point north-west of Pozières. All around Thiepval there was close fighting in which this brigade acted in close liaison with the 50th Brigade. In this struggle many gallant deeds were done, and it is recorded, among others, how Lieutenant Griffiths of the Welsh

Regiment advanced using his Lewis gun as if it were a rifle. He is said to have slain sixteen Germans in this novel fashion before his own wounds brought him fainting to the ground. According to the plan the two converging brigades left a large central section untouched, which was promptly mopped up by the 115th Brigade, so that every man of the Thirty-eighth Division was engaged in this fine operation.

Farther to the left the 6th Dorsets of the 50th Brigade, in spite of gas clouds and machine-guns had crossed the Ancre in its narrowest reach, where some sort of bridges had been prepared. With great energy and initiative they cleared up the front trenches and pockets so as to give room for a deployment, pushing their patrols out towards Thiepval, but they were driven in again by an attack from the Schwaben Redoubt. The rest of the 50th Brigade (Gwyn-Thomas) had followed, most of the infantry wading across in the dark up to their waists in mud and water. Pushing on, as part of the general advance, all three battalions of the 50th Brigade went forward, capturing several hundred prisoners, but deviating so far from their course that when they thought and reported that they had captured Courcelette it was really Pozières which they had got. In the early afternoon Allason's 52nd Brigade was pushed in on the right of the 50th Brigade, connecting them up with the Welshmen. The mistake in the direction of the 50th Brigade was not an unmixed evil, for while it left the Twenty-first Division with its right flank exposed and in considerable difficulty, it made a pocket of a large number of Germans in front of the Welshmen, 900 of whom were captured. General

Robertson saved the situation on the left by pushing in his reserve brigade, the 51st (Dudgeon), and so filling the gap between his division and that of General Campbell.

CHAPTER IV.

The Attack of Byng's Third Army. August 24.

The latter division, especially the 64th Brigade, which had pushed on to Miraumont the night before, had some desperate fighting. The whole brigade was passed in single file over two foot-bridges. At 11.30 P.M. they were assembled upon the south bank and ready to start. A barrage had been arranged for their attack, but owing to changes in plan it was not thick or effective. The advance was made by the 15th Durhams on the right and the 9th Yorkshire Light Infantry on the left with the 1st East Yorks in support, the column being guided by means of compass bearing, and by the presence of the Ancre on the left flank. This nocturnal march in the face of the enemy was a very remarkable and daring one, for the ground was pitted with craters and there were two ravines with sheer sides at right angles to the advance. Touch was kept by shouting, which seems to have confused rather than informed the enemy, who only fought in patches. Grandcourt was overrun with 100 prisoners, 20 machine-guns, and 4 field-pieces. Early in the morning General M'Culloch, who had conducted the operation, was badly wounded and the command passed to Colonel Holroyd Smith of the Durhams. When full daylight came the brigade was deeply embedded in the German line, and the enemy closed in upon it but their attacks were repulsed. The soldiers were compelled to lie flat, however, in order to escape from the heavy fire. The 110th Brigade of the same division had advanced on the right, but it was acting in close liaison with the Seventeenth Division, and independent of the isolated unit, which was now completely alone on the hill south of Miraumont, their East Yorkshire supports being at Grandcourt, and so much out of touch with the advanced line that the Officer Commanding imagined the stragglers to be all that was left of the brigade. The first intimation of the true state of affairs was given by the wounded Brigadier as he passed on his way to the casualty station. About 10.30 Captain Spicer, the Brigade Major, got back by crawling, and reported that the advanced line still held, though weak in numbers. Aeroplane reconnaissance confirmed the report. All day the valiant band held out until in the evening the advance of the Forty-second Division on their left, and of their own comrades of the 110th Brigade on their right, rescued them from a desperate situation. Their work had been exceedingly useful, as their presence had partially paralysed the whole German system of defence. Great credit in this remarkable affair was due not only to General Campbell and his staff, upon whom the initial responsibility lay, but to the gallant and inspiring leading of General M'Culloch and of the battalion leaders, Holroyd Smith and Greenwood. It was indeed a wonderful feat to advance three miles over such country upon a pitch-dark night and to reach and hold an objective which was outflanked on both sides by the successful German defence. The troops had been heartened up by messages with promises of speedy succour which were dropped by aeroplanes during the day.

The 62nd Brigade had now pushed in between the 64th on the right and the Forty-second Division on the left, touching the latter in the neighbourhood of Pys, so that by the late afternoon of August 24 the whole line was solid and the crossing of the Ancre with the capture of the ridge were accomplished facts. There have been few more deft pieces of work in the war. The German fixed line had been driven back and the remaining operations consisted from this date onwards in a pursuit rather than an attack. It was a pursuit, however, where the retreat was always covered by an obstinate rearguard, so that there was many a stiff fight in front of the Fifth Corps in the days to come.

CHAPTER IV.
The Attack of Byng's Third Army. August 24.

Divisions had been instructed that the pursuit was to be continued in a relentless fashion, and Corps cavalry, drawn from the 8th and 20th Hussars, were told off to throw out patrols and keep in close touch with the German rearguard. The immediate objectives of the infantry were Longueval and Flers for the Welshmen, Gueudecourt for the Seventeenth, and Beaulencourt for the Twenty-first Division. The general movement was extraordinarily like the advance in the spring of 1917, but the British were now more aggressive and the Germans were less measured and sedate in their dispositions. On August 25 the pressure was sustained along the whole line, and the Germans, fighting hard with their machine-guns which swept the exposed ridges, were none the less being pushed eastwards the whole day. The Welsh took Contalmaison and reached the edge of Mametz Wood, where so many of their comrades had fallen just two years before. The Seventeenth, fighting hard, captured Courcelette and Martinpuich. The Twenty-first got Le Sars and the Butte de Warlencourt, that strange old tumulus which now marked the joining point with the Fourth Corps still advancing on the left. At no point was there a battle and at no point was there peace, but a constant ripple of fire rose and fell along the thin fluctuating line. It is noted in the diaries of some of the British Generals as being the first day of purely open warfare in offensive fighting which their troops had ever experienced.

On the morning of August 26 the Welsh overran Bazentin-le-Grand, but the 115th Brigade were held up for a time at the old stumbling-block High Wood. Later in the day it was taken, however, while the 113th Brigade got as far as the edge of Longueval, meeting a severe counter-attack which was rolled back in ruin by rifles and machine-guns. The Seventeenth Division gained some ground, but both brigades, the 51st and 52nd, were held up by a withering fire before reaching Flers. The 64th Brigade on their left met with equal opposition and could not get forward. Everywhere there were signs of a strong German rally for the evident purpose of covering the removal of their guns and stores. It was well maintained and well organised, so that the object was attained. It became clearer with every day that an artillery barrage was still a necessity for an infantry advance.

On August 27 the advance was continued. Outside the Fifth Corps boundaries the Fourth Corps on the left was encircling Bapaume and pushing advanced guards on to Maplecourt and Frémicourt, while Rawlinson's men on the right were facing Trones Wood and the Guillemont Ridge. In the early morning, with a moon shining brightly, the whole front of the Fifth Corps was on fire once more

BYNG'S THIRD ARMY

and rolling eastwards. By 9 A.M. the 113th Brigade were through Longueval and in touch with the Fourth Army near the Sugar Refinery. The 114th Brigade attempted to pass north of Delville Wood, but after some confused fighting were held on the line of the Flers—Longueval Road. Flers, however, had been taken by the 50th Brigade, though the Germans made a strong fight of it and at one time reoccupied the village. Whatever the general morale of the enemy may have been there was no immediate weakening in the actual fighting power of his line. The Twenty-first Division made only a moderate advance, but they got ahead of their neighbours. The 6th Dragoon Guards, who were now furnishing the patrols, were withdrawn, as it was clear that the Germans meant to stand.

On the morning of August 28 they were still in position, and the day was mainly devoted to reorganising the infantry and bombarding the German lines, together with all the roads which lay eastwards. Early next morning the Welsh advanced once more, the 113th Brigade on one side of Delville Wood and the 114th on the other, with the result that this sinister graveyard was surrounded and the line carried definitely to the east of it. Morval still held out, but Lesbœufs was overrun. There was weakening all along the German line, which meant no doubt that they had completed the withdrawal of their more essential impedimenta. Flers and Gueudecourt both fell to the Seventeenth Division, almost without a battle. The Twenty-first Division was also able to move forward with no great difficulty as far as Beaulencourt and the line of the road from that village to Bapaume. This new line was held

Chapter IV.

The Attack of Byng's Third Army.
August 27.

August 28.

CHAPTER IV.

The Attack of Byng's Third Army.
August 30.

with great determination by the enemy, who were still, as must be admitted, masters of the situation to the extent that though forced to retire they would still retire in their own fashion. The Welsh attacking Morval that night found the place was strongly held and no progress possible.

August 30 was to show that the German rearguards were by no means demoralised and were not to be unduly hustled. It is impossible not to admire the constancy in adversity of Hans and Fritz and Michel, whatever one may think of the mentality of the Vons who had placed them in this desperate position. Morval still held its own against the Welsh, and the Seventeenth Division could not reach the clear line in front of them which is furnished by the Peronne—Bapaume Road. Beaulencourt was also retained by the enemy, as the patrols discovered to their cost. The line was still strong and menacing. There was inaction on August 31, which was spent in bombardment and preparation.

Sept. 1.

At 2 A.M. on September 1 the Twenty-first Division attacked Beaulencourt and carried it with a rush, and a strong attempt to regain it after dawn cost the enemy heavy losses. During the morning the Welshmen on the right flank attacked Morval and were at last successful in taking this strong position. There was very heavy fighting all day round Sailly-Sallisel, where the 113th and 115th Welsh Brigades made repeated efforts to envelop and capture the village. There were several checks, but the gallant Welshmen stuck to their task, and before evening the place had fallen and the general British line was well to the east of it. On the other hand, the Seventeenth and Twenty-first Divisions had a bad day in front of Le Transloy and the Sugar Factory, having nothing to show for considerable losses, the 9th West Ridings being especially hard hit. None the less the Seventeenth was hard at it again next morning, for it was imperative to keep up the pressure without any relaxation. On this day, September 2, the plan was that the 50th and 52nd Brigades should work round on each side of the village while the artillery kept the defenders from interfering. This attack, though delayed for some time, eventually succeeded, the 6th Dorsets clearing up the ruins, while the Twenty-first Division, after several brave attempts, drove the tenacious German garrison out of the Sugar Factory. The 10th West Yorkshires, under Colonel Thomas, did particularly good work in linking up the two divisions. Altogether it was a very satisfactory morning's work, and the 50th Brigade added to it in the evening by capturing in a fine attack the village of Rocquigny, and pushing patrols on into Barastre, which was found to be empty. On this day, as the Corps front had contracted, the Twenty-first Division was drawn back into reserve. It may be remarked that in all these operations Robertson's Seventeenth Division had the supreme satisfaction of hurling the enemy out of a long series of villages which they had themselves been forced to relinquish under the pressure of the great March advance.

CHAPTER IV.

The Attack of Byng's Third Army. Sept. 1–3.

It was clear now that the Germans, either of their own will or driven by the constant pressure, were withdrawing their rearguards, so that in the early morning of September 3 no touch could be gained by patrols. By 6 A.M. the British advance guards were well on their way, streaming forward to the

Sept. 3–6.

CHAPTER IV.
The Attack of Byng's Third Army.
Sept. 3–6.

Canal du Nord, from the eastern bank of which the eternal machine-guns were rapping away once more, stopping the 50th Brigade in an attempt to make a direct advance. There were no bridges left, so nothing further could be done that day, which brought the corps front up to the western bank from Manancourt to the north-east of Etricourt. On September 4, however, the crossing was effected without any very great difficulty, and bridge-heads established by both the divisions in the line.

On September 5 the 114th Brigade attacked the trench system round Equancourt without success. The 51st Brigade had better luck to the north of the village and gained a good bit of ground. The 7th Lincolns were held up with considerable loss in the first advance on account of some misunderstanding about the starting-point and insufficient touch with the Forty-second Division on their left. The 7th Borders, a battalion made up of Cumberland and Westmoreland Yeomanry, carried on the attack and found the village deserted. The day ended with the right flank of the Fifth Corps in touch with the Third Corps to the northwest of Nurlu, while the left flank joined the Fourth Corps north of Vallulart Wood. That night the Twenty-first Division came back into line, taking the place of the Welshmen who had done such splendid and strenuous service since August 22.

September 6 and 7 were occupied in a slow but steady advance which absorbed Equancourt, Fins, and Sorel-le-Grand. On September 8 matters were less one-sided, as the Twenty-first Division, acting in close liaison with Rawlinson at Peizières, attacked Vaucelette Farm and Chapel Crossing. It

BYNG'S THIRD ARMY 95

must have been with peculiar ardour and joy that
General Campbell and his men flung themselves
upon the positions which they had held so heroically
upon March 21. Here after six months were their
complete vindication and revenge. The fighting
was carried on into September 9, the Seventeenth
Division joining in on the left in close touch with
the New Zealanders of the Fourth Corps. It was
clear that the Germans meant standing if they could
and the struggle was a very hard one, but before
evening much of the ground had reverted to the
two divisions which were both, by a peculiar coincidence, more or less in their old positions. There
were attack and counter-attack, and a good price
paid for all that was gained. There are days when
land is cheap and days when it is the dearest thing
upon earth. At the end of this fight the Germans
were in a continuous trench on one side of the ridge
and the British in a corresponding position on the
other. It became more and more clear that the
days of pursuit and rearguard actions were over,
and that the whole British front in this quarter
was up against a fixed battle position of the enemy
—or at the least against the strong outposts in
front of a fixed battle position. This important fact
regulates the whole situation up to the great attack
of September 29.

Chapter IV.
The Attack of Byng's Third Army.
Sept. 6–10.

September 10 and 11 were spent in local encounters
in the Chapel Crossing and Vaucelette Farm district,
the Germans striving hard by these outpost engagements to prevent the British line from getting within
striking distance of the old Hindenburg position,
behind which they hoped to rally their dishevelled
forces. The British were equally eager to break

Sept. 10–18.

down this screen and get at the solid proposition behind it. The weather was terrible, rising at one time to the height of a cyclone, which disarranged the assembly. On September 12 there was a more serious British advance, the Fourth Corps on the left attacking the Trescault Spur, while the Welsh, who had now relieved the Seventeenth Division, were to go forward on their flank. The Germans clung desperately to their ground, however, and after a long day of alternate advance and retreat the British line was where it had been in the morning. A position called African Trench lay in front of the Welshmen, and it was not possible to carry it in face of the very severe machine-gun fire. From this date until September 18 there was no advance and no change on the front of the Fifth Corps save that Pinney's Thirty-third Division came in to patch its worn array.

On September 18 the Fifth Corps attacked once more in conjunction with Rawlinson's Army on its right, the final objective being the trench lines south of Villers-Guislain—Gauche Wood. The advance was made by the Welsh Division opposite to Gouzeaucourt, the Seventeenth in front of Gauche Wood, and the Twenty-first to the immediate south. It was preceded by field barrage, heavy barrage, machine barrage, trench mortar bombardment, and every refinement of artillery practice as elaborated in this long war. The results of a hard day's fighting were rather mixed. The Welsh Division was held near Gouzeaucourt and finished up in its own original line, leaving the left flank of the 52nd Brigade exposed. The two other divisions were able, after hard fighting, to reach their objectives, including Gauche Wood.

The Twenty-first Division had a particularly trying and yet successful day, all three brigades being heavily engaged and enduring considerable losses in capturing the very ground which they had held on March 21. Their advance was complicated by a mine-field, laid down by themselves and so well laid that it was still in a very sensitive condition, while the dug-outs had been so undisturbed that the 1st Lincolns actually found their own orderly papers upon the table. In the fighting the 62nd Brigade led the way with complete success, and it was not until the 64th and the 110th Brigades passed through it and began to debouch over the old No Man's Land that the losses became serious, Epéhy and Peizières being thorns in their flesh. Colonel Holroyd Smith of the 15th Durhams was killed, but the 64th Brigade made good its full objective, the 1st East Yorks capturing a German howitzer battery, together with the horses which had just been hooked in. At one time the Germans got round the left flank of the Division and the situation was awkward, but Colonel Walsh of the 9th Yorks Light Infantry, with his H.Q. Staff, made a dashing little attack on his own, and drove the enemy back, receiving a wound in the exploit. The Twenty-first Division, save on the right, had all its objectives. The left of the Third Corps had not prospered equally well, so that a defensive line had to be built up by Campbell in the south, while Robertson did the same in the north, the whole new position forming a marked salient. Two efforts of the enemy to regain the ground were beaten back. The southern divisions had been much troubled by flanking fire from Gouzeaucourt, so an effort was made that night to get possession of this place, the

6th Dorsets and 10th West Yorkshires of the 50th Brigade suffering in the attempt. This attack was led by General Sanders, who had succeeded Gwyn, Thomas as Brigadier of the 50th, but he was himself killed by a shell on September 20. Some 2000 prisoners and 15 field-guns were the trophies taken in this operation by the Fifth Corps. Gouzeaucourt was shortly afterwards evacuated, but there was no other change on the front until the great battle which shattered the Hindenburg Line and really decided the war. All of this fighting, and especially that on September 18, has to be read in conjunction with that already narrated in the story of the Fourth Army on the right.

Having brought Shute's Fifth Corps up to the eve of the big engagement we shall now ask the reader to cast his mind back to August 21, the first day of General Byng's advance, and to follow Haldane's Sixth Corps on the northern flank of the Army during these same momentous and strenuous weeks. It will then be more easy to trace the operations of Harper's Fourth Corps, which was intermediate between Shute and Haldane.

Haldane's Sixth Corps, like its comrades of the Third Army, had gone through the arduous days of March and had many a score to pay back to the Germans. It was a purely British Corps, consisting upon the first day of battle of five fine divisions, the Second (Pereira), Third (Deverell), Sixty-second (Braithwaite), Fifty-ninth (Whigham), and the Guards. With four Regular units out of five, Haldane's Sixth Corps might have been the wraith of the grand old Mons army come back to judgment. The First Cavalry Division, also reminiscent of Mons,

BYNG'S THIRD ARMY

was in close support, ready to take advantage of any opening.

The first advance in the early morning was made by the 99th Brigade of the Second Division on the south, and the 2nd Guards Brigade on the north, the latter being directed upon the village of Moyenneville, while the 99th Brigade was to carry Moyblain Trench, the main German outpost position, 1000 yards in front of the line. The right of the line was formed by the 1st Berks and the left by the 23rd Royal Fusiliers, the latter having a most unpleasant start, as they were gas-shelled in their assembly places and had to wear their masks for several hours before zero time. Any one who has worn one of these contrivances for five consecutive minutes will have some idea what is meant by such an ordeal, and how far it prepares a man for going into battle. Only a very expert man can keep the goggles clean, and one is simultaneously gagged, blinded, and half smothered, with a horrible death awaiting any attempt at amelioration.

At five o'clock nine tanks moved forward behind a crashing stationary barrage, and the infantry followed eagerly through a weak German fire. In spite of all precautions the Fusiliers had lost 400 men from gas, but otherwise the casualties were very small. It may be remarked that many of these serious gas cases occurred from the reek of the gas out of the long grass when the sun dried the dew, showing how subtle and dangerous a weapon is this distillation of mustard. Some small consolation could be gained by the British soldier suffering from these hellish devices, by the knowledge that our chemists, driven to retaliate, had in mustard gas, as in every other

CHAPTER IV.

The Attack of Byng's Third Army. August 21.

CHAPTER IV.

The Attack of Byng's Third Army.
August 21.

poison, produced a stronger brew than the original inventor. Well might the German garrison of Lens declare that they wished they could have dropped that original inventor into one of his own retorts.

The advance of the Guards kept pace on the left with that of the Second Division. The 2nd Brigade went forward with Moyenneville for its immediate objective. The 1st Coldstream in the north were to carry the village, while the 1st Scots were to assemble in the low ground north of Ayette, and to carry the attack to the Ablainzeville-Moyenneville Ridge. The 3rd Grenadiers were then to pass through the Scots and to capture the line of the railway. The opening of the attack was much the same as in the case of the troops on the right, save that no difficulty was experienced from gas. There were few losses in the two leading battalions, which took many prisoners, and it was only the 3rd Grenadiers who, as they neared the railway, met a good deal of machine-gun fire, but pushed on in spite of it and made good the line of their objective.

In the meantime the 9th Brigade of the Third Division had moved through the ranks of the 99th Brigade, and had carried on the advance in the southern area. They advanced with the 1st Northumberland Fusiliers on the right and 4th Royal Fusiliers behind them. The latter had the misfortune to lose Colonel Hartley and 50 men from a shell-burst while moving into position. The left front of the brigade was formed by the 13th King's Liverpools. The whole line advancing in open order passed on without a check, save from mist which caused loss of direction and constant reference to the compass. Over a series of trenches the line plodded its way, clearing up occasional machine-guns and their crews. By 9.15 they were on the railway embankment.

The 8th Brigade (Fisher) of the Third Division had also advanced on the left of the 9th, keeping pace with it so far as the fog would allow. The 7th Shropshires were on the left, in touch with the Guards. The 1st Scots Fusiliers were on the right and the 2nd Royal Scots in support. The attack was directed upon Courcelles, which was carried by the Scots Fusiliers and mopped up by the 8th Royal Lancasters. From the village a sharp slope leads down to the railway line and here the opposition was very strong, the ground being closely swept by rifle and machine-gun fire. Behind two tanks the leading battalions rushed forward and the railway was rushed, with 200 prisoners. The position was organised, and touch established with the Guards on the left and with the 9th Brigade on the right. The 9th Brigade found it difficult, however, to get touch with the Sixty-third Naval Division on their right, that unit having experienced considerable difficulties and losses. The 76th Brigade, the remaining unit of the Third Division, had the 2nd Suffolks and 1st Gordons close up to the line, and all of these battalions were much mixed up owing to the persistent fog.

A very determined pocket of German infantry and machine-gunners had remained in front of the left flank of the Sixty-third Division, formed by the 188th Brigade. These men were now on the right rear of the 9th Brigade, but the situation was obscure and nothing was certain save that the British line was not yet continuous and solid. In spite of a

Chapter IV.

The Attack of Byng's Third Army. August 21.

concentration of artillery the Germans were still holding out next morning, being the only hostile units to the west of the railway line on the Sixth Corps sector.

An attempt had been made to get forward to Achiet-le-Grand, in which part of the Sixty-third Division on the right and two companies of the Gordons participated. The Ansons and the Gordons both lost considerably in this attack and were unable to reach the village, though they advanced the line by 500 yards. Lack of artillery support, while the enemy guns were numerous and active, was the cause of the check.

The night of August 21 was quiet on most parts of this new front of the Third Army, but at early dawn a counter-attack developed before the Sixty-third Division and before the 8th Brigade. An S.O.S. barrage was called for and promptly given in each case, which entirely extinguished the attack upon the Sixty-third. On the 8th Brigade front some of the German infantry got as far forward as the railway line but were quickly hurled back again by bombs and the bayonet. At 7.45 A.M. the enemy again made a rush and occupied one post of the railway, from which, as well as from the posts on the right of the 9th Brigade where the railway line was not yet in British hands, he enfiladed the front defences during the day, causing many casualties, until in the evening the post was retaken by the 1st Northumberland Fusiliers. Among the gas cases sent to the rear this day, though his injuries had been incurred during the assembly, was General Fisher of the 8th Brigade.

The Guards in the north had also encountered the attack of the early morning of August 22, which seems to have been general along the line, though at no part very vigorous. This particular section of it was delivered near Hamelincourt by the Fortieth Saxon Division, who suffered terribly in the venture. The rest of the day was comparatively quiet and was spent in arranging the attack for the morrow. This attack was planned with the idea of outflanking the German position at Achiet-le-Grand, which had shown itself to be dangerously strong. It was determined to outflank it both upon the north and the south. With this intention the Third Division was to capture Gomiecourt during the night of August 22. Farther north two fresh divisions, the famous Fifty-sixth London Territorials, and the Fifty-second from Palestine, were ordered to prolong the line of the Guards, all under General Haldane, and to capture Hamelincourt, Boyelles, and Boiry Becquerelle, with as much more as they could get, on the early morning of August 23. On the front of the Fourth Corps on the right the advance was entrusted to the Thirty-seventh Division and to the Forty-second Division on the bank of the Ancre.

The attack upon Gomiecourt, which was to be the prelude of the day's work, since all advance to the south was impossible while that village was in German hands, was carried out by the well-tried 76th Brigade, the 8th Royal Lancasters and 2nd Suffolks in the front line, with the 1st Gordons in close support. Tanks were to lead the van, but they were unable to get across the railway embankment in time. The assault, which began at 4 in the morning, was preceded by a short crashing bombardment of heavy shells upon the doomed village. It had hardly ceased before the Suffolks and Lancasters were swarming

CHAPTER IV.

The Attack of Byng's Third Army.

August 22, 23.

Chapter IV.

The Attack of Byng's Army.

August 22, 23.

down the street, and the place was secured with little loss. Whilst this brisk and successful affair was going on, the 13th King's Liverpools of the 9th Brigade on the right made an advance to keep the line level, taking some prisoners and three guns. This was the more important as the weak point of the situation had always been to the south and most of the damage sustained was by enfilade fire from this direction.

The 8th Brigade, now under the command of Colonel Henderson, kept pace with the 76th Brigade in their advance, occupying the ground north of Gomiecourt. The 2nd Royal Scots and 7th Shropshires were in the lead. There was very heavy fire and the losses were considerable, but the machine-gun nests were rooted out with the bayonet, and the full objective was attained. Farther north the attack was carried on by the 3rd Grenadier Guards and the 1st Scots. These were successful in taking the village of Hamelincourt and the trench system south of it, while keeping in touch with the Fifty-sixth Division to the north of them. The 1st Coldstream was then pushed through and crossed the Arras — Bapaume Road, gaining a position eventually from which they looked south upon Ervillers.

Farther north still both the Fifty-sixth and the Fifty-second Divisions had joined in the advance, moving forward to the line of the great high road which runs from north to south. Bridges had been thrown over the Cojeul River by the sappers of the Fifty-ninth Division, who had held this front—the workers having to wear gas masks during their labours. To the 470th Field Company R.E. belongs the credit of this most difficult job, under the direction of Colonel

Coussmaker. Over these bridges passed the Fifty-second Division, while south of them the attack was urged by the 168th Brigade of the Fifty-sixth Division, with several villages for their objective. The 13th London (Kensingtons) were on the right, the 4th London in the centre, and the 14th London (London Scottish) on the left. The advance went without a hitch, save that touch was lost with the Guards on the right. This was regained again in the evening, however, when the Brigade found itself to the north of Croisilles and close to the old Hindenburg Line. The Fifty-second Division had also reached the line where it runs across the Sensée valley.

The main advance in front of Haldane's Corps had been entrusted to the Second Division, who advanced through the ranks of the Third Division after the capture of Gomiecourt. This advance was on a three-brigade front. On the right was the 99th Brigade, in touch with the 63rd Brigade of the Thirty-seventh Division to the south of them. This Brigade was told off to keep the flank, but it captured 500 prisoners in the process. On the left was the 6th Brigade, which had been ordered, with the help of eight whippets, to attack Ervillers. In the centre the 5th Brigade with ten whippets was to carry Behagnies and Sapignies. This considerable attack was timed for 11 o'clock.

Gomiecourt having fallen, the 5th Brigade used it as a screen, passing round to the north of it and then turning south to Behagnies. The 2nd Highland Light Infantry headed for that village, while the 24th Royal Fusiliers advanced to the storm of Sapignies. The 2nd Oxford and Bucks were in reserve.

106 THE BRITISH CAMPAIGN, 1918

CHAPTER IV.

The Attack of Byng's Third Army. August 23.

The ten light tanks which led the attack had a series of adventures. Three were knocked out by a gun on the railway. The other seven under heavy gun-fire swerved to the right, got out of the divisional area, and on the principle that any fight is better than no fight, joined with the Thirty-seventh Division in their attack upon Achiet-le-Grand, where they did good service. In the meantime, the tankless 5th Brigade moved round Gomiecourt, coming under very heavy fire on their left flank. Colonel Brodie, a most gallant V.C. officer of the Highland Light Infantry, was killed, and Colonel Cross of the Oxfords wounded, by this fire. The day was very hot, the men exhausted, and the losses severe. The new position was organised, therefore, and the advance suspended for the present.

The 6th Brigade had advanced on the left of the 5th, heading for Ervillers, with the 1st King's Liverpools and the 2nd South Staffords in the lead. The front waves, assisted by light tanks, rapidly broke down all opposition, and Ervillers was taken about 2 P.M. All movement beyond the village was checked by very heavy fire from the high ground to the northeast, so that Mory Copse, the next objective, was found to be unattainable. The object of the British Commanders was never to pay more for a position than it was worth, or buy a machine-gun at the cost of half a battalion. On the other hand, papers captured during the day showed beyond all doubt that the object of the Germans was to make an orderly retreat as far as the Hindenburg Line, so that it was clearly the game to hustle and bustle them without cessation.

August the 24th was a heavy day in the Sixth

BYNG'S THIRD ARMY

Corps, who were ordered to push on and gain ground to the utmost extent along the whole front. In order to strengthen the movement, the Canadian Corps had been very quietly and deftly removed from the right wing of Rawlinson's Army and transferred to the left wing of Byng's Army, in touch with the Fifty-second Division.

Chapter IV.

The Attack of Byng's Third Army. August 24.

It will be remembered that the Second Division, though they had taken Ervillers, had been pinned down there by German fire, while they had failed to take Behagnies or Sapignies. Both these movements were now resumed. In the night of August 23–24 the 1st King's Liverpools advanced from Ervillers upon Mory, but were held up by very heavy fire. The 3rd Guards Brigade on the north was advancing successfully upon St. Leger and this had the effect of outflanking the Mory position on that side. St. Leger was taken by the 2nd Scots Guards and the 1st Welsh, who cleared it in the course of the afternoon. They could get no farther, however, until the Second Division had completed its task at Mory. This was now in the hands of the 99th Brigade, who, headed by the 1st Berkshires, with the 1st Royal Rifles behind them, and a spearhead of tanks in front, broke down all opposition and captured Mory Copse, a very formidable position full of emplacements and dug-outs. By this success the threat was removed from the right of the Guards, and all was clear for their further advance upon Ecoust.

The Sixty-second Yorkshire Division had now moved up to relieve the Second Division, but the latter were determined before their withdrawal to complete their unfinished tasks. In the early morning of August 25 the attacks upon the two obdurate villages were resumed, after a very heavy bombardment. The new venture was splendidly successful. The 2nd Highland Light Infantry and the 24th Royal Fusiliers rushed into Behagnies while it was still dark and cleared out the whole village. This enabled the force to get to the rear of Sapignies, which was stormed by the 2nd Oxfords—a battalion with such proud traditions that even now in semi-official documents it is still the 52nd Light Infantry. 300 prisoners and 150 machine-guns were taken in the village, a proportion which illustrates how far machines were taking the places of men in the depleted German Army. Having gloriously tidied up its front the Second Division now stood out while the Sixty-second took its place.

It will be remembered that the Fifty-second and Fifty-sixth Divisions had fought their way to the Hindenburg Line on August 23. This was too formidable an obstacle to be taken in their stride, and the most that could be hoped was that they should get into a good position for the eventual attack. The Fifty-second Division had shown the metal of the Palestine Army by a very fine advance which made them masters of Henin. On their right was the 167th Brigade, with the 1st London and the 7th and 8th Middlesex in the line. These troops pushed right into the outskirts of Croisilles, but it was clear that new German divisions were in the line, and that the resistance had very much hardened. The Londoners were unable to hold the village, and the Fifty-second Division was also held up on Henin Hill by very strong fire. Matters seemed to have come to a stand in that quarter.

Early on the morning of the 25th the Guards 3rd

Brigade and the 186th and the 187th Brigades of the Sixty-second Division made a resolute advance to clear their front and get nearer to that terrible paling which was meant to enclose the German domain. It was a day of very hard fighting for all three brigades, and they had ample evidence that the German line had indeed been powerfully reinforced, and had no intention of allowing General Byng to establish himself in the very shadow of their fortifications if they could hold him off. The opening was inauspicious, for by some mistake there was an error of half an hour in starting-time between the two divisions. As a result the Guards found themselves on the line of road between Mory and St. Leger with an open flank and under heavy enfilade fire, which made many gaps in the ranks of the 1st Grenadiers. At the same time the leading tanks were put out of action on that flank. In the centre the tanks lost their way in the mist, but the 2nd Scots Guards pushed ahead in spite of it. Banks Trench, however, in front of them was very strongly held and the assault was not pressed. On the left the 1st Welsh were in St. Leger Wood, but Croisilles was still untaken and the advance could not be carried forward as the machine-guns from this village swept the country. About 9 A.M. the enemy buzzed out of the Hindenburg Line and fell upon the Scots Guards, but were shot back again into their cover. During these operations the Guards captured a battery of field-guns.

The Sixty-second West Yorkshire Territorials on the right of the Guards had an equally arduous day. They had found the same difficulties in getting forward, but at 5 P.M. the enemy had the indiscretion to counter-attack, and when once he masks his own

CHAPTER IV.

The Attack of Byng's Third Army. August 25.

machine-guns he has ceased to be formidable. His attack was near Mory Copse and aimed at the junction between the two divisions, but it was heavily punished and shredded away to nothing. About 7 P.M. he tried another advance upon the right of the Sixty-second Division and won his way up to the line, but was thrown out again by the 5th West Ridings and driven eastward once more. The 186th Brigade, forming the right of the division, co-operated with the Fourth Corps in their attack upon Favreuil, which place was captured.

On the evening of August 25 Haldane's Sixth Corps, which had become somewhat unwieldy in size, was limited to the north on a line just south of Croisilles, so that the Fifty-second, Fifty-sixth, and Fifty-seventh Divisions all became Fergusson's Seventeenth Corps, which was thus thrust between the Sixth Corps and the Canadians, who had not yet made their presence felt upon this new battle-ground. The Seventeenth Corps was now the left of the Third Army, and the Canadians were the right of the First Army. The immediate task of both the Sixth and Seventeenth Corps was the hemming in and capture of Croisilles, and the reoccupation of the old army front line. August 26 was a quiet day on this front, but on August 27 the Guards and the Sixty-second Division were ordered forward once more, the former to attack Ecoust and Longatte, the other to storm Vaulx-Vraucourt. The First German Division encountered was easily driven in. The second, however, the Thirty-sixth, was made in a sterner mould and was supported by a strong artillery, large and small. The 2nd Grenadiers and 2nd Coldstream in the front line of the Guards

1st Brigade got forward for nearly a mile on each flank, but were held up by a withering fire in the centre, so that the flanks had eventually to come back. The Fifty-sixth Division of the Seventeenth Corps had not yet captured Croisilles, from which a counter-attack was made upon the left flank of the 2nd Coldstream, which was handsomely repulsed.

Chapter IV.

The Attack of Byng's Third Army. August 25.

On the whole, however, it had been an unsatisfactory day and the Sixty-second had been equally unable to get forward, so that none of the objectives had been gained. The Seventeenth Corps and the Canadians in the north were both advancing, however, and it was possible that the position in the south might alter as a consequence.

Such was indeed found to be the case on August 28, for the Fifty-sixth Division was able this day to get possession of Croisilles, which eased the situation to the south. The Guards and the Sixty-second pushed forwards, following always the line of least resistance, so that by evening they were 1200 yards forward at some points, though the right of the Sixty-second Division was still pinned to its ground. That evening the Third Division replaced the Guards, and the same tactics were pursued on the following day. The 76th Brigade was now in the front line to the south of Croisilles, with the hard-worked Sixty-second Division still on their right. A sugar factory was the chief impediment in front of the latter. The right of the division got forward during the day and occupied the old army trenches.

August 30 was once again a day of heavy fighting, the Seventeenth and Sixth Corps, represented by the Fifty-sixth, Third, and Sixty-second Divisions, closing in upon the Hindenburg Line and attacking the last villages which covered its front. The tanks had miscarried, and the infantry at 5 A.M. had to go forward alone. On the right the 185th and 186th Brigades of the Sixty-second Division both made good progress, the obnoxious sugar factory was taken, and though Vaulx could not be cleared it was partly occupied. Next day saw the dour Yorkshiremen still sticking to their point, and fighting with varying success in and out of the village. At times they had flooded through it, and yet again they were beaten back. By the morning of September 1 the 186th Brigade had possession of Vaulx-Vraucourt and were on the high ground to the east of the village. Next morning they had Vaux Trench as well, but about ten o'clock in the forenoon of September 2 a strong counter sent them reeling back in some disorder. Gathering themselves together in grim North Country fashion they went forward again and cleared Vaulx Wood before evening. That night, after a very desperate and costly term of service, the Sixty-second was relieved by the Second Division.

The experiences of the Third Division from the August 30 attack were as arduous as those already described. On that morning the 76th Brigade, with the Suffolks and Gordons in the lead, got forward well at the first, though they lost touch with the Londoners to the north. The Suffolks were on that side and the gap enabled the Germans to get round to their left rear with disastrous results, as the losses were heavy and the battalion had to fall back. The Gordons had to adjust their line accordingly. This rebuff had lost most of the ground which had been gained early in the day. General Deverell now sent up the 9th Brigade, as the 76th was much worn, but the 1st Gordons remained in the fight.

On August 31 the 9th Brigade attacked the Vraucourt position, with the 1st Gordons, battle-weary but still indomitable, on the right, the 4th Royal Fusiliers in the centre, and the 13th King's Liverpools on the left. It was known that no less than three new German divisions had been thrown in, and however the fighting might turn it was certain that the attrition was going merrily forward. The assembly was unfortunately much disturbed by the German barrage, which fell with particular severity upon the Fusiliers in the centre. At 5.15 A.M. the line moved forward, but again the luck was against the Fusiliers, who were opposed by a particularly dangerous machine-gun nest in a sunken road. One company endeavoured to rush it, but all the officers save one, and most of the men, were mown down. A tank which endeavoured to help them met with a strange fate, as a German officer managed, very gallantly, to get upon the top of it, and firing through the ventilation hole with his revolver, put the whole crew out of action—a feat for which in the British service he would certainly have had his V.C.

The Fusiliers were hung up, but the King's on the left had carried the village of Ecoust, getting in touch with the right of the Fifty-sixth Division in Bullecourt Avenue. Many hundreds of the enemy were taken, but some pockets still remained on the southern edge of the village, and fired into the flank of the unfortunate Fusiliers. The King's then attempted during the long day to throw out their right flank and get in touch with the left of the Gordons so as to obliterate the sunken road, which

CHAPTER IV.

The Attack of Byng's Third Army. August 31.

was the centre of the mischief. The ground was absolutely open, however, and the fire commanded it completely. Under these circumstances Colonel Herbert of the 1st Northumberland Fusiliers, which was in reserve, suggested that the attack be postponed until dusk. This was done, and at 8 P.M. Herbert's men overran the sunken road, capturing the guns. Ecoust was also completely cleared of the enemy. So ended this day of vicissitudes in which the 9th Brigade, with heavy loss, had struggled through many difficulties and won their victory at the last. A further advance during the night by both the 9th and the 76th Brigades straightened the whole line from Ecoust to the south.

On the morning of September 1 the Fifty-second Division had relieved the Fifty-sixth Division, both of the Seventeenth Corps, in the Croisilles sector, and was in close touch with the Third Division to the south. Both divisions went forward with no great difficulty at the appointed hour, the three battalions of the 9th Brigade being all in the line once more. The important trench known as Noreuil Switch was captured in this advance. It may well seem to the reader that the gains were tardily and heavily bought at this stage of the operations, but it is to be always borne in mind that Fergusson and Haldane in particular were up against the old intricate trench system, and away from that open fighting which can alone give large results. To others there was always some way round, but here there was an unbroken obstacle which must be frontally attacked and broken down by pure persistence. In these operations the new machine-gun organisation proved to be particularly efficient, and B Company of the

3rd Battalion Machine-Gun Corps did essential work in winning the way for the 9th Brigade. The whole battle was a long steady contest of endurance, in which the Germans were eventually worn out by the persistence of their opponents.

CHAPTER IV.

The Attack of Byng's Third Army. Sept. 2.

The advance was renewed along this area on September 2, the object of the Fifty-second Division being to encircle Quéant from the south and west, while that of the Third and Sixty-second Divisions was to gain the east of Lagnicourt and the high ground east of Morchies. The fortunes of the Sixty-second Division have already been briefly described. On the front of the Third Division the 8th Brigade, strengthened by one battalion from each of the other brigades, took up the heavy task, the 7th Shropshires, 2nd Royal Scots, and 1st Scots Fusiliers forming from right to left the actual line of battle. The last-named battalion by a happy chance joined up on the left with its own 5th Battalion in the Fifty-second Division. They assembled under heavy shelling, some of which necessitated the use of box-respirators. No sooner had the advance begun than the Shropshire men came under machine-gun fire and lost the three tanks which led them. They had gained some ground, but were first brought to a halt and then compelled to retire. In the centre the Royal Scots took Noreuil, which was found to be lightly held. In attempting to get on to the east of this village they found the trenches strongly manned and the fire, both of rifles and machine-guns, so murderous that it was impossible to get forward. The Scots Fusiliers were also faced with strong resistance, including a belt of wire. Three company and eight platoon commanders were down before this obstacle and the sunken road behind it were crossed. Without the aid of tanks the depleted battalion moved on under very heavy fire, and eventually halted in a line with the Royal Scots on their right. To the right of these, as already shown, the Sixty-second Division had also been brought to a stand. A formidable trench, called in the old British days Macaulay Avenue, barred the way and had only been reached by a few of the assailants. It is a fact, however, that Lieutenant R. R. MacGregor of the Scots Fusiliers with five men did force their way in upon this morning, and tenaciously held on to their position until after dark, forming just that little nucleus of determined men by whom great battles are so often won.

There was a momentary check, but it was retrieved by Captain Nagle's company of the 2nd Suffolks, who charged with two companies of the Royal Scots and won a section of the trench. The utmost difficulty was experienced by the Brigadier in keeping in touch with the action, as the ground was so exposed that nearly every runner sent back from the front line was killed or wounded. Colonel Henderson came forward, therefore, about three o'clock and reorganised his dispositions, with the result that before evening the line had been straightened and advanced, with the capture of many prisoners and machine-guns. Meanwhile Quéant to the north had been captured by the Fifty-second Division, and the whole German system of defence was weakening and crumbling, the Seventeenth Corps strongly co-operating with the Canadians upon their left. The enemy's purpose during all this very hard contest was to sacrifice his rearguards if necessary, in order to cover

the retreat of his main body across the Canal du
Nord. There were few more difficult problems in
local fighting during the whole war than how to carry
these successive positions, bravely held and bristling
with machine-guns. That it was finally done was
a great achievement upon the part both of those
who commanded and those who obeyed. Colonel
Vickery's guns, covering the infantry, had much to
do with the final success. How great that success
was could only be judged upon the following morning
when the new divisions which had taken over the
front, the Guards on the left and the Second on the
right, found that all the kick had been taken out of
the Germans, and that a substantial advance could
be made with little loss.

Neither the Guards nor the Third Division encountered serious opposition upon September 3, and a steady, if cautious, forward movement went on all day. The Seventeenth Corps upon the left had turned south in order to clear Mœuvres and Tadpole Copse. By midday the Second Division had cleared both Hermies and Demicourt. Before evening the 2nd Guards Brigade was in the old British front line, which was held during the night. The Canal du Nord was just ahead, and it was realised that this would mark what the Germans intended to make their permanent line. It was all-important to push the rearguard across it and to get any bridges with their eastern exits, if it were in any way possible.

The advance on September 4 was resumed in the face of some sporadic opposition, but by the evening of the 6th the enemy was all across the Canal, and the Sixth Corps was awaiting developments elsewhere. On September 11 steps were

Chapter IV.

The Attack of Byng's Third Army. Sept. 2.

taken, however, to get into striking position for the final fracture of the Hindenburg Line, in view of which it was necessary to gain the Hindenburg front system west of the Canal. On September 12 the main attack was delivered, though on September 11 the Second Division had secured the western ends of the Canal crossings. The centre of the new operation was the attack upon Havrincourt by Braithwaite's Sixty-second Division. This operation was carried out by the 186th and 187th Brigades, the pioneer battalion, 9th Durham Light Infantry, being attached to the former, while eight brigades of field-guns and three groups of heavies lent their formidable assistance. The right of the Sixty-second was in close touch with the Thirty-seventh Division, which was attacking Trescault. The advance of both brigades was uninterrupted, though strongly opposed. The 2/4th Hants and 5th West Ridings on the right, and the 2/4th York and Lancasters with the 5th Yorkshire Light Infantry on the left, trampled down all opposition. The individual is almost lost to sight in the scale of such operations, but a sentence must be devoted to Sergeant Calvert of the last-named battalion, who attacked two machine-guns, bayoneted four and shot three of the crews, taking the rest prisoners. At 7.30, the western edge of the village of Havrincourt had fallen, but the fortified château on the south, in the area of the 186th Brigade, still held its own. It was attacked by the 2/4th West Riding Battalion, who had a most difficult task in the tangled gardens which surrounded the house. At the same time the 2/4th Hants pushed into the village and fought their way right through it. They had to sustain a heavy counter-attack delivered about

7 in the evening by the Twentieth Hanoverian Division, supported by a flight of low-flying aeroplanes. This attack was broken up with great loss by the steady fire of the men of Hampshire and Yorkshire.

In the early morning of September 13 the village was strongly attacked by the enemy, who effected a lodgment in the cemetery and pushed back the British line for 200 yards. A fine return was made by the 5th Devons of the 185th Brigade, who cleared the village once again. Two of the divisional machine-guns held out close to the posts occupied by the Germans—so close that the sergeant in charge shot the battalion leader of the enemy with his revolver. From this time the Sixty-second were left in possession of Havrincourt, which they had thus won for the second time, since it was carried by them in the Cambrai battle of November 20, 1917. General Braithwaite, who was the victor upon each occasion, remarked that if his men had to take it a third time they should, on the cup-tie principle, be allowed to keep it for ever.

Meanwhile the Second Division on the left had made its way slowly but without any serious check as far as London Trench, which brought them nearly level with the Sixty-second, while the Thirty-seventh in the south had captured Trescault and were also well up to the Hindenburg Line. There was no further serious fighting for several days on this front save that the 185th Brigade advanced its line to Triangle Wood on the morning of September 14. This attack was carried out by the 2/20th Londons and was completely successful, as was their subsequent defence against a brisk counter-attack. On September 16 the Sixty-second Division was

Chapter IV.

The Attack of Byng's Third Army.
Sept. 13-14.

relieved by the Third, and the Second Division by the Guards. There was no further fighting until September 18, that general day of battle, when a very severe German attack was made about 6 o'clock in the evening, which covered the whole front of the Third Division and involved the left of the Thirty-seventh Division in the area of the Fourth Corps. After a heavy bombardment there was a determined advance of infantry, having the recapture of Havrincourt for its objective. A number of low-flying aeroplanes helped the German infantry. The attack fell chiefly upon the 1st Scots Fusiliers and 2nd Royal Scots, and some gain was effected by a rush of bombers aided by flame-throwers, but they were finally held and eventually driven back, while 100 prisoners were retained. C Company of the Royal Scots particularly distinguished itself in this action, forming a solid nucleus of resistance round which the whole defence was organised. Nothing further of importance occurred until September 27, the day of the general advance, in this northern portion of the British line.

In order to complete this account of the doings of Byng's Third Army from August 21 onwards, some account must now be given of what was originally the central unit, Harper's Fourth Corps, though its general progress has already been roughly defined by the detailed description of the two Corps on its flanks.

The first task set for this Corps on August 21 was to capture the general line between Irles in the south and Bihucourt in the north, while the flank of this main attack was to be guarded by a subsidiary advance along the valley of the Ancre, and between Puisieux and Miraumont. The first objective of the main attack was Bucquoy, Ablainzeville, and the important high ground to the immediate east of these villages.

The advance commenced in a thick mist, and was undertaken in the case of the main attack by Williams' Thirty-seventh English Division. It was completely successful, and aided by the fire of six heavy and fifteen field brigades of artillery, it swept over its first objectives, the tanks helping materially to break down the opposition. The moral effect of a tank in a fog can be pictured by the least imaginative. Two field-guns and many lighter pieces were taken. The veteran Fifth Division on the right and the Sixty-third Naval Division on the left then passed through the ranks of the Thirty-seventh to enlarge the opening that they had made, carrying the advance on to the limit of the field artillery barrage, and halting at last just west of Achiet-le-Petit. The naval men met with a blaze of machine-gun fire from the edge of Logeast Wood, but they rooted out the nests and occupied the position, though the passage through the tangled brushwood and trees disorganised the units, and progress became slow. The railway line ran right across the front, and this, as usual, had become a formidable and continuous obstacle, which could not be turned. The reserve brigade of the Fifth Division on the right carried Achiet-le-Petit, but could not get over the railway. The Sixty-third was also unable to reach the railway, and found a considerable concentration of Germans opposite to them in the brickworks and cemetery west of Achiet-le-Grand. The tanks had wandered off in the mist, and for the moment the advance had reached its limit. Many of the tanks, as the mist lifted, were hit

CHAPTER IV.

The Attack of Byng's Third Army. August 21.

by the anti-tank guns of the enemy, though some most gallantly crossed the railway line and penetrated the German positions, doing such harm as they could, until they were eventually destroyed.

Meanwhile, the subsidiary attack on the right flank had also been successful up to a point. The New Zealanders on the immediate south of the Fifth Division had gone forward in their usual workman-like fashion, and had taken Puisieux. Upon their right, and next to the Fifth Corps who were beginning their arduous crossing of the Ancre, was the Forty-second Division (Solly-Flood), an ex-Palestine unit of Lancashire Territorials which had won laurels in the March fighting. It had come away with a flying start, and had got as far as the important point named Beauregard Dovecote. There it remained until the early morning of August 22, when the enemy regained it by a spirited attack from a new division. The total effect of the day's work along the whole front of the Fourth Corps had been the capture of 1400 prisoners, of a number of guns, and of an extent of ground which was important, though less than had been hoped for. The main resistance had always been the railway, and the German guns behind it, so that to that extent his line was really inviolate. Indeed from his point of view the whole work of the Third Army on that date might be represented as an attack upon a false front, the real position remaining intact.

The enemy was by no means abashed, and early in the morning of August 22 he showed that he did not propose to surrender the field until he had fought to regain it. At dawn the Fifty-second German Division deployed through Miraumont and fell upon the left of the Fifth Division in one direction, and the Forty-second in the other. As already stated they succeeded in driving back the latter, and Beauregard Dovecote remained as a prize of victory. Some three hundred Germans pushed through between the Fifth Division and the New Zealanders, but were at once attacked by a party of the 1st Devons, assisted by some of the New Zealanders. Corporal Onions of the Devons showed great initiative in this affair, which ended in the capture of the whole of the intruders. He received the V.C. for his gallantry.

Chapter IV. The Attack of Byng's Third Army. August 22.

It was a day of reaction, for the Sixty-third Division in the north was strongly attacked, and was at one time pushed as far as Logeast Wood. They rallied however and came back, but failed to regain the railway at Achiet-le-Grand. Early in the morning of August 23 the Beauregard Dovecote was finally captured by units of the Forty-second and New Zealanders, the enemy falling back to Miraumont. About the same hour in the morning the Sixth Corps in the north had taken Gomiecourt as already described, which strengthened the general position.

Early on August 23 the Thirty-seventh Division came up on the left and relieved the Naval Division. Guns had been pushed into position, so at 11 o'clock in the forenoon it was possible to deliver a strong attack under an adequate barrage upon the line of the railway. The result was a complete success, in spite of the formidable nature of the defences. The imperturbable English infantry flooded over every obstacle, took its inevitable losses with its usual good humour, and established itself upon the farther side of the position, while the tanks, taking advantage of a level crossing, burst through and did very great work. Both Achiet-le-Grand and Bihucourt fell to

August 23.

the Thirty-seventh Division, while the Fifth captured the high ground overlooking Irles, and subsequently pushed on eastwards as far as Loupart Wood. Since Miraumont was still German the flank of Ponsonby's Division was scourged by the machine-guns, and an attempt by the Forty-second Division to relieve the pressure by taking the village had no success, but the Fifth maintained all its gains in spite of the heavy enfilading fire. In this fine operation the Thirty-seventh Division alone captured 1150 prisoners. There were signs, however, of German reaction, especially on the southern flank, where a new division, the Third Naval, had been brought into line.

August 24 was another day of victory. The New Zealanders passed through the depleted ranks of the Fifth Division and made good not only the whole of Loupart Wood, but also Grevillers to the north-east of it. An even more useful bit of work was the storming of Miraumont by the Forty-second Division in the south. This village, which had been nearly surrounded by the advance on the flanks, gave up 500 prisoners and several guns. The Forty-second continued its career of victory to Pys, which they took, and were only stopped eventually by the machine-guns at Warlencourt. This advance greatly relieved the situation on the right flank, which had been a cause for anxiety, and it also, by winning a way to the Ancre, solved the water problem, which had been a difficult one. This day of continued victorious advance was concluded by the occupation of Biefvillers by the united action of the Thirty-seventh and of the New Zealanders.

At 5 A.M. upon August 25 the advance was

resumed, with the Sixty-third Division on the right, the New Zealanders in the centre, and the Thirty-seventh on the left. The naval men found a head wind from the first, for the Germans were holding Le Barque and Thilloy in great strength. No great progress could be made. On the left the New Zealanders and the Thirty-seventh both reached the very definite line of the Bapaume—Arras Road, where they were held by very heavy fire from Bapaume on the right and Favreuil on the left. The splendid Thirty-seventh, with some assistance from the New Zealanders on their south, rushed the wood and village of Favreuil and helped to beat off a German counter-attack by the fresh Hundred and eleventh Division, which was so mauled by aircraft and artillery that it never looked like reaching its objective. Many dead and some abandoned guns marked the line of its retirement.

On August 26 these indefatigable troops were still attacking. It was indeed a most marvellous display of tenacity and will-power. The general idea was to encircle Bapaume from the north and to reach the Cambrai Road. In this the Fifth Division and the New Zealanders were successful, the former reaching Beugnatre, while the latter got as far as the road, but sustained such losses from machine-gun fire that they could not remain there. In the south Thilloy still barred the advance of the Naval Division, which was again repulsed on August 27, when they attacked after a heavy bombardment. There was a pause at this period as the troops were weary and the supplies had been outdistanced. On August 28 the Sixty-third left the Fourth Corps and the Forty-Second took over their line and repeated their experi-

CHAPTER IV.

The Attack of Byng's Third Army. August 25, 26.

ence, having a setback before Thilloy. On August 29 there was a general withdrawal of the German rearguards, the whole opposition dissolved, Thilloy fell to the Forty-second Division, and the New Zealanders had the honour of capturing Bapaume. Up to this time the advance of the Fourth Corps had yielded 100 guns and 6800 prisoners.

Chapter IV.
The Attack of Byng's Third Army.
August 28–31.

On August 30 the whistles were sounding once more and the whole British line was rolling eastwards. It will mark its broader front if we say that on this date the Fifth Corps on the right was in front of Beaulencourt, while the Sixth Corps on the left had taken Vaulx, Vraucourt. The Forty-second Division on this day was unable to hold Riencourt, but the rest of the line got well forward, always fighting but always prevailing, until in the evening they were east of Bancourt and Frémicourt, and close to Beugny. Always it was the same programme, the exploring fire, the loose infantry advance, the rapping machine-guns, the quick concentration and rush—occasionally the summoning of tanks or trench mortars when the strong point was obstinate. So the wave passed slowly but surely on.

On August 31 the Germans, assisted by three tanks, made a strong attack upon the New Zealanders, and a small force pushed in between them and the Fifth Division. They were surrounded, however, a German battalion commander was shot and some sixty of his men were taken. The whole line was restored. On this day the Lancashire men on the right took Riencourt with some prisoners and a battery of guns.

September 2 was a day of hard battle and of victory, the three Corps of General Byng's Army attempting to gain the general line Barastre—Haplincourt—Le Bucquière. The Forty-second Division captured Villers-au-Flos and advanced east of it, while the New Zealanders made good the ridge between there and Beugny. Some 600 prisoners were taken. There was some very fierce fighting round **Beugny** in which the Fifth Division lost six tanks and many men with no particular success. The place was afterwards abandoned.

<small>CHAPTER IV.

The Attack of Byng's Third Army. Sept. 2-9.</small>

The British line was now drawing close to the Hindenburg position, and the Fourth Corps like all the others was conscious of the increased effort which the Germans were making in order to prevent the attackers from gaining all the outlying posts, and being able to carry the main line before every preparation had been made for its defence. For several days there were wrestles for this position or that, which culminated on September 9 in a very sharp tussle between the New Zealanders and a German Jaeger Division at African Trench on the ridge west of Gouzeaucourt. It was a very desperate fight, which some of the old New Zealanders declared to have been the most intense and close which they had experienced since they met the Turks at Gallipoli—a compliment to the Jaeger, but somewhat a reflection upon other units of the German army. In the end the New Zealanders were unable to hold African Trench and had to be content with African Support. The Fifth Division shared in this fighting. This engagement was part of a local co-operation in an attack made by the Fifth Corps in the south.

On September 12 there was a combined attack, which has already been mentioned, by which the Fourth and Sixth Corps should capture Trescault Spur and

Havrincourt. It will be remembered that the latter was captured by the Sixty-second Yorkshire Division. The New Zealanders advanced upon the Spur, where they met with very vigorous opposition from their old enemies, the Jaeger, who fought with great tenacity. The Thirty-seventh Division turned the Spur from the south, however, capturing both Trescault and Bilhem. Two guns and 500 prisoners were captured. On September 18 the Fifth Division together with the Welsh Division of the Fifth Corps undertook a local operation against African Trench, but the indefatigable German Jaeger still remained masters of the situation. At 5.20 P.M. on that day the initiative passed to the enemy, who broke suddenly into a very heavy bombardment, followed by a furious attack upon the left of the Thirty-seventh Division. It made some progress at first and the British losses were heavy, especially in the case of the 1st Herts, a battalion which has many times shown great steadiness and gallantry. Lieutenant Young of this unit rallied his men and counter-attacked at a critical moment, dying single-handed amid the German ranks but winning a posthumous V.C.

We have now brought the record of the Fourth Corps level with that of the Fifth to the south and of the Sixth to the north. It is necessary to give some fuller account of the Seventeenth Corps which had been formed on the left of the Sixth. This will complete the account of General Byng's operations with his Third Army from their inception on August 21 until the eve of the great general battle which was to break out at the end of September.

It has already been stated that on August 25 Sir Charles Fergusson's Seventeenth Corps was formed on the left of General Byng's Third Army and became the northern unit in that force, having the Sixth Corps on its right and the Canadian Corps on its left. It contained at first three divisions, the Fifty-second (Hill), Fifty-sixth (Hull), and Fifty-seventh (Barnes). Two of these had already been heavily engaged in the new advance before becoming part of the Seventeenth Corps. Indeed on the day preceding the entrance of the Corps into the line, the evening of August 24, the Fifty-sixth Division had attacked the Hindenburg Line at Summit Trench and Hill Switch, near Croisilles, without effect. They had now established themselves near their objective and were waiting orders to try again.

Chapter IV.

The Attack of Byng's Third Army. August 25.

The Fifty-second Division, one of the fine units which had been released from Palestine owing to the reinforcements of Indian troops in that country, had also tried for the Hindenburg Line and taken a bit of it upon August 24, but they had found it too hot to hold. They were now lying low on the western borders of Henin Hill, hoping to co-operate with the Canadians of the First Army on their left at some later date. A line of British divisions was now crouching in front of Hindenburg's bars all ready for a spring.

In the new attack it was planned that the Fifty-sixth Londoners should co-operate with the Sixth Corps on their right, and clear the village of Croisilles by outflanking it, while the Fifty-second Division should work on the north of the Cojeul stream in close touch with the big Canadian attack, advancing towards Fontaine-les-Croisilles. The effect of these movements would be that the portion of the Hindenburg Line which faced the Seventeenth

K

130   THE BRITISH CAMPAIGN, 1918

<small>CHAPTER IV.</small> Corps would be attacked from the rear instead of the front.

<small>The Attack of Byng's Third Army. August 26.</small> On August 26 at 3 A.M. the Canadians went forward, as will be told under the head of their operations. The Fifty-second Division kept its place on their right flank, working up along the Cojeul River, and carrying all the objectives allotted to them. By 10.35 A.M. their task had been completed and they were still in close touch with the Canadians. In the afternoon the 155th Brigade on the extreme left, consisting of Scottish Territorials, attacked Henin Hill from the north-west, capturing a succession of machine-gun positions. The crews of these guns got—and indeed accepted—little quarter, fighting staunchly to the last. By 4 o'clock the Fifty-second Division was well into the Hindenburg Line from the Cojeul northwards; and by 5 o'clock the 155th Brigade was across Henin Hill, moving south-east. The whole of this very important position was now in British possession, though there were pockets of the enemy scattered here and there who were holding out to the last. The Fifty-sixth Division on the right was still in front of Croisilles, sending out occasional patrols which reported that the village was still strongly held. Its orders were to maintain pressure but not to advance until the development of the movement in the north should shake the enemy's resistance.

<small>August 27, 28.</small> On August 27 Croisilles and the strong trenches around it were kept under bombardment. The Fifty-sixth Division began to thrust forward its left flank, and made some progress, but was eventually held by very heavy fire from the south. At midday the Fifty-second Division was driving down from the north,

getting to the Sensée River about Fontaine and endeavouring to help the left of the Fifty-sixth Division by moving along the Hindenburg Line. This was partly accomplished, but it was impossible for the Fifty-sixth to get ahead as the troops on their right in the Ledger Trenches had also been held up. That evening the Fifty-second Division after a fine term of service was drawn out and the Fifty-seventh took its place.

The Attack of Byng's Third Army. August 27, 28.

Early on August 28 it was evident that the scheme for pinching out Croisilles had been successful. At 8 A.M. a contact aeroplane reported the village to be empty, and at 8.30 the London patrols were in the main street. There now lay Bullecourt in front of the Fifty-sixth, and Hendecourt and Riencourt in front of the Fifty-seventh Division. At 12.30 the attack was in full swing, lines of the gallant Territorials of London and Lancashire streaming across the low dun-coloured curves which are cut by the famous trenches. It was a long uphill fight, but by 4.30 in the afternoon the 169th Brigade, containing the London Rifle Brigade, the 2nd Londons, and the Westminsters, had fought their way into Bullecourt. There they were held, however, for there were numerous pockets of Germans in their rear, and the machine-guns pelted them from every side, while the village was far from clear. The 167th Brigade on the right had also been held up by machine-guns, all three battalions, the 1st London and the 7th and 8th Middlesex, having heavy losses and being forced back for a time. The Fifty-seventh Division on the left of the line encountered the same desperate resistance, which could only have been overcome by troops who would take no denial. Hendecourt was not reached, but all the gains of the morning were held as a basis for a future advance. The liaison on either flank with the Sixth Corps and the Canadians was complete. It had been a day of very hard and expensive fighting and of no very marked success.

The battle was renewed about midday on August 29, the morning having been devoted to re-pulverising the powder-heap of Bullecourt with heavy artillery, and to clearing up some of the pockets in the immediate front of the advance. The Fifty-sixth Division advanced once more, the 168th Brigade having taken the right of the line. The machine-guns were still very destructive, and the right and centre were held up, though the left made some progress. The general result was to get the British line all round Bullecourt, but the village itself was still defiant. The Fifty-seventh Division on the left had another day of desperate fighting, in which the Lancashire Territorials showed their usual valour. At 4.30 some of them had got through Hendecourt and had penetrated, with great difficulty and suffering heavily, into Riencourt. It was afterwards found that some ardent spirits had even forced their way into the Drocourt—Quéant line, and left their dead there as a proof for those who followed after. The line in the evening was the western outskirts of Hende-court, where they were in touch with the right of the Canadian Division.

At 5 A.M. on the morning of August 30 the Germans, who had a perfectly clear vision of the fact that the loss of the Hindenburg Line must entail the loss of the war, attacked in great force along the general line Ecoust—Bullecourt—Hendecourt, and made some considerable dents in the British front, especially at Bullecourt, which had to be evacuated. The Fifty-seventh were pushed back to the line of the Hendecourt—Bullecourt Road, and abandoned the ruins of an old factory, which is a marked position. This attack corresponds with the one already detailed when the Third Division were driven out of Ecoust, and it is heavy weather indeed when the Third Division begins to make leeway. The Fifty-sixth tried very gallantly to regain Bullecourt by a bombing attack, but it could not be done. The Germans got a footing in Hendecourt, but could not clear it, and the evening saw the Lancashire Territorials and their enemy at close grips among the ruins.

CHAPTER IV.

The Attack of Byng's Third Army. August 30.

On the morning of August 31 the indefatigable Londoners attacked once more, the 4th Londons, London Scottish, and Kensingtons of the 168th Brigade carrying on the work. The factory was soon retaken and so was the Station Redoubt, but Bullecourt itself, squirting flames from every cranny, was still inviolate. On the right the Third Division had recaptured Ecoust, which relieved the general situation. The British bombers got into Bullecourt in the afternoon and before evening they had made good the greater part of the ruins, a handful of Germans still clinging manfully to the eastern edge. That night the Fifty-second came to the front and relieved the Fifty-sixth. In the five days' battle the London division had lost 123 officers and 2600 men. On the other hand they had captured 29 officers and over a thousand men, while they had inflicted very heavy losses upon the enemy.

September 1 saw this long-drawn battle still in full progress. There is nothing more amazing than the way in which the British divisions at this stage

CHAPTER IV.

The Attack of Byng's Third Army. Sept. 1.

of the war without reinforcements carried on the fight from day to day as though they were sustained by some prophetic vision of the imminent victory which was so largely the result of their heroic efforts. With the early morning the Fifty-seventh Division was into Hendecourt, and before seven o'clock the 171st Brigade had completely cleared the village and joined hands with the Canadians on the farther side. There was a great deal of actual bayonet work in this assault, and Lancashire came out triumphant. On the right the Fifty-second Division had a busy morning in clearing out the dug-outs and cellars of Bullecourt. In the afternoon they advanced eastwards and cleared another 500 yards of ground, when they came under very heavy fire from Noreuil on their right flank. The 155th Brigade was lashed with a pelting rain of bullets, one battalion, the 4th Scots Borderers, losing 10 officers and 140 men in a few minutes. The advance was continued, however, until Tank Avenue, the immediate objective, was reached and cleared. It was a splendid example of indomitable perseverance.

The 171st Brigade, which was still advancing on the left, had also undergone the torment of the machine-guns, but some skilful flanking movements by supporting platoons enabled progress to be made and the German posts soon surrendered when there was a danger of being surrounded. Riencourt fell, and by 6.30 the extreme objectives had been gained and touch established on either flank.

The success of this spirited attack, with the heavy losses inflicted, seemed to have cowed the enemy before the Fifty-seventh Division, for the night passed quietly on that front, which was very helpful in allowing the preparations to go forward for the considerable operation planned for next morning.

September 2 was the date for the main attack by the First Army upon the Drocourt—Quéant line south of the Scarpe, to which all the fighting which has been detailed was but a preliminary. The rôle assigned to the Seventeenth Corps was to co-operate with the Canadians by thrusting forward their left flank so as to gain position for an attack upon Quéant from the north. The Sixth Corps on their right was ordered to attack Morchies and Lagnicourt and then push forward vigorously towards Beaumetz. The First Canadian Division, with Gagnicourt for its objective, was on the immediate left of the Seventeenth Corps. The orders to the Seventeenth Corps were that the Fifty-seventh Division should support the Canadian attack, that the Fifty-second Division should conform to the movements of the Fifty-seventh on its left and of the Third on its right, and finally that the Sixty-third Naval Division, now added to the Corps, should move up in support and improve whatever advantages were gained.

At 5 A.M. the barrage fell and the troops moved forward upon one of the critical battles of the war. The grand part played by the Canadians in the north is described elsewhere. The 172nd Brigade of the Fifty-seventh Division advanced splendidly towards the gap which had been formed, a storm of gas shells bursting among their stolid ranks. The leading battalion, the 1st Munster Fusiliers, followed the men of the Dominion through the breach which they had made in the Drocourt—Quéant switch, and then according to plan swung sharply to the right, smashing their way with bomb and bayonet down the whole line of the German position and so clearing the front for their comrades. It was a fine exploit and worthy of the great battalion which carried it out. They were strongly counter-attacked at the moment when, panting and weary, they had reached their full objective, and yet they retained sufficient vitality to drive back the German stormers.

Other elements of the 172nd Brigade had worked south on the right of the Munsters, and got forward as far as Possum Lane, so that they formed a useful defensive flank on the left of the Fifty-second Division. Meanwhile the 171st Brigade had advanced directly from Riencourt Ridge and had cleared up the trenches opposite, which were enfiladed by their comrades.

The Sixty-third Division was now brought forward to play its part, with the 188th Brigade, consisting of Ansons, Marines, and Royal Irish, in the van. At 9 A.M. it passed through the left of the Fifty-seventh Division about a mile south of Gagnicourt. From this point it was continually advancing during the day, being in touch with the First Canadians on the left and with the Fifty-seventh on the right. By nine in the evening it was seated firmly in the Hindenburg Line. The switch line of Drocourt—Quéant had been ruptured as early as 8 in the morning, which was the signal for the Fifty-second Division on the south to advance upon the main Hindenburg Line south-west of Quéant. The 156th Brigade was in the van. Some few parties reached the main objective, but by 10 o'clock the advance had been suspended, as operations had not yet progressed sufficiently elsewhere. The Fifty-second continued, however, to exert pressure at the point of junction between the switch and the Hindenburg support line. All day progress was being made in proportion as the attack drove down from the north, so that by 3 P.M. the front line had been cleared, and before midnight the whole of the German defences, a perfect maze of trenches and wire, were in the hands of the British infantry. At this hour patrols had penetrated into Quéant and found it clear. Such was the close, so far as the Seventeenth Corps was concerned, of one of the most decisive days' fighting in the whole of the war. Late that night the tireless Sixty-third Division had reached Pronville, where they added more prisoners to their considerable captures. Altogether about a thousand were taken by the Corps during the day, with a large amount of material.

CHAPTER IV.
The Attack of Byng's Third Army. Sept. 2.

September 3 saw the Sixty-third Division still adding to its gains. In the morning it occupied Tadpole Copse and advanced upon the Canal du Nord. It then captured Inchy, but was held up in front of Mœuvres by strong enemy rearguards. This marked a definite line of equilibrium which was maintained until the general dispositions of the Army allowed a further advance. For a considerable time the only fighting upon this Corps front was in connection with Mœuvres, a village which remained as a sort of No Man's Land until, on September 19, a spirited attack by the 155th Scottish Brigade of the Fifty-second Division put it finally into British hands. After this there was quiet on the left flank of the Third Army until the great operations at the end of the month.

CHAPTER V

THE ADVANCE OF HORNE'S FIRST ARMY

From August 26 to September 27

The indefatigable Fifty-first Division—Capture of Greenland Hill—Fine advance of the Canadians—Breaking of the Drocourt–Queant line—Fine work of the Sixty-third Naval Division—Great day for the Dominion—Demeanour of German prisoners.

CHAPTER V.

The Advance of Horne's First Army.

ON August 8 Rawlinson had attacked on the south with the Fourth Army. On August 22 Byng followed on his left with the Third Army. Four days later Horne took it up in turn south of the Scarpe with his First Army. The general function of that Army was to co-operate with the attack of the Third Army on its right, and to cover the flank of that Army from the north. Therefore the First and Eighth Corps stood fast, while the Canadians, who had been brought up from the southern sector, advanced. They formed the right unit of the First Army, and were in touch to the south with Fergusson's newly formed Seventeenth Corps, which was the left unit of the Third Army. As only the Canadians were seriously engaged up to the end of September the narrative of the First Army can be easily summarised.

It will be necessary first to explain some preliminary operations. After its return from its hard fighting in the French line, where it had co-operated

HORNE'S FIRST ARMY

with the Sixty-second Division in attacking the great German salient upon the Ardres, the famous Fifty-first Highland Division had only a few days' rest before it was in action once more. It was now placed on the north bank of the Scarpe in the Arras sector. The 170th Brigade of the Fifty-seventh Lancashire Territorial Division lay to the south of the stream, and this was placed under the command of Carter-Campbell, General of the Fifty-first, so that he had four brigades under him, with instructions to advance along the line of the river, as opportunity served, in order to screen the left of the attack now about to break out in the south. Carter-Campbell covered from Feuchy in the south to the east of Bailleul, about 8000 yards.

CHAPTER V.

The Advance of Horne's First Army.

It was known that the enemy was withdrawing its advanced positions in front of the Army, and it was therefore very necessary for Fergusson's Seventeenth Corps to keep in touch with the Germans in that region. With this object in view the 170th Brigade in conjunction with the Fifteenth Division on their right moved along the south bank of the river to seize the advanced German trenches. This was done at 1 A.M. of August 19, when a considerable stretch of ground was occupied with little opposition. An endeavour to increase their gains on the next night was met by a sharp counter-attack. On the same night two brigades of the Fifty-first Division pushed forwards north of the river, but met with very strong resistance. On August 20 there was another German attack upon Moray Trench, south of the Scarpe, but the Lancashire men broke it up by artillery and rifle-fire. By 9 P.M., however, the 170th Brigade were ordered back from their advanced position, having been badly harried all day. On August 24 in the early morning the Fifty-seventh Division advanced with good results, the 153rd Brigade capturing Pippin Trench and other important points. The 152nd Brigade lay to the immediate west of Fampoux, and did not move, but the advance was again carried on upon the left on August 25 with some gain of ground.

Meanwhile the Canadian Corps had quietly taken the place of Fergusson's Seventeenth Corps to the south of the Scarpe, pushing them to the south, and all was ready for the big battle which broke out on August 26, and was a continuation to the north of the large movement already going on down the line. In this important attack, the Third Canadian Division was on the left, and the Second on the right, the two of them bridging the space between the Scarpe and the left of the Third Army. It was stated by prisoners that the attack had been foreseen, and that they had withdrawn 2000 yards the day before. However that may be, everything went very well, and the men of the Dominion showed their usual determined valour. The 7th and 8th Canadian Brigades, just south of the river, swept along with hardly a check, save for a time when the 8th was held up behind Orange Hill. At 7.35, Monchy, important as a place of observation, was in British hands once more. At 10.45, the 4th Canadian Brigade had captured Guémappe, and in the afternoon, Wancourt Ridge had also fallen to the Second Canadian Division. Here, as elsewhere, a single day had given what weeks of effort had once failed to achieve; 2000 prisoners were taken.

On the north bank, the Fifty-first Division, which

was now part of the Canadian Corps, made a similar advance, both the 152nd and 153rd Brigades sweeping forward, and occupying Rœux, Gavrelle and the Chemical Works, with little opposition. The Eighth Division was to the north of the Fifty-first, and it also pushed forward its line, its patrols occupying Oppy after dusk.

Chapter V.

The Advance of Horne's First Army. August 26.

The Eighth Division, reconstituted under its veteran commander, General Heneker, after its murderous and heroic experience upon the Aisne, was the right-hand unit of Hunter-Weston's Eighth Corps, which was the next unit of the First Army. The front of this Corps was formed by the Twentieth Division in the north and the Eighth in the south, and its rôle at this period was to stand fast, but by a succession of well-conducted enterprises the Eighth Division was continually encroaching upon the German lines. Presently, as will be seen, when the line was advanced on the south, the Eighth Corps was unleashed and sprang forward in combination with the general advance on either flank. On its left, and following its general movements, was Holland's First Corps, which was allotted, after September 20, to the Fifth Army, so that instead of being Horne's northern unit it became the southern Corps of Birdwood.

On August 27 the Canadians went forward once more, the 9th Brigade on the left near the river, while the 4th and 5th were on the right. Again there was a day of steady advance, which was rather a slow pursuit than a battle. In the evening the line ran east of Cherisy, but west of Pelves and Haucourt. In the north the Fifty-first Division attacked Greenland Hill, which was a most important piece of high ground—so important that it may be said to be the point on which the whole great advance to the Canal du Nord pivoted. The attack was delivered with great spirit by the 7th Gordons and 6th Black Watch of the 153rd Brigade, but they were unable to get the summit; while the 6th Seaforths to the south of them were also held up by machine-gun fire. Some advance was made, however, by the 154th Brigade, which had now come in on the north of the line. That night the 25th Brigade of the Eighth Division took over this northern section.

August 28 saw the Canadians still continuing their slow but inexorable advance. On that morning their 7th Brigade took Pelves and Boiry. There were two strong counter-attacks upon the Second Canadian Division in the evening near Artillery Hill, and for a time the front line was pushed back, but it soon recovered and held firm. There was quiet now on the Canadian front, but on August 29 the 154th Brigade of the Highland Division made a fresh attack upon Greenland Hill, which was captured by the 4th Gordons and 7th Argyll and Sutherlands with only slight losses. This important success caused the evacuation by the enemy of several positions commanded by the hill, especially Delbar Wood. This capture screened the left flank of the Canadians and drew from their General a generous message of thanks, in which he said, "That your division after its continuous fighting for the last year was able to take and keep the strong position of Greenland Hill, testifies to the fact that the fighting qualities of the Fifty-first are second to none in the Allied armies."

There were some changes of troops at this date in

preparation for the big attack upon the Hindenburg switch line which was impending. The Twenty-second Corps (Godley) now formed on the left of the Canadians, took over the Fifty-first Division, and also occupied the south bank of the Scarpe with the Eleventh Division. It retained the Forty-ninth Division (Cameron) in reserve. On the other hand, the Fourth British Division was attached to the Canadians, and came into their centre at Remy and Haucourt. At dawn on August 30 the Canadian First Division attacked Upton Wood and the trenches near, with the object of straightening the line and maintaining close touch with the Seventeenth Corps on the right. This movement was splendidly successful, and 500 prisoners were taken. The Fourth British Division advanced at the same time and their line in the evening was just east of Eterpigny. Next day they were held up once at St. Servin Farm, but took it at the second attempt. Meanwhile, the Eleventh Division was moving steadily forward on the south bank of the river. It was relieved on October 1 by the Fifty-sixth London Division, acting under the Twenty-second Corps.

On September 1 the Canadian Corps was outside the Arras—Cambrai Road, with the Fourth British Division forming its left flank, the Fourth Canadian its centre, and the First Canadian on the right. It was a day of local attacks and bickerings, but great preparations were on foot for the morrow. The first light of dawn had hardly begun to glimmer in front of the eager lines of infantry before the signal was given for the advance upon the Drocourt—Quéant line. This line is not the main Hindenburg Line, but it is a northern extension of the Hindenburg system.

CHAPTER V.

The Advance of Horne's First Army. August 30.

144   THE BRITISH CAMPAIGN, 1918

CHAPTER V.
The Advance of Horne's First Army.
Sept. 2.

and it may be said to cover the towns of Douai and Cambrai. The advance of the First Army was on a front of five brigades—one belonging to the British Fourth Division on the left, and two of each first line Canadian Division to their right. The general idea of the day's operations—among the most important of the war—was to break through the German line upon a narrow front, and afterwards to roll up the flanks of the enemy, both north and south. This having been done, the main attack was to push through, seize the higher ground overlooking the Canal du Nord, and if possible cross the Canal and seize the farther bank.

The attack should be from the Sensée River, southwards, and the function of the Twenty-second Corps was to form a defensive flank on the left of the attack, taking up consecutive positions eastwards along the River Sensée, and working in close collaboration with the British Fourth Division.

There was a preliminary bombardment, but the guns had been busy wire-cutting during the last three days, so that the great metal aprons which extended from the German position were ragged and torn. Hence they offered small impediment to the infantry who dashed through at the first rush, and easily captured the outlying trenches which stretched across a low hill. The village of Gagnicourt lay imbedded in the German trenches, and this was a centre both of attack and resistance. By 8 o'clock the Canadian infantry of the First Division had carried the village, while the Canadian Fourth Division was in Dury on the left, and had made its way into Dury Wood. The advance had already covered about 3000 yards. Both the barrage and the tanks were admirable, and the combination beat down the German defence which at first was not formidable—indeed many of the German front-liners escaped the shrapnel by running in front of it and surrendering the moment the battle began.

As the advance progressed the German resistance grew stiffer, especially in front of the Fourth Canadian Division at Dury Wood, where there was some very desperate fighting. All along the line, pockets of German snipers and machine-gunners did what they could to redeem the honour of the German Army. Astride the Cambrai Road there was a particularly strong point of opposition. The defenders were numerous all along the line—so much so that prisoners from six different German divisions were captured, including the First and Second Guards Reserve, and the Third Division which had only arrived the night before with orders to advance into the Canadian area. Many of them did so as far as the prisoners' cage.

This splendid advance of the Canadians had been covered and supported on the right by the Fifty-seventh Lancashire Division of Fergusson's Seventeenth Corps, which had cleared up the villages of Riencourt and Hendecourt in a preliminary operation on September 1. The Lancashire men made good the Canadian flank, and then the Sixty-third Naval Division of the same Corps skirted the southern edge of Gagnicourt, passing the Canadian troops, and pushed on to Buissy, nearly two miles further east. This advance was on a front of a mile, and brought the victors into contact with six other German divisions, each of which provided samples for the cages. Not content with this fine performance, the Naval Division, who were now ahead of their guns

CHAPTER V.

The Advance of Horne's First Army.
Sept. 2.

and without tanks, pushed on again in the evening, and inclining to the south they captured the village of Pronville, thus getting to the east of Quéant, which was still held by the Germans. The Drake, Anson, Hood, and Hawke battalions, together with the Royal Marine units, were all heavily engaged during this long day of fighting.

Meanwhile the Canadians had carried on along the original line of advance, the First Canadian Division clearing the woods of Loison and Bouche. On the extreme left the Fourth British Division added to its great fighting record another strenuous day of battle. It had in front of it a very strong position, Prospect Farm, which offered a desperate resistance, but was eventually taken. It was afternoon, however, before the place fell, which prevented the attainment of the full objectives of the day. They were still advancing in the morning of September 3, and before noon they had taken all their original objectives, including Etaing and Lecluse, while on the same morning the Fourth Canadians got as far forward as Rumancourt.

It was a fine victory, which will make September 2, 1918, memorable to Canadians. Great work was done by the British divisions on either side of them, but the stress of the attack and the consequent credit lay with our comrades from across the Atlantic. More than 10,000 prisoners were taken during the day. Their demeanour as described by Mr. Perry Robinson, the well-known correspondent of *The Times*, is of interest as reflecting the softening and disintegrating influences in the German Army. " As the newcomers arrived they were greeted with shouts of laughter and welcome by their comrades already behind the wires, and greetings and badinage and names were called back and forth. Those inside were mostly eating, and held up bully-beef tins and biscuits for the new arrivals to see, and the latter cheered responsively. . . . Many were very tired, but the whole scene suggested a new train-load of revellers at some annual bean-feast being welcomed by fellow-holiday-makers."

The Germans had dammed the river which flows down the Trinquis valley in front of the Twenty-second Corps, and this had now formed a considerable lake which hampered operations to the north. The Fresnes—Rouvroy line when tested by patrols seemed to be still strongly held. It soon became evident, however, that on the south the Germans had withdrawn behind the Canal du Nord. The Canadians on September 3 closed up to the western bank, occupying with little resistance Recourt and Baralle. During the day the First British Division relieved the Fourth British Division, while the Second and Third Canadians relieved respectively the First and Fourth Canadians. The Canal was found to be full, and all the bridges down, so that progress was for the time suspended, and a period of inaction followed, which was accompanied by a bad spell of boisterous weather, lasting for more than a week. During this time the First British Division was sent south to form part of the Ninth Corps on the extreme south of the line next to the French. The Fifty-sixth London Division took its place on the right of the Twenty-second Corps, and on September 19 it extended so as to take over the ground held by the Third Canadians, thus contracting the Canadians' front on that flank, while it was extended to the south, where it took over from the

Chapter V. The Advance of Horne's First Army. Sept. 3.

Chapter V.

The Advance of Horne's First Army.

Fifty-second Division on the left of the Seventeenth Corps. The Cambrai Road became the dividing line between the British and the Canadians. To preserve uniformity of treatment we shall now return to Rawlinson's Fourth Army in the south, and we shall carry each successive Army forward from the end of September to the date of the German surrender.

CHAPTER VI

THE OPERATIONS OF RAWLINSON'S FOURTH ARMY

From the Battle of the Hindenburg Line (September 29) to the Battle of the Selle, October 17

The first American operations—The rupture of the Hindenburg Line—Predicament of Twenty-Seventh American Division—Their gallant resistance—Great Australian attack—Remarkable feat by the Forty-Sixth North Midland Territorial Division—Exeunt the Third Corps and the Australians—Entrance of the Thirteenth Corps—Rupture of the Beaurevoir line—Advance to the Selle River.

TURNING to Rawlinson's Fourth Army, which were last seen in contact with the old Hindenburg Line along its formidable front from Vandhuile on the left to Gricourt on the right, it will be remembered that it consisted of Butler's Third Corps on the left, the Australian Corps in the centre, and Braithwaite's Ninth Corps on the right in contact with the French. The time had now come for an attack on the largest scale in order to endeavour to carry this Chinese Wall of Germany by storm. The part assigned to the Third Corps in this important operation was not a large one, and their front was now contracted to 2000 yards, while two of their divisions, the Fifty-eighth Londoners and the Seventy-fourth Yeomanry, were transferred to another area. There remained only the Twelfth and Eighteenth Divisions in line, which had to cover the left flank of the main attack which was to be made by the Australian and Second American Corps, and by Braithwaite's Ninth Corps to the south of them.

At this point the great Canal de l'Escaut passes under a tunnel which is nearly six miles in length. Thus it is the only place in the whole line where tanks could be used to advantage. The general plan was that this section of the line should be carried by the Second American Corps as far north as the northern entrance of the tunnel. This done they would extend their gains to the left in a north-easterly direction beyond Vandhuile, so as to open up a way for the Fifth Corps. After the line had been taken Australian Divisions were to move forward through the Americans and push the advantage to the east. The rôle of the Third Corps was to cover the left of the Americans, and then, when the latter had moved northwards, to mop up Vandhuile, establish bridge-heads east of that point, and bridge the canal for the Thirty-eighth Welsh Division on the right of the Fifth Corps to get across.

Before the general attack which took place on that *dies irae*, September 29, the Americans had a brisk fight of their own, which deserves some special mention as it was the first large operation of an American force acting as part of a British Army. The Second American Army Corps (General Read) had been specially selected to lead the attack on September 29, and as a preparation for this great effort they were ordered to make some advance along their whole front in order to gain an advantageous point from which to start. They lay roughly along

RAWLINSON'S FOURTH ARMY

the front of the Hindenburg outpost line, but they needed to draw up closer to the main line before the day of battle. On the night of September 24, General O'Ryan's Twenty-seventh American Division from New York on the left relieved the Eighteenth and Seventy-fourth British Divisions, taking over a front of 4500 yards opposite to Gouy. The defences immediately before them were particularly strong, including the notorious danger points, the Knoll, Quinnemont Farm, and Guillemont Farm. The 53rd American Brigade (Pierce) took over the line, with the 106th Infantry Regiment in front and the 105th in support. The entire American front was from near Vandhuile in the north to Bellicourt in the south.

CHAPTER VI.

The Operations of Rawlinson's Fourth Army. Sept. 27.

The tunnel, which formed a special feature in the next great battle, deserves some description, as it was a remarkable feature dating back to the First Empire, and still bearing upon its arches the laconic N of the great Corsican. It is 6000 yards long and averages 50 feet below the surface, with a breadth of about 70 feet. The Germans had converted it into an extraordinary military work, for it was stuffed with barges in which a whole division could take absolute refuge from the heaviest barrage ever launched. There were all sorts of bolt-holes in every direction for getting in or out, and there were powerful machine-gun emplacements along the top. Altogether it was as awkward a nut to crack as any military engineer could conceive. The main Hindenburg Line lay a couple of hundred yards west of the tunnel, a heavily-wired system of trenches. About a mile farther east was a strong support line joining the villages of Nauroy and Le Catelet, while two or three miles farther on was yet another strong position, known as the Beaurevoir line. The way in which Americans, Australians, and British combined with equal valour to hunt the Germans out of this terrific series of positions is a story which will go down in the common traditions of the English-speaking race.

At 5.30 A.M. on September 27 there was the preliminary operation, already mentioned, which should gain the ground necessary for the jumping-off place. This was done by General Lewis' Thirtieth American Division on the right with little difficulty. It was different with the Twenty-seventh on the left. On this flank a depth of about 1100 yards had to be gained, coinciding roughly with the rearmost trenches of the Hindenburg outpost line. This task was carried out by the 106th Infantry with all three battalions in line and four tanks ahead of each battalion. The leading companies, following the barrage, reached their objectives in most cases, but were involved in desperate fighting at the points already mentioned, which were connected by cross-cuts with the main German line, from which there flowed an endless supply of reinforcements. All day attack and counter-attack followed each other, both parties fighting with great valour and enduring heavy loss. By night the 53rd American Brigade was well advanced on its right, but its left was still battling hard to reach the allotted line: 8 officers and 259 Germans had been taken in the fighting. That night the 54th Brigade (Blanding) took over the new front and lay ready for the coming battle, with the 108th Infantry on the right and the 107th on the left. On the front of the Thirtieth Division the 60th Brigade (Faison) was in line, with the 119th and 120th Infantry in the van, the latter to the right, in touch with the British Ninth Corps to the south of them.

The task which lay before the New Yorkers of the Twenty-seventh American Division was particularly difficult, because the men were so scattered over 1100 yards of depth that the barrage had to be thrown forward to cover that area of ground. Thus the main body of the stormers had to cross that space before getting the full protection of the artillery. There were no American guns in action, but the British artillery was as splendidly efficient as ever, crashing down at 5.30 A.M. upon the starting line, where it lingered for four minutes and then advanced at the rate of 100 yards in every four minutes. The German barrage came down instantly in reply, and though it was not very heavy it inflicted considerable damage upon the supporting troops. What with fog and smoke it was difficult to see more than a few feet in any direction, and this was a great advantage to the stormers, the more so to troops who are so individual as the Americans. The Thirtieth Division on the right, a unit raised in the Carolinas and Tennessee, dashed through the main Hindenburg Line in the most gallant fashion, capturing Bellicourt on the way, while the veteran Australian Fifth Division passed through their cheering ranks after they had reached their allotted limit. The 117th American Regiment on the right was in close touch to the south with the Forty-sixth British Division, whose fine advance is chronicled elsewhere, so that the British, American, and Australian dead lay along the same battle-line.

CHAPTER VI.

The Operations of Rawlinson's Fourth Army. Sept. 29.

CHAPTER VI.
The Operations of Rawlinson's Fourth Army.
Sept. 29.

The 120th American Regiment on the left had taken and held Nauroy, but had been forced to bend its line back at the north end as far as the tunnel, on account of the fire which beat upon them on that flank.

The Twenty-seventh Division had met with grave difficulties from the start, for the tanks encountered mines and traps, while the infantry as already explained had practically no barrage, and found a strongly posted enemy in front of them. The men behaved with the utmost gallantry and the officers led them with great devotion, but no troops in the world could have carried the defences under such circumstances. For a thousand yards north of the inter-divisional boundary, near the village of Bony, they got into the main line, and from point to point all along the front bold parties pushed forward as far as Gouy and Le Catelet, many of whom never got back. The more successful were ruined by their own success, for as the mist rose it was found that in their swift advance they had left many pockets and strong points behind them which fired into their backs when they rose to advance. The Third Australians, following up the attack, could do little to make matters better, for all this part of the field of battle was such a complete mix-up, and the two armies were so dovetailed into each other, that it was impossible to use artillery, and yet the situation was such that without artillery it was quixotic madness for the infantry to advance. The reinforcing Australians were held up on the line between the Knoll and Guillemont Farm. Groups of brave men gathered together from time to time, and stormed up to Guillemont and Quinnemont Farms, which were among the most deadly of the German strongholds. A British Divisional General assured the present chronicler immediately after the action that he had never seen the dead lie so thick at any spot during the war as the Americans lay round Guillemont Farm. Neither the blue-clad infantry of Grant nor the grey Confederates of Lee showed a higher spirit than the khaki-clad lads who fought alongside the British that day. The best that could be done, however, was to hold such ground as had been gained, and to wait until the advance of the Fifth Australians from the south, and of the Eighteenth British Division from the north, should make all their section of line untenable for the Germans. The Twenty-seventh Americans and Third Australians had in the meantime held on to every inch of ground they had gained, and also to every prisoner whom they had taken. On the night of September 30, the Americans, shattered in numbers, but with unabated spirit, were withdrawn from the line. Altogether 40 officers and 1100 men had been taken from the enemy.[1]

It is necessary now to state the difficult and confused events of September 29 from the point of view of the Fifth Australian Division, who had almost as severe a day as their compatriots on the left. General Hobbs' Division went forward with the 8th Brigade on the right, which was in constant touch with the British troops. On the left was the 15th Brigade, which eventually found its northern flank in the air on account of the hold-up

CHAPTER VI.

The Operations of Rawlinson's Fourth Army.
Sept. 29.

---

[1] It was the privilege of the present writer to see the actual operations during this decisive action which broke the Hindenburg Line. His account, written at the time, of his personal experience is too slight for the text, but has been reproduced in the Appendix, where it can be consulted or avoided by the reader.

in that quarter. At 9.40 the line of the 8th Brigade passed Bellicourt, which the Americans had cleared. As they advanced, however, they were scourged by a very heavy fire from the direction of Nauroy. At midday the 32nd Battalion of Australians on the right were in touch with the 4th Leicesters on Knobkerry Hill. As the Brigade advanced they came upon concrete pill-boxes of the familiar type behind Nauroy which caused heavy losses. Joncourt on the right was taken by the 32nd Battalion, and at 8 in the evening the general line of Nauroy—Le Catelet had been reached.

The 15th Brigade on the left had the harder task. The fog and the rapidity of the American advance had combined to leave a number of machine-guns still active, and there was constant opposition. Touch was maintained with the 44th Battalion of the Third Australian Division on the left. A great many scattered groups of Americans were reached, most of whom came on with the Australians. The Brigade had been well provided with tanks, but in the space of fifteen minutes all the heavies and most of the whippets had been knocked out. So mixed were the conditions and so thick the clouds over the battlefield that for a time the 59th Australian Battalion on the left was altogether lost, but the 57th and 58th fought on together, and with their American friends reached the Le Catelet line, a bunch of Germans remaining in the trench between the two battalions. The 59th was afterwards found to have trended northwards and to be in close liaison with the right of the Third Australian Division.

The fighting had been mixed on September 29, but it became still more so next day, and it will tax the industry of some Antipodean historian to trace each unit, Australian or American, and define their relations to each other. The rôle of the 15th Brigade was simple as it was directed to make good the rest of the Nauroy—Le Catelet line, which was in time accomplished. The 14th Brigade was ordered to attack northwards in order to help the left flank which had encountered such difficulties on the first day, while the 11th Brigade was also directed towards the north-east, and ordered to take a strong impediment called the Knob, which was eventually done. The 53rd Battalion which led the 14th Brigade distinguished itself greatly, advancing with a steady persistence which always gained its ends, and overflowing the German field-guns. It was finally held up, however, and a strong counter-attack drove it to take refuge in that part of the Le Catelet—Nauroy line which was already in British hands. There was a good deal of close fighting in this quarter but the gains were held by the 15th Brigade, which failed, however, to get Cabaret Wood Farm. On October 1 the 56th Australian Battalion, with the aid of tanks, carried Estrées.

We shall now follow the work of General Braithwaite's Ninth Corps on the extreme right of the whole British Army on this great day of battle. This Corps consisted now of the First, Sixth, Thirty-second, and Forty-sixth Divisions. Of these, the Sixth Division (Marden) was in touch with the French, the First (Strickland) was in the centre, and the Forty-sixth (Boyd) was on the left. Opposite the Corps lay the broad and deep St. Quentin Canal, and the storm troops of the Forty-sixth Division were fitted up with 3000 life-belts, having proved

CHAPTER VI.

The Operations of Rawlinson's Fourth Army.
Sept. 29.

by experiment that they were buoyant enough to support a fully-equipped man. Since the Spanish infantry of Alva waded out neck-deep to attack the Dutch defences on the Frisian Islands there has surely never been a more desperate enterprise than this, when one remembers that on the farther side of the Canal was every devilment which German sappers could construct, while no tanks could lead the van of the stormers. The general plan was that the Forty-sixth North Midlanders should take the whole position between Bellenglise and Riqueval; that the Thirty-second Division (Lambert) should then pass through their ranks and push onwards to Tronquoy and beyond; while the First Division should carry out a difficult turning movement by swinging its left flank north-east to form a defensive line between Pontruet and the Canal at the right of the Forty-sixth Division's advance. The Sixth Division was to make threatening demonstrations.

The very special obstacles which lay in the path of the Ninth Corps had led to a reinforcement of their artillery, so that it was after a two days' bombardment from 500 pieces of all calibres that the assault was made at the same hour as that of the Americans on the left. The Stafford men of the 137th Brigade led, with the 1st Regular Brigade covering their right flank. An advance line of German trenches intervened between the British and the Canal. Favoured by the thick mist the attackers were able to overrun these without any great loss, killing most of the garrison who fought bravely for every inch of ground, and winning their way to the Canal. In the meantime the 1st North Lancashires cleared the trenches on their right, while farther south the 1st Black Watch pushed forward from Pontruet, cleared the trenches north-east of that place, and finally, squeezing out the North Lancashires, fought their way down to the right flank of the Stafford stormers.

The 3rd Infantry Brigade had also become strongly engaged on the right of the First Division. The 1st Gloucesters were pushed along the high ground a mile south-east of Pontruet. Here they were held up for the time, but the 1st South Wales Borderers came in on their left and connected up with the Black Watch. All day the 3rd Brigade threw back a long flank north of Gricourt to the Sixth Division, which was ordered to hold its ground.

The 137th Brigade having fought its way to the banks of the St. Quentin Canal proceeded now to force the passage. The 6th South Staffords on the right found the water low and there was little swimming to be done, but the 5th South Staffords in the centre, and the 6th North Staffords on the left were hard put to it to get across. The men dashed backwards and forwards on the bank, like hounds that are balked, looking for the most hopeful spot, and then springing into the water, sink or swim, with their gallant officers trailing ropes behind them as they got across. In a few minutes the whole smooth surface of the Canal for a mile or more was dotted with the heads of the English infantry, while cables, broken bridges, extempore rafts, and leaking boats were all pressed into the service. Within a few minutes the dripping ranks were into the trenches on the eastern bank, where the moral effect of their dashing achievement took all the iron out of the defenders. At Riqueval the bridge was intact and the enemy pioneers in the act of blowing it up when the British sappers and infantry swarmed in upon them and bayoneted them with the lanthorns in their hands. This bridge and a second pontoon bridge made later by the engineers and pioneers of the Forty-sixth and Thirty-second Divisions, were invaluable as a means of communication.

The trenches and the tunnel entrance at Bellenglise were soon occupied and the perilous passage had been safely made. The advance then continued, the teams of four guns being shot down as they tried to get away. The 138th Lincolns and Leicesters with the 139th Sherwood Forester Brigade had relieved the Stafford battalions, which dropped back after having performed one of the most notable feats of the war. These two brigades began to go forward preceded by twelve tanks which had made their way round over the solid ground on the Australian front. The advance was much impeded, however, by some German guns on the west side of the Canal, to the south of the point where it had been crossed. These guns, firing into the back of the 139th Brigade on the right, knocked out by direct fire every one of the six tanks allotted to it. A party of the Foresters then recrossed the Canal, shot or bayoneted these gunners, and extinguished the opposition in the rear.

The 138th Brigade on the left advanced well, and by 12.30 was near Magny and Le Haucourt, but it was necessary to call a halt, as the failure to hold Nauroy upon the left had exposed the north flank of the division, while the south flank had always been somewhat in the air. During the delay the barrage got ahead, but the infantry soon overtook it once more, racing eagerly for the protection of that slowly-moving cyclone. By 3 P.M. all objectives allotted to the Forty-sixth Division had been taken, and by 4 P.M. the Thirty-second Division had passed through their ranks—a glorious military picture on a day of victory—with the old 14th Brigade in the van. The leading lines of the infantry were now well up with the German guns, and it is on record that the German gunners fought with the greatest valour and continued to fire their guns at point-blank range up to the last. Many great deeds were done as small bodies of infantry closed in on these guns, often dashing through their own pelting barrage in their determination that the enemy should not have time to limber up and get away. Nauroy had now fallen save only the north end, which was still a scourge to the left flank of Braithwaite's Corps. Late in the afternoon the 97th Brigade captured the southern half of Joncourt, and before night Le Tronquoy had fallen also. From there the final line ran west of Le Vergies, and then back to Etricourt, where it was in touch with the Thirtieth American Division.

Chapter VI.

The Operations of Rawlinson's Fourth Army. Sept. 29.

Late at night the Sixth Division on the extreme right, which had endured heavy fighting all along its front during the day, was relieved by the extension northwards of the Fifteenth French Corps. The Sixth Division went into reserve. All night there was a bickering of machine-guns and rifle-fire along the front, and before morning the 14th Brigade had completed the mopping up of the villages which it had captured.

It was a most glorious day's work which reflects great credit upon General Braithwaite and his men,

M

who were allotted a task which it seemed presumptuous to demand and yet carried it out to the last inch. The stormers captured 90 guns and 5400 prisoners during the day, the vast majority of which (70 guns and 4000 prisoners) fell to the Midland Territorials. It was fitting that in so intimate a struggle as that between Great Britain and Germany it was men from the very inner heart of England who at the critical moment struck the most deadly blow.

On September 30 there was a continued forward movement on the front of the Ninth Corps. The First Division took Thorigny and the Thirty-second Division took Le Vergies during the day, with some 700 prisoners. The general movement of troops was from the south, the French taking ground to the left in order to release the British for that north-eastern movement which promised the more decisive results.

On the morning of October 1 the Thirty-second Division, in close liaison with the Australians, completed the capture of Joncourt, and made progress towards Sequehart. During the afternoon the glad news arrived that the French were progressing splendidly in the south and that their pioneers were in St. Quentin. All day the Thirty-second Division was flowing slowly onwards, taking Sequehart and establishing its van in the Fonsomme line, which extends from that village to Beaurevoir. The Germans had given fanciful names to all of these lines which were taken with such unfailing regularity by the Allies. There were the Siegfried line, the Wotan line, and other Wagnerian titles, which led some wit to remark at the time that if they went far enough through the list of that composer's operas, they would certainly come, sooner or later, to the Flying Dutchman. There was some confused fighting in the line south of Ramicourt, but the setting sun found the Thirty-second Division in full possession. It was clear, however, that heavy fighting was ahead, as the Intelligence Department learned that three fresh divisions, the Eighty-fourth, Two hundred and twenty-first, and Two hundred and forty-first, had come forward to buttress the line of defence. These new-comers were strong enough to bar the way successfully to the weary Thirty-second Division on the morning of October 2. In the evening the Germans passed to the attack and, backed by strong gun-fire, they got temporary possession of Sequehart, the British line being drawn across the high ground to the west of that village. We must now pause to consider what was going on in the north.

CHAPTER VI.

The Operations of Rawlinson's Fourth Army.

Sept. 30–Oct. 1.

As regards the part played by the Third Corps in these operations it was mainly limited to the action of the 54th and 55th Brigades of the Eighteenth Division, with elements of the Twelfth Division. On the left the 54th Brigade attacked the position known as the Knoll, which was occupied by the 6th Northants who repelled several severe counter-attacks. Any further movement was hampered, however, by the deadly fire of the enemy from Guillemont Farm. The 55th Brigade was unable, as planned, to get down the Macquincourt valley as the Hindenburg Line, which commanded it, was still intact. Next morning, however (September 30), it was found possible to get forward as far as Guillemont Farm and Vandhuile village, which were occupied with little loss, but the enemy was still in force in the Hindenburg Line behind it, and attempts to cross the Canal were checked by the German machine-guns.

Sept. 29.

CHAPTER VI.

The Operations of Rawlinson's Fourth Army.

Oct. 1.

The 37th Brigade of the Twelfth Division held the front line to the north-west of Vandhuile, with outposts along the Canal, which they also were unable to cross. On October 1 it was realised that the Australians working north had got in contact with the remains of the Twenty-seventh American Division, and also with the 55th Brigade in the Macquincourt valley. On the left the Fifth Corps had also reached the Canal. At noon on October 1 the long term of service of the Third Corps was at an end, and their section was taken over by Morland's Thirteenth Corps. The work of the Third Corps during that time had been very brilliant. Between August 8 and September 30 the five divisions which composed it met and overthrew twenty German divisions, including a number of the very best troops which the enemy retained in the field. They pushed them back over 25 miles of difficult country, and captured 15,700 prisoners in all with 150 guns. The achievement was the more remarkable as the troops employed were mostly young and untried, the successors of those veterans who had laid the foundations of the great reputation of these grand divisions. 1100 officers and 24,000 men in the list of casualties attest the severity of the service. In estimating the work of the latter period it is to be remembered that the Germans were in the line which they had been taught to consider impregnable, with very heavy artillery support, so that it is not surprising that it took six days to drive them back 4000 yards to the main outpost line, and another week to gain the Canal 2000 yards farther east. This remark applies equally to the Corps on either side.

Braithwaite's Ninth Corps having passed the St.

Quentin Canal in the dashing way already described, had established itself firmly upon the other side during the first two days of October. On October 3 it made a further forward movement in close liaison with the Australians on the left. The two very tired divisions which had fought incessantly for four days, the Forty-sixth on the left and the Thirty-second on the right, were still in the van. There was some hope of a break from these repeated hammer-blows, so the Fifth Cavalry Brigade were close behind the infantry, waiting hopefully for the developments of the day. The First Division on the right was told off to keep in touch with the French Fifteenth Corps which was joining in the attack.

CHAPTER VI.

The Operations of Rawlinson's Fourth Army. Oct. 1.

Both divisions, starting at 6.25 in the morning, made excellent progress. Ramicourt was carried by the Midlanders in the first rush, and it had been cleared before 7.30. By 8, Sequehart, with 200 prisoners, had fallen to the Thirty-second Division. The final objective was the village of Montbrehain and Mannequin Hill. On the left the Second Australian Division, advancing with irresistible dash, had occupied Wiancourt and were making good progress towards Beaurevoir. By 11, some of the Forty-sixth Division were on Mannequin Hill, and some on the left were in the outskirts of Montbrehain, but the Australians had been held up to the north of that village, which made the situation very difficult. By 3 P.M., however, the whole of this important point had fallen, with the large capture of 70 officers and 2000 men. There was very severe and close fighting in the village all day, and the northern flank of the Midland Territorials was still bare to enfilade fire, so they were drawn back to the western outskirts, which are on the reverse slope of the hill east of Ramicourt. At 7 P.M. the Germans counter-attacked on the British right and for a time regained the crest of Mannequin Hill, but they were pushed off again after dark. Another counter-attack against the Thirty-second Division about the same hour at Sequehart was a complete failure. During the night one brigade of the First Division and a dismounted section of the 5th Cavalry Brigade reinforced the utterly weary Forty-sixth Division on the left. In the meantime the French Fifteenth Corps, which had attacked with no marked success during the day, elongated its line to the north so as to relieve the First Division.

The breach made during this day's fighting in the Beaurevoir—Fonsomme line, together with the action of the New Zealanders, presently to be described, in keeping their grip of Crevecœur in the north, had completely destroyed the resistance of the last of the great organised defences of the Hindenburg system to which the enemy had trusted as being impregnable. Officers who went over these works immediately after the fighting were amazed at the breadth and strength of the wire and the depth of the dug-outs and trenches. Their final destruction was due to the action of many forces, British, American, and Australian, all equally heroic, but the historian of the future surveying the whole field with the detailed facts before him, will probably agree that the outflanking forces at either end, the New Zealanders in the north and the Englishmen of the Midland Division in the south, stand pre-eminently out in this wonderful achievement. Sir Douglas Haig visited the Ninth Corps on October 4 and congratulated it upon the vital work which it had accomplished.

RAWLINSON'S FOURTH ARMY

October 3 had been a day of desperate fighting for the Second Australian Division on the left of the Ninth Corps, which had taken the place of the Fifth Australians, while the Eighteenth British had relieved the Third. Their attack was upon the Beaurevoir line, including the village of Beaurevoir, and though the latter was not taken considerable progress was made. The advance was made with Martin's 5th Brigade on the right, while the 7th Brigade (Wisdom) was in touch with the Fiftieth British Division on the left. Sixteen tanks lumbered in front of the line of infantry. The honours of the day rested with the 18th, 19th, and 25th Battalions, in that order from the right, who swept forward against the formidable German position. So terrible was the fire and the wire that the two right-hand battalions drew back and lay down while the guns were again turned on. They then rushed the line almost before the flying fragments of splintered wire had reached the ground. Two hundred prisoners and eighteen machine-guns were the fruits, while the 25th on the left got the village of Lormisset. The first phase of the action ended with the possession of the German line from this village to the divisional boundary on the right, and the formation of a defensive flank by the 7th Brigade, facing north. The 17th and 20th Battalions then pushed in and got Wiancourt. Altogether 11 battalions, with an average strength of 200, were concerned in this operation, and they took 6500 yards of double-trenched system. They lost roughly 1000 men, but killed as many Germans, besides taking 1200 prisoners, 11 guns, and 163 machine-guns. A German officer summed up the enemy view by saying, " You Australians are all

CHAPTER VI.

The Operations of Rawlinson's Fourth Army.

Sept. 30–Oct. 3.

bluff. You attack with practically no men and are on the top of us before we know where we are."

The total effect of the fighting on October 3 in this section of the line had been extraordinarily good, though all objectives had not been taken. As the net result the British held the line for 10,000 yards from Sequehart to the west of Beaurevoir. At one time the gains had been greater but the enemy had countered with great valour, the Twenty-first Reserve Division, Twenty-fifth, and One hundred and nineteenth all making very strong attacks, so that the advanced line was retaken all along. On October 5, however, the division in the north got Beaurevoir while the 6th Australian Brigade carried out a very dashing attack by which the village of Montbrehain, which had already been taken and lost, was now permanently occupied. This hard struggle was begun by the 21st and 24th Battalions, but both were very worn, and there was not sufficient weight and impetus to drive the attack home. It was at this crisis that the 2nd Australian Pioneer Battalion, which had never been in action, made a fine advance, losing 400 of its number but saving the situation and capturing the village with 600 prisoners.

Immediately after this battle the Second American Corps took over the whole line from the Australians, who retired for a rest which proved to be a final one. So exit from the world's drama one of its most picturesque figures, the lithe, hawk-faced, dare-devil man of the South. His record had always been fine, and twice on a day of doom his firm ranks stood between the Empire and absolute disaster. The end of March on the Somme, and the middle of April in Flanders, are two crises in which every man who speaks the English tongue the whole world over owes a deep debt of gratitude to the men who stemmed the rush of German barbarism which might have submerged the world. But their supreme effort lay in those last hundred days when, starting from the Abbé Wood, west of Villers-Bretonneux and close to Amiens, they carried their line forward in an almost constant succession of battles until they were through the last barrier of the desperate and redoubtable enemy. The men were great; the officers, chosen only by merit, were also great; but greatest of all, perhaps, was their commander, Sir John Monash, a rare and compelling personality, whose dark, flashing eyes and swarthy face might have seemed more in keeping with some Asiatic conqueror than with the prosaic associations of a British Army. He believed in his men, and his men believed in him, and their glorious joint history showed that neither was deceived in the other. So exit Australia. *Ave et vale!*

It has been already stated that Morland's Thirteenth Corps took over the sector which formed the left of Rawlinson's Fourth Army, after the Third Corps which had occupied this position was drawn out for a rest and reorganisation. The same relative positions were maintained, so that from October 1 when they first came into action till the end of the war the Thirteenth Corps had the Fifth Corps of the Third Army on their left, and the Australians and their successors on their right. They came into line at that very critical moment when the great Hindenburg Line had been broken on their south by the Americans and Australians, but when the situation was difficult on account of a large body of the former, the remains of the Twenty-seventh Division,

CHAPTER VI.

The Operations of Rawlinson's Fourth Army.
Oct. 3–6.

being embedded in the German lines, having advanced with such speed that the trenches had not been cleared, so that they found themselves with as many enemies on their rear as in their front. That under these circumstances there was no great surrender speaks volumes for the spirit and constancy of the men.

The Thirteenth Corps took over Lee's seasoned Eighteenth Division from the Third Corps. It contained also the Twenty-fifth Division (Charles), which had been practically annihilated in the three desperate battles described in the previous volume, but had now been rebuilt largely of men from the Italian front where the reduction of brigades to the three-battalion scale had liberated a number of trained and veteran soldiers. It was now commanded by General Charles, an officer who had signalised his professional youth by riding round the rear of the Boer army in the company of young Captain Hunter-Weston. There was also the Fiftieth Division (Jackson) which has so often been described in the van of the battle. It had also been reconstituted after its practical destruction, and now contained no less than six Regular battalions from the East, full of experience and also, unfortunately, of malaria. Finally there was Bethell's Sixty-sixth Division, a Lancashire Territorial unit which had played a fine part on several historic occasions. The South African Brigade now formed part of this Division. Altogether General Morland had a sound hard-working team under his hand, with a strong backing of artillery.

The Fourth Army was now across the line of the Canal de l'Escaut, but it was necessary to clear a way for General Byng's Third Army to cross on the north. With this object it was wise to push the

RAWLINSON'S FOURTH ARMY

attack in the south and so to outflank the Germans that they would have to abandon the whole position. It was with this object that the Ninth Corps and the Australians were ordered to attack on October 3 as already described in order to secure the high ground east and north of Beaurevoir and the villages of Montbrehain and Sequehart, while the Thirteenth Corps conformed, pivoting on its left, and capturing, as will be shown, the villages of Gouy and Le Catelet and the rising ground known as Prospect Hill. The two villages which lie in a basin surrounded by hills were powerfully held and fortified. To the west of Le Catelet the St. Quentin Canal runs between steep banks, which rise 50 feet above the water at that part, but come down to the normal at Vandhuile.

On the front of Morland's Corps only one division, the 50th, was in line, the others being arranged in depth behind it. Sugden's 151st Brigade was on the right in close touch with the Australians, the 149th on the left. The latter was to hold its ground and form a hinge round which everything in the south should swing.

Early on October 3 the attack started in a thick mist, which made observation impossible—not an unmixed evil when a strong defensive position is to be stormed. The troops went forward with splendid dash, meeting with varied experiences as they encountered the strong posts of the enemy, but continually getting forward, though they had not attained the level of the Australians when about 9 A.M. the latter had occupied the Masnières—Beaurevoir line. The 6th Inniskilling Fusiliers who had been told off to take Prospect Hill had been drawn

CHAPTER VI.

The Operations of Rawlinson's Fourth Army. Oct. 3.

CHAPTER VI.

The Operations of Rawlinson's Fourth Army.

Oct. 3.

into the fighting in the village of Gouy, but the 1st Yorkshire Light Infantry pushed in on their right and sweeping past the village, caught up the barrage and captured the hill which it at once consolidated. By 10 o'clock the whole of the original objective, including both villages, had been occupied, while the Australians were in Estrées to the south. The rest of the day was spent, however, in holding the new line against very vigorous counter-attacks which drove down from the north-east and pushed the 4th King's Royal Rifles of the 150th Brigade (Rollo), who had already lost heavily, out of Gouy. They rallied, however, and reinforced by the 2nd Northumberland Fusiliers they restored the situation after some heavy fighting which came to close grips among the houses. The Second Australian Division on the right had also lost its hold of Beaurevoir and been driven by a heavy counter-attack to Beaurevoir Mill. The night closed down upon these lines, the British having failed to hold all their furthest points, but having greatly enlarged their foothold on the far side of the St. Quentin Canal, which had now been crossed and held from a point 400 yards south-east of Vandhuile. The Fiftieth Division had used seven battalions and incurred heavy losses, but it had won Gouy, Le Catelet, and Prospect Hill, with some 300 prisoners. The tactical success was complete, but the strategic aim was not yet attained, as the Germans still held the Canal in front of the Third Army to the left. It was decided, therefore, to renew the operations at once, bringing in the Twenty-fifth Division on the right. There was a marked salient in the German line which included the villages of Beaurevoir and Ponchaux. The plan was to cut in to the north and south of this salient and pinch it out. The 151st Brigade came into line on the left and Hickie's 7th Brigade of the Twenty-fifth Division on the right, while it was arranged with General Shute on the left that the Thirty-eighth Welsh Division should support the attack of the 151st Brigade. There were nests of trenches upon the high ground north of Gouy and Le Catelet and these were the main obstacles in front.

At 6 o'clock on October 4 the attack went forward in thick fog, so thick that it was not until 11 that the position of the Divisions could be defined. At that hour it was learned that the right of the 7th Brigade was in the high ground west of Ponchaux and in touch with the Australians on the Torrens Canal. They were also holding the line of railway near the cemetery, but were under very heavy fire from the villages which raked their position. Neither of the villages had fallen, so that the attack on the left seemed to have miscarried. The reports from the Fiftieth Division were that some progress had been made towards La Pannerie, but that the left was held up by heavy fire. At 1 o'clock La Pannerie was reported as taken, but the situation was still unsatisfactory, and the troops were under the guns of the Germans to the north, especially from Hargival Farm, which, however, was taken in the late afternoon. About 6 o'clock the glad news came in from General Jackson that the enemy appeared to be weakening, and he suggested a farther advance. This was held over until the Welsh Division should be available, while all preparations were made for a fresh attack upon the salient and the villages next morning.

CHAPTER VI.

The Operations of Rawlinson's Fourth Army.

Oct. 4.

CHAPTER VI.

The Operations of Rawlinson's Fourth Army.

Oct. 5.

At 6 A.M. on October 5 the untiring infantry were off once more, through the usual dense obscurity which shrouds that region of marshes and canals. At 9 it cleared. The 7th Brigade had been held on the right, but the 74th Brigade of the Twenty-fifth Division under Craigie-Hackett, had fought its way past Beaurevoir Mill, and its left-hand battalion, the 11th Sherwood Foresters, had reached its objective in a sunken road north-east of Guisancourt Farm. Some small parties were reported by the aeroplanes to be on the east side of Beaurevoir, but the Germans were still in the village. They were fighting with fine resolution, and a heavy counter-attack once more re-established their line, save that Bellevue Farm remained in the hands of the 74th Brigade. Further British efforts met with no better success, so it was decided to reorganise and attack again at dusk. The glad news had arrived that in the north the Welsh Division had found all clear in front of it and that the Fifth Corps was streaming across the Canal. The Fiftieth Division then fell into line, with the Welsh sharing in their advance. Fryell's 75th Brigade was now assembled in the dead ground west of Beaurevoir, and about 6.30 dashed at it with levelled bayonets and a determination which would take no denial. The enemy were swept out of it and the line carried forward 500 yards to the east of it, while junction was established with the Australians upon the Estrées—Le Cateau Road. Nearly 600 prisoners were taken during this day. That night the Second American Corps took over from the Australians on the right of the Thirteenth Corps.

There was now in front of General Morland a high waterless plateau extending from the St. Quentin

Canal to the Selle River. As it is a country of large, open spaces intersected with sunken roads, it offers great facilities for the use of machine-guns. It is dotted with villages nestling in their orchards, but the wide stretches between are given over to beet-root cultivation. As the German rearguards were still hanging on to their position, a big attack was arranged for October 8 which would entail an advance of the Thirteenth Corps to the Premont—Serain—Walincourt Road, meaning a depth of 6000 yards on a 4000-yard frontage. The Twenty-fifth Division had one brigade on the right in touch with the Americans, the Sixty-sixth were in front of Serain with two brigades, while the Fiftieth Division with one brigade was on the left.

CHAPTER VI.

The Operations of Rawlinson's Fourth Army. Oct. 5.

The general fight was preceded by a local attack by units of the Fiftieth Division, at 1 o'clock in the morning of October 8, upon the strong German post called Villers Farm which overlooked their line. This was successfully taken, but a simultaneous attack by the Thirty-eighth Division upon the village of Villers-Outreaux to the north was held up, with the unfortunate sequel that a heavy German barrage fell upon the troops as they assembled for the main attack. They endured tragic casualties with silent patience, carrying through their preparations with absolute disregard of the shower of projectiles. The attack was launched at 5.20, the order of brigades from the right being the 7th, the South Africans, the 198th, and the 151st.

Oct. 8.

This attack was a complete success. There was a stiff fight at Ponchaux, but the village was soon carried. The whippet tanks moved up with great daring in front of the infantry but suffered severely

CHAPTER VI.
The Operations of Rawlinson's Fourth Army.
Oct. 9.

from shells and anti-tank rifles. The 2nd Cavalry Brigade, who were eagerly awaiting a chance to be unleashed, found no opening during the day. The infantry got forward finely, however, and by 11 A.M. all objectives were held save on the front of Hunter's 198th Brigade, which was badly handicapped by the fact that Villers-Outreaux was still in German hands. By 3 P.M. the Fifth Corps had taken this village and the left of the Thirteenth Corps got forward to its extreme point. The Twenty-fifth and Sixty-sixth Divisions were at once ordered to push forward and improve the success in every way, and the final line was from the eastern outskirts of Premont and Serain up to the distillery on the Elincourt—Malincourt Road. Some 800 prisoners had been taken.

The battle was continued on the morning of October 9 with a prompt vigour which was amazing considering the continual exertions of the troops. It was speedily evident that these attacks had shaken the enemy and that he had been unable to get his roots down in his new positions. Much ground was gained with little loss, Elincourt, Avelu, and Maretz all passing into British hands. It was hoped at one time that the passages of the Selle River might be seized that day, but the infantry were too exhausted and the distances too great. The Canadian Cavalry Brigade, pressing forward in small parties, got past Reumont and cut off some of the Germans, but larger bodies of cavalry were faced always with murderous machine-gun fire from scattered positions. The Sixty-sixth Division had overtaken the Canadian Cavalry before evening, and the line of the Corps was west of Escaufort but clear of the eastern edge of Honnechy towards Bertry Station. They were coming at last into the old battle-ground of 1914. The wheel had swung full circle.

At 5.30 on October 10 these indefatigable soldiers were off again. They made good progress until the western slopes of the Selle valley were reached. Here the Twenty-fifth Division was checked by the fire from St. Benin, which appeared to be strongly held. At noon the Sixty-sixth Division was in Le Cateau, but under heavy fire from the south-west of Forest. About 2 P.M. the 74th Brigade, consisting of the 9th Yorkshires, 11th Sherwood Foresters, and 13th Durhams, made a very dashing assault upon the village of St. Benin, and drove the enemy at the point of the bayonet across the river. It was a fine achievement but led to no immediate advance, as the stream was unbridged and strongly defended. The Sixty-sixth Division meanwhile attacked the ridge to the east of Le Cateau, going forward with the 6th Connaught Rangers on the left and the 18th King's Liverpools on the right. The Irishmen rushed the town with great gallantry and got through to the railway cutting on the far side. The latter battalion got as far as Montay, but found the banks of the river heavily wired and were unable to cross. The Connaught men were ordered back, therefore, after dusk, as both their flanks were in the air. They continued to hold the western bank of the Selle, where it passes through the town of Le Cateau.

There we may leave them preparing for the important battle of the Selle River, while we bring up the Second American and Ninth British Corps on the right until they also are in line upon the Selle. These two Corps worked in close liaison, forming the extreme right of the whole line of the British Armies, which was now rolling forward in an unbroken wave more than a hundred miles in length, gathering speed and volume as it went. Some half-cynical Italian critic had remarked early in the war that the British may only win one battle in a war but it is always the final one. The hour had now struck and the line was irresistible in its cold and purposeful determination.

October the 8th was a great day of battle, in which the Second Americans on the left, the Ninth British in the centre, and the Fifteenth French on the right were all heavily engaged, the men advancing with ardour from the knowledge that at last the open land of France lay before them, and that the nightmares of barbed wire and permanent lines were behind. Taking the line from the north, the immediate object of the Americans was to capture Brancourt and Premont, including a total advance of 6000 yards. The attack was made by the 59th Brigade of the Thirtieth Division, with the 60th Brigade in support. The advance was supported by a number of heavy tanks and of whippets. The machine-guns were numerous and deadly, but the Americans would take no denial, fighting with that grim earnestness which is as much their national characteristic in battle, as is the débonnaire light-heartedness of the British, or the exalted abandonment of the French. By evening both villages had fallen and all objectives attained. Early next morning the 59th American Brigade advanced once more, maintaining the fight until the early afternoon when the 60th American Brigade passed through their thin ranks, taking the towns of Busigny and Becquigny. To carry on a

RAWLINSON'S FOURTH ARMY 179

connected narrative of the American Corps it may be added that they were still attacking on October 10, endeavouring to secure the command of the Selle River and the high ground beyond. The 119th American Regiment in the north captured Escaufort and St. Souplet, and in collaboration with Morland's Corps got possession of St. Benin in face of a very hot fire. Finally the 119th Regiment forced its way to the western bank of the Selle. The 120th American Regiment on the right had been checked by enfilade fire near Vaux Andigny, and had to throw out a defensive line to the south, being for the moment ahead of the general line. This regiment had suffered very heavily in its fine advance, and it was relieved on the early morning of October 11 by the 118th Regiment, who found their comrades so stretched out that they were covering a front of 5000 yards. The left American sector then remained stationary, but the 118th Regiment swept forward and took at the point of the bayonet the villages of Vaux Andigny and La Haie Manneresse, making an advance of 1000 yards. That night the Twenty-seventh Division came forward and relieved the Thirtieth. We shall now return and follow the movements of the Ninth Corps on the right during these five days of battle.

This Corps had joined vigorously in the attack on October 8, advancing with the 71st Brigade of the Sixth Division on the left, the 16th Brigade in the centre, and the 139th Sherwood Foresters Brigade on the right, the function of the latter being to keep in touch with the French. The line sped forward without a check for 2000 yards, a squadron of whippets leading them gallantly on. The 16th Brigade had

Chapter VI.

The Operations of Rawlinson's Fourth Army.

Oct. 8.

the hardest task, but they forced their way eastwards, and by midday Mannequin and Doon Hills with Beauregard Farm were all within the British lines. The cavalry tried to get through, but the machine-guns were still their masters, and it could only have been done at the cost of unjustifiable losses. Cerise Wood was a serious obstacle, but the resistance there suddenly collapsed before the stern insistence of the 16th Brigade, and 190 prisoners gave themselves up. Mericourt also was taken. Out of Mannequin Wood 200 more Germans were extracted. Altogether it was a very successful day, as 4 guns, 35 machine-guns, and 1200 prisoners remained with the victors. The Corps line on the left was well forward on its objectives, though on the right the advance had not been as far as was expected.

In order to strengthen the right the Forty-sixth Division was put in between the Sixth Division on the left and the French. With this greater weight of attack things went very much better on October 9. The new-comers captured Fresnoy-le-Grand, while the Sixth Division took Jonnecourt Farm which had been a lion in the path upon the previous day. A railway lay across the front and the Germans tried to build up a fresh line upon it, but in the afternoon they had lost their grip. The usual organised retreat of the Germans showed signs now of hurry and demoralisation. Late in the evening the Sixth Division occupied Bohain, which was found to contain several thousands of civilians, many of whom had not touched food for three days, but who forgot their hunger in the joys of liberty.

The next day, October 10, the whole Corps front was moving forward, but resistance thickened as it advanced, and finally in the evening they appeared to be once more faced by an organised line of battle. The Sixth Division was now in touch with the Thirtieth Americans at Vaux Andigny. On October 11 a fresh German division, the Fifth Reserve, had come into line, and it was very difficult to get forward in face of their fire. The casualties were low, however, and indeed it may be remarked that the greater tactical skill acquired by years of practice showed itself now, not merely by the defeat of the enemy but also by the cheapness of the cost. The iron front of the tank took many a bullet which in earlier days would have found the breast of the stormer, for brain work in England had come to the aid of valour in France. Up to now, in all these momentous operations from the 18th of September, the total casualties of the Ninth Corps had only been 6000, less than those of many a futile trench attack in the early years. On the other hand their prisoners were 12,000, a most remarkable record.

CHAPTER VII

THE OPERATIONS OF RAWLINSON'S FOURTH ARMY

From the Battle of the Selle, October 17, to the end

Attack upon the line of the Selle River—Stubborn work by the Second American Corps—Success of the Ninth Corps—Hard fighting at Le Cateau—Great feat of the South Africans—Continued advance—Delay-action mines—Capture of Landrecies—Dramatic exit of the German machine-gunner—Splendid work of the First Division.

<small>CHAPTER VII.
The Operations of Rawlinson's Fourth Army.
Oct. 17.</small>

THERE was a pause now on the front of the Fourth Army, and a period for preparation and reorganisation which was badly needed after the rapid and unremitting advance. The Selle River in front of the American section of the line had been carefully reconnoitred and was found to be fordable except for occasional deep holes. The position opposite to this Corps was very difficult, the enemy holding the east bank strongly, with outposts near St. Souplet in the north and Molain in the south. Across the stream and parallel with it was the railway, which had an embankment rising in places as high as thirty feet. Behind the railway was rising ground.

The Americans attacked with both their divisions in the line, the Thirtieth being on the right. The 301st American Tank Battalion led them on. The attack was on a three-brigade front, the Twenty-seventh Division having both its units in the fighting line. It should be explained that an American division has only two brigades as against the three in the British system, but that each brigade is very much stronger, consisting nominally of 6000 bayonets. These particular brigades, however, were already very worn, and a great strain was thrown upon them by the failure of the reinforcing organisation which, for some reason, had been unable to make good the very serious casualties already incurred.

CHAPTER VII.

The Operations of Rawlinson's Fourth Army. Oct. 17.

The battle began at 5.20 in the morning of October 17. The left of the American line had its jumping-off place in the partially destroyed village of St. Souplet, and it was no easy matter to get forward from the beginning. None the less the whole line fought its way across the stream and up to the high railway embankment beyond. This, as in the area of the Thirteenth Corps, proved to be a very formidable obstacle, the more so as the fog made cohesion of attack and accurate observation equally impossible. Bandoval Farm on the left of the line poured out a destructive volume of machine-gun fire, but it was eventually rushed by the American Infantry. The right of the Twenty-seventh Division got the village of Arbre Guernon. The difficulties of this unit were greatly increased by the fact that their tanks could not ford the stream, and though it had been arranged that they should join them from the south, where there was a crossing, only two did eventually arrive, both of which were destroyed by shell-fire. In spite of everything, however, the Twenty-seventh Division fought their way forward to the Le Cateau—Arbre Guernon

Road, where they finally halted, as both of their flanks were, for the moment, in the air.

The Thirtieth American Division had encountered a fierce resistance from the start at the villages of Molain and St. Martin, so that they were held up in crossing the river. After taking these villages they were faced by heavy fire from the ridge across the river. They formed a defensive flank, however, up to the point which their comrades had reached on the left. The total achievement of the Second American Corps was a fine one, for their prisoners amounted to nearly 1500 men, while their front had been advanced for 4000 yards.

Next morning, October 18, the attack was renewed by General Read, the Thirtieth Division bringing up the 60th Brigade which had been in reserve on the day before. In front of it was a line of well-fortified villages, two of which, Ribeauville and Ecaillon, were captured before evening, while a third, Mazinghien, was ringed round and American patrols were in the streets. This success represented a further advance of 1500 yards. The last-named village was completely cleared by the bayonet on the morning of October 19 and the advance was carried on for a further distance of 3000 yards. The objective of this day's attack was the high ground overlooking the Canal, and by night the west slope of this ridge had been reached all along the divisional front.

The Twenty-seventh Division had advanced on the left and had taken Jonquière Farm, pushing its patrols across the St. Maurice River and up to the ridge beyond, behind which lay Le Catillon. A pause was now ordered while fresh dispositions were

RAWLINSON'S FOURTH ARMY

made all along the British front, and during this pause the two American divisions, which had fought a succession of severe actions ever since September 27, were drawn out. Their losses had been very heavy, and as already stated no replacements had been received. In their term of service the Second American Corps had taken 81 German guns, 6000 prisoners, and a large amount of material, while their own casualties amounted to the very honourable total of 364 officers and 12,826 men. They left the line with the deep respect and affection of their British comrades, who well appreciated the difficulties which new-comers, however brave, must meet with in work which calls for so terrible an apprenticeship.

We will now return to the operations of the Ninth Corps, on the right flank of the Americans, from October 17 onwards. The action was started with the Forty-sixth Division on the right and the Sixth on the left, while the First Division was in close support, ready to come through when needed. A great forest lay on their front and the general idea was that the Ninth Corps should encircle this from the north and join beyond the wood with the Fifteenth French Corps, General Braithwaite coming forward with his headquarters to the immediate rear of the battle so as to keep control of what would be a delicate and difficult operation. One battalion of the 139th Brigade, attacking on the right of the British line, lost its direction in the fog and got into so false a position that upon the fog suddenly lifting it was exposed to very heavy loss from the German machine-guns. The splendid Sherwood Foresters have seldom had a more severe ordeal. The left of the battalion swung round, however, and

CHAPTER VII.

The Operations of Rawlinson's Fourth Army.
Oct. 18.

changed direction, with the result that the situation was restored. Without any loss of spirit the brigade rushed on and captured Regnicourt, driving back a heavy counter-attack which rolled in from the east about 11.30. The other three brigades in the line, which were, counting from the right, the 138th, 18th, and 16th, all made good progress, though in the fog they left several lively machine-guns in their rear. Each captured all the objectives in front, including the wood of St. Pierre.

The First Division was now coming up behind the Sixth with the intention of passing through them, but they ran into very heavy fire before they had reached their allotted positions. Both the 1st and 2nd Brigades had to advance for 2000 yards under the constant thrashing of the machine-guns, in spite of which these veteran battalions maintained their cohesion and direction, arriving at their starting-point in the battle line at the time arranged. Passing through the Sixth Division they continued the advance, with the 1st Brigade on the right and the 2nd in touch with the Americans on the left. The village of La Vallée Mulatre was very sternly defended, but nothing could stop the fire of the attack, and by 2.30 it had been entirely occupied. The Forty-sixth Division on the right had fought their way through the woody country, and had finally completed the whole scheme by joining hands with the French at the outskirts of the great Forêt Domanial just northwest of Mennevret. It was a good day for the Ninth Corps, and the prisoners amounted to 150 officers and 1500 men, a proportion of officers which suggests that the demoralisation of the German Army had not stopped at the ranks. Among the prisoners were samples from 6 divisions, 13 regiments, and 31 battalions, indicating the urgency with which reinforcements had been hurried up to prevent a complete fracture of the line.

In the early morning of October 18 the Forty-sixth Division in co-operation with the French captured Mennevret and Le Repas. On the same morning the 3rd Brigade advanced in co-operation with the Americans on the left and pushed the line forward as far as Ribeauville. The French had come on well in the south and were now in touch with the 1st Brigade, while the Forty-sixth and Sixth Divisions were drawn out of the line. By evening on October 19 the First Division had made its way forward and was lining the western bank of the Canal. The Sixth Division now came in again on the left, and got touch with the Thirteenth Corps, thus covering the gap left by the withdrawal of the Americans.

Returning to the Thirteenth Corps, who were on the left of the Fourth Army at the battle of the Selle River on October 17, the weary Twenty-fifth Division had been drawn into reserve, while the Fiftieth, their heavy losses made good by reinforcements, were put into the right of the line once more, while the Sixty-sixth carried on to the left. The river was at once reconnoitred and found to be a serious impediment, especially in the immediate neighbourhood of Le Cateau, where it had been dammed and deepened, while it was commanded by high ground in the east and also by numerous strongly-built houses in the town. Arrangements were made, therefore, that the main attack should be lower down where the facilities were greater. The Fiftieth Division held this right sector, with St. Souplet as

CHAPTER VII.

The Operations of Rawlinson's Fourth Army.

Oct. 18.

Oct. 17.

CHAPTER VII.
The Operations of Rawlinson's Fourth Army.
Oct. 17.

its southern limit for the 151st Brigade, while the 149th was near St. Benin. The Sixty-sixth covered the ground up to Le Cateau, the South African Brigade under General Tanner being north of the town. The South Africans with great skill and daring arranged their assembly within fifty yards of the German outposts on the other side of the stream, at a point where they were absolutely commanded by the German guns in case of discovery. There they lay in silence until, at the first twinkle of dawn, they sprang to their feet and rushed forward to the eight bridges which the sappers with their usual splendid efficiency had prepared for them during the night. So well had the bridge-makers worked, that in the region of the main attack they had actually been able to throw across bridges which would carry forward the ten tanks allotted for the assault.

The fog was so dense and the communications so precarious that the officers in charge of the operations had the nerve-trying experience of seeing their whole force vanish into the gloom and knowing nothing of what had become of them, save that the deafening roar of guns told of a deadly struggle. Soon there came news of disasters to the tanks. Three drove into a morass and were embedded there. Two developed engine trouble and collapsed. One never got across. The others lost their place in the fog and all hope of useful co-operation with the infantry was at an end. Then came belated news of the storm troops. The leading battalions of the Fiftieth Division had got across in safety but had been swallowed up in the fog, shrouding several German posts containing machine-guns, which opened on the supports after the front files had passed them.

On the left the formidable obstacle of the station with its heavy loop-holed out-buildings held up the flank battalion of the 151st Brigade, and the whole advance was stopped and greatly disorganised at this point. The railway was a strong line of German resistance, and especially a wooded mound on its eastern side, which bristled with guns. The attack being held, the reserve of the Fiftieth Division, the 150th Brigade, was thrown into the fight which in the early afternoon was still in a condition of equilibrium.

In the meanwhile a great deed of arms had been wrought in the northern part of the line. Tanner's South African Brigade, having reached the eastern bank of the river, had penetrated the German wire and stormed through the fog up the hill on the north of the town. The second wave was held by the concentrated fire, and the first wave was so utterly lost that the patrols could find no trace of where it had got to. Just as all hope had been given up, and it had been arranged to restart the barrage, a brave runner got through with the news that the leading South Africans were right through the town and engaged in a desperate hand-to-hand fight in the deep cutting on the farther side. In order to reach this place they had been compelled to force their way through another broad apron of untouched wire, a most remarkable achievement. Gradually the very strenuous German resistance was overcome, small bodies of South Africans dribbling up in support of their comrades. By noon this part of the German line had fallen, with a corresponding weakening along the rest of their front, for the bravest man is less brave when he begins to think that the

> Chapter VII.
> The Operations of Rawlinson's Fourth Army.
> Oct. 17.

day is already lost and that his self-sacrifice is manifestly vain.

With a view to helping the Fiftieth Division the 198th Brigade of the Sixty-sixth was now ordered to cross the river to the south of the town, and to strike in on the left of the long-drawn struggle at the station, where the assailants were now so mixed up that the two brigades were telescoped into one and all battalion order had been lost. A strong counter-attack had developed about 3 o'clock on the right of the line, where the British and American Corps joined, and this had some success, though the 4th King's Royal Rifles held on desperately to their ground. It was necessary to send in the 150th Brigade to steady the line. The 7th Wiltshires and the Munster Fusiliers were the reinforcing battalions and by their aid the position was once more restored. It was a dangerous crisis, for with the river in the rear any sort of retreat would have been disastrous.

There was now a concentrated bombardment of the obdurate station, and this seems to have broken down finally the spirit of the brave defenders. Shortly after dusk patrols forced their way into the buildings, and by 8 P.M. the whole place was in British hands, and Le Cateau, save for the extreme eastern outskirt, was cleared of the enemy. It had been a very desperate battle, the laurels of which rest with the South African Brigade, who had carried out so remarkable an assault, and also with the Fiftieth Division which had held on with such a bulldog grip to its purpose.

The day's work had not been quite completed, as the neighbouring village of Bazuel had not been captured, and this was undertaken on October 18 by the Fiftieth Division, strengthened by the inclusion of the 75th Brigade. This operation was carried out with perfect success. There was considerable opposition from scattered machine-gun posts, but before noon Bazuel and the whole ridge to the east of Le Cateau had been secured, while the Sixty-sixth Division had cleared up the suburbs of the town. Thus the whole capture and command of the Selle River had been triumphantly accomplished. To get a complete view of the battle these operations are to be read in connection with the fighting of the Third Army, as later recounted, on the left, and that of the remainder of the Fourth Army on the right.

After a pause of a few days for reorganisation and readjustment the active operations of the Thirteenth Corps were resumed in the country between the Selle and Mormal Forest, a district which was less open than the plains to the west, but presented special difficulties of its own, for it was well wooded and was also cut up into numerous small compounds with thick hedges which presented serious obstacles to any advance. However, the obstacle had never yet been found in France or Belgium which would stop a British Army, so the troops moved forward with a high heart to this new attack. The Ninth British Corps had taken the place of the Americans on the right, and was to advance to the line of the Sambre and Oise Canal, while the Thirteenth, in conjunction with the Fifth Corps of the Third Army on the left was to reach the main Le Quesnoy—Landrecies Road, near the western edge of Mormal Forest. The larger aspect of this movement was that it should cover the right flank

CHAPTER VII.

The Operations of Rawlinson's Fourth Army.
Oct. 23.

of the Third Army while it carried out its own important attack.

The attack was launched in bright moonlight at 1.20 in the morning of October 23. The 7th Brigade advanced on the right, with the 53rd and 54th Brigades of the Eighteenth Division in the order given on its left. The first objective was the village of Pommereuil, and it was attained in the face of heavy fire from the mills and farms along the banks of the Richemont River. On the right the 7th West Kents did particularly well, especially an independent company under Captain MacDonald which attacked with such vigour that it captured Garde Hill and Garde Copse, extending its gains outside the divisional area, and taking many prisoners. The 10th Essex and 2nd Bedfords were also in the leading line. The second objective facing the Eighteenth Division was Les Tilleuls Farm, with the great Bois l'Évêque beyond it, which covered four square miles. By 9 o'clock the Eighteenth Division had got the farm and was established in the north-east corner of the wood. Wood's 55th Brigade coming through had got well forward and was advancing upon the village of Bousies in close co-operation with the Thirty-third Division of the Fifth Corps. By 11.30 the Twenty-fifth Division was also in Bois l'Évêque and the British infantry was crashing through the brushwood which makes up the greater part of the plantation. All these various points were made good, but it was found that beyond them the enemy had a fixed line of defence with wire and every other defensive arrangement, so, as the soldiers were much exhausted from a long day's labour, the attack was pushed no further. Bousies had been taken after a hard fight among the surrounding orchards, by those old battle-comrades, the 7th Buffs and 8th East Surreys of the 55th Brigade, and the woods were completely cleared. Two field-guns had been captured near the Richemont River, and the bodies of 30 men of the 8th Royal Berks within 60 yards of their muzzles showed how fierce had been both attack and defence. Altogether 50 guns and nearly 1000 prisoners had been taken.

The attack was resumed before dawn on October 24. On the right, the village of Malgarni was the first objective and this was carried and passed by the 74th Brigade. Fontaine-aux-Bois was also captured, but the Germans held part of their line on the Englefontaine—Landrecies Road and could not be dislodged. On the left, the Eighteenth Division, using the same brigades as the evening before, took Robersart and some scattered farms, but had to fight very hard for everything they got. The 7th Queen's were the first into the captured village. The new ground was consolidated and patrols thrown out to report any weakening of the enemy line. That night General Wood, who had done such long and fine service with the 55th Brigade, was invalided and Colonel Irwin of the East Surreys took over the command.

On October 26, a day of rain and mist, the Fifth Corps was attacking Englefontaine, and the Eighteenth Division conformed by throwing forward its left, which involved the 7th West Kents and 8th Berkshires in some hard fighting. Much work was thrown upon the Thirteenth Corps on this and the following days in evacuating the civilians who swarmed in the villages, and who had no protection against the noxious fumes of the gas shells which the Germans with their usual thorough-going brutality showered amongst them. If in the peace terms the Germans found that the hearts of the Allies were hard and their thoughts stern, they have only to read the details of their own military history in order to understand the reasons.

A very large attack had now been planned in which the First French Army, the Fourth, Third, and a portion of the First British Armies should all participate. The Germans were known to be tottering and one more good blow might bring them down. It was necessary to act at once, for the German delay-action mines, which were usually in the shape of one shell set to explode among a dump of shells by the road or railway, were making the communications almost impossible. Fortunately the ingenuity of the British sappers discovered the private mark—a small star upon the cap of the fuse—by which the danger-shell could be distinguished among its neighbours, and so many a disaster was averted. It should be mentioned that on October 30 two gallant senior officers of the gunners, Colonels Thorpe and Burnyeat, were both killed by the same shell.

The general line of advance of the Fourth Army, which had been north-east, was now changed to east. The orders given to the Thirteenth Corps were to advance in that direction, astride of the Sambre and Oise Canal, to the line of the Cartignies—Dompierre —Bavai Road. The Ninth Corps was to cross the Canal simultaneously on the right of the Thirteenth at Catillon and Ors, advancing on the same objective. The general proposition before the Thirteenth Corps was a total advance of about ten miles, part of it through the south end of Mormal Forest, with the forcing of the Canal crossings thrown in.

CHAPTER VII.
The Operations of Rawlinson's Fourth Army.
Nov. 4.

The frontage of the Corps attack was 7500 yards, narrowing down as it advanced, so three divisions were put into the line. On the right was the Twenty-fifth Division, with the task of forcing the passage of the Canal opposite Landrecies, of capturing that town, and of clearing the country up to Maroilles. The Sixty-sixth Division was then to carry on the advance to the ultimate objective.

The Fiftieth Division was in the centre and was to fight a way through Mormal Forest, while the Eighteenth Division on the left was to storm the village of Sassegnies. The desperate determination of the Army may be gauged from the fact that a large number of life-belts were served out to the leading brigade in case it should be necessary to swim the Canal for want of bridges.

The attack, the last great concerted movement of the war, was launched at 6.15 in the morning of November 4—a day of thick, all-pervading mist. The order of brigades from right to left in the initial advance was 75, 149, 150, 54, and 53. Good progress was made from the beginning all along the line, and the news from the Ninth Corps was uplifting. They were across south of Catillon and Ors, but the Thirty-second Division, on the immediate right of the Twenty-fifth Division, had been held up, so that they were ordered to move south and pass by the crossings already established. The Twenty-fifth and Fiftieth Divisions both got well away, the former at 9 A.M. being within 300 yards of Landrecies, while the latter was well up to the old bugbear, the Englefontaine—Landrecies Road, though Robinson's 149th Brigade, and especially the 13th Black Watch, had lost heavily. The Eighteenth Division had also attained its first objectives and drove off a half-hearted counter-attack. The 7th West Kents had a desperate house-to-house fight in the village of Hecq, which remained in their hands, while the 2nd Bedfords had a similar hard victory in Preux, where they were much helped by the 10th Essex.

The 75th Brigade had forced its way down to the Canal bank. The 5th Gloucesters had the good fortune to discover two German foot-bridges and poured across. It was indeed a proof of German deterioration that such an oversight should have occurred, for it is in attention to detail that the merit of German soldiering lies. The 8th Worcesters followed their comrades and these two battalions began to encircle the town from the south. There was no bridge higher up the Canal, but a fine feat of arms was performed by a small party of the 122nd Tunnelling Company, who dashed forward, seized the lock gates, and cut the wires which were meant to blow them up. On the extreme left some of the 1/8 Warwicks discovered another forgotten bridge and pushed across to the north of the town, which was now practically surrounded so that the garrison was soon taken or killed. The official report remarks: " The capture of Landrecies was an operation which might well have absorbed the energies of a whole division. Success was accomplished with a single brigade and was due to the spirited leading of the officers, the bravery of the troops, and that element of good fortune which any well-planned and boldly-executed enterprise deserves."

The Eighteenth and Fiftieth Divisions had pushed on through the forest with hardly a check and surrounded a considerable number of Germans, who for the most part put up a very resolute resistance. About two o'clock there were signs, however, that the whole line was shaking, but it was impossible to advance farther until the Ninth Corps was in line. The final position on this most successful day was east of Landrecies, through Le Preseau, along the west bank of the Sambre to Hachette, and on to Locquignol.

The Operations of Rawlinson's Fourth Army. Nov. 4.

It was guessed that the enemy was in a bad way, but on this evening it was confirmed by the capture of a cavalry orderly bearing a message ordering the troops to withdraw to the Sambre during the night, and to continue the retirement upon Maubeuge. Their skeleton rearguards still hung on, however, and put up a spirited resistance. Next morning, November 5, the corps advanced once more, the 74th Brigade taking La Rosière, while Maroilles fell before noon to the same division. The Eighteenth Division had pushed ahead and occupied Sassegnies, while the Fifth Corps were in Berlaimont on their left and were crossing the Sambre. The Fiftieth Division had more difficulty as the ground was very water-logged and the resistance considerable. The day's advance finished by the 74th Brigade, still in the van, capturing Basse Noyelle, while at dusk the 149th Brigade got across the Grande Helpe, a stream behind which the Germans were expected to build up a new line.

Nov. 5.

A steady advance was maintained next morning, November 6, though the constant tapping of machine-guns in front told of the German sporadic resistance.

That night the line of the Thirteenth Corps was east of Marbaix and Dompierre. It was found that the small enclosed fields were very helpful in dealing with German machine-guns, as a concealed flank attack could always be carried out. Armoured cars on the roads were also found to be of great help to the infantry. On November 8 there was a sharp fight on the line of the Avesnes—Maubeuge Road. After the road was won there was a very spirited counter-attack, the German machine-gunners coming forward with great heart, though the infantry would not face the fire. The 6th Inniskilling Fusiliers and 1st Yorkshire Light Infantry bore the brunt of this engagement, which lasted several hours.

The state of supplies made it impossible for the Corps to advance farther, but the 12th Lancers went on as cavalry, supported by small mobile columns. A line was reached which ran north and south through Hestrud, and this proved to be the farthest east of the Thirteenth Corps, as it was gathering itself there for an attack when the final white flag was hoisted. Up to the last moment there was local skirmishing and even a small German attack, which was driven back and added a few more to the monstrous death-roll of the war. The whole British Army has an admiration for the German machine-gunner, and one closing incident of the war may be recorded. At two minutes from the moment of the Armistice a machine-gun opened up about 200 yards from the British line, and fired a whole belt without a pause. The gunner was then seen to stand up beside his weapon, take off his helmet, bow, and turning about walk slowly to the rear. In his person there vanished from the stage a brave and

RAWLINSON'S FOURTH ARMY

formidable character in the war. His last action was as typical of the remorseless valour of his corps as that of the British infantry who refrained from shooting him was characteristic of their chivalrous and sporting instincts. When the hour of fate struck, the line of the vanguard of the Thirteenth Corps was just west of Montbliart and Sautain, being the most eastern point of any troops in the British Armies in France.

During the five weeks that Morland's Corps had been in the line it had captured 8554 prisoners and 340 guns, while its take of machine-guns was at least 2500. It had engaged units of no less than forty-four divisions, which gives a vivid idea of the state of disruption which the German Army had reached. From thirteen of these divisions prisoners varying from 100 to 1000 had been taken, showing that these at least had been substantially engaged.

Having brought Morland's Thirteenth Corps to the goal of all its hopes and efforts, we shall now turn back to the days after the battle of the Selle River and carry the Ninth Corps on the right on to the same goal.

On October 23 broke out the general engagement which will be known as the battle of the Oise—Sambre Canal. The order of battle of the Ninth Corps on this day was the First Division on the right, with the 2nd and 3rd Brigades in the line, and the Sixth Division on the left, with the 18th and 71st in the line. It was a night attack launched at 1 in the morning, and though a heavy German barrage, mixed with gas, beat upon it, none the less both divisions made good progress at first, though many obstinate strong points had to be reduced. By 8

CHAPTER VII.

The Operations of Rawlinson's Fourth Army. Nov. 8.

Oct. 23.

Chapter VII.

The Operations of Rawlinson's Fourth Army.

Nov. 2.

in the morning the First Division was reported as being on all its objectives from Catillon southwards, with patrols pushed into the town. The Sixth Division had great difficulty on its left flank while endeavouring to clear Bois l'Évêque, but late in the afternoon they got forward again. It was clear by night, however, that the Germans, who were battling hard, still held some parts of the west bank of the Canal, including Catillon and Ors. Next morning the Sixth Division, working in close liaison with the Twenty-fifth Division on the flank of Morland's Corps, got well forward, but were still short of their full objective on the left. Every day after this in a series of minor operations the Corps improved its footing on the west side of this great obstacle, which was of a most formidable nature, 60 feet wide, unfordable, with steep slippery banks and wire mixed with wooden abattis along the farther edge. Such was the new line of defence behind which the German Army had rallied, and which offered a fresh problem to the victorious British leaders.

Most of the western bank had been occupied by November 2, including the village of Ors, but there were points where deep marshes and German redoubts on this side had prevented the assailants from reaching the edge of the Canal. There was also a spur at the bend of the Canal which enfiladed the line, but this was taken as a preliminary operation by the Thirty-second Division. It was retaken, however, by the Germans in a very strong counter-attack supported by an overwhelming drum-fire. On November 3 the British again got the spur known as Happe-Garbes, but once again in the afternoon of the same day the Germans regained it in a very determined advance. This heavy fighting fell upon the 96th Brigade and specially upon the 15th Lancashire Fusiliers, who were exposed to great pressure all day. Among many brave records that of Sergeant John Clarke of this battalion is pre-eminent, who took four machine-guns single-handed, bayoneting the crews, and fighting with desperate courage at the head of his platoon from morning till night. The idea of capturing the place before the general attack of November 4 was then given up, and other steps were taken to neutralise it. The main crossing of the Canal was planned to be at Ors, just south of Ors, and at two other points.

This the last great battle of the war broke out as already stated at 5.45 on November 4, the infantry advance being covered by a tremendous barrage. The First Division attacked on the right, the Thirty-second on the left, while the Forty-sixth was in close support. On the left and in the centre of the Thirty-second Division two bridges were thrown across the Canal under intense machine-gun fire, only to be destroyed immediately, before any large number of troops could get across. On the right of the division, however, the 14th Brigade gained a considerable success, the 1st Dorsets getting across over a bridge of kerosene tins which was most cleverly constructed by the Engineers and laid down in the darkness and mist, so that it was a complete surprise to the enemy. A smoke barrage and a concentration of machine-guns helped the stormers to get across. No praise can be too great for the sappers who worked amid clouds of poison gas in the completion of this essential bridge upon which the fate of the battle might depend. To one of them, Sapper Adams, of the 21st Field Company, the V.C. was awarded, but there was not a man round him who did not deserve the same honour.

In the meantime the First Division had advanced under cover of a thick mist, and four bridges having been thrown across, the two leading battalions got over the Canal, just escaping the German barrage which came roaring down behind them. The further experiences of this division, and especially of the 3rd Brigade at Catillon, should be told in some detail.

A special task was assigned to the brigade, which was to clear the outlying portion of the town, to occupy the rest of it, and to force the crossing of the Sambre Canal at the broken bridge. The order of the battalions on the east side of the Canal was that the 2nd Welsh were on the right, the 1st Gloucesters in the centre, and the 1st South Wales Borderers on the left, good old comrades who had fought together from the first. There were still strong enemy posts on the west of the Canal, and the enemy had fought tenaciously for every inch of ground. On the far side of the Canal were many houses which contained machine-guns, and their fire was always heavy and accurate. The actual attack upon the town began at 5.45 in the morning of November 4, and was carried out in the midst of a very dense fog by the 1st Gloucesters under Major Guild. The portion of the town to the west of the bridge was first conquered, with the efficient aid of an aggressive tank. Many machine-guns were taken in the suburban orchards and in the town itself. The bridge was commanded by a heavy machine-gun, but its position was spotted and the tank put it out of action by accurate fire. The British barrage was falling thickly across the Canal, and the British regimental leaders, those wonderful men on the spot who adapt themselves to every emergency, crossed at once, so that when the Germans emerged from their cellars as the barrage lifted they were received into the expectant arms of the Gloucesters. Over a hundred were taken at this spot. The battalion then, having formed a bridge-head, pushed on through the town, mopping up as they went, while the Welshmen cleared the orchards on both sides. The captures in this well-managed affair amounted altogether to 550 Germans, while of the British only 70 casualties were reported. No less than ten different German regiments were identified by the 2nd Brigade during this operation, which indicates how mixed and broken the hostile army had become under the constant pounding.

At the same time as the 3rd Brigade were capturing Catillon, the 2nd Brigade on their right had shown great gallantry in forcing their section of the Canal. They had been ordered to cross by a lock south of the town, but it was a desperate business, for the lock itself was hard to reach, with banks and water in front of it, all strenuously defended. The infantry, with their attendant bridging parties of sappers, were held up for a time, but Colonel Johnson of the 2nd Sussex restored the situation, personally leading the assault forward. It was again checked by the hurricane of fire, but he again rallied it and eventually led it across. In the subsequent official report attached to his V.C., it was stated that the offensive spirit that he had inspired in his Sussex men was entirely responsible for the successful crossing.

<small>Chapter VII.

The Operations of Rawlinson's Fourth Army. Nov. 4.</small>

CHAPTER VII.

The Operations of Rawlinson's Fourth Army.

Nov. 4.

By 8.45 the Thirty-second Division reported that their right brigade had got across, but owing to the enfilade fire two battalions of the left brigade had been unable to do the same. About midday, however, they were all over and had established themselves in a position south-west of Landrecies. The First Division was now touching Mezières with its left, where it was pushing on to Fesmy, while the German line seemed to be dissolving in front of it. It was a great day for the old division which had fought so gallantly from the first gunshot of the war to this which was so nearly the last one. Much of the credit of the victory is due to General Cartwright, the Corps Engineer, upon whom the weight of these various arrangements had fallen.

The Germans were now so fluid that a light cavalry screen was pushed out in front of the Corps, and the Forty-sixth Division advanced on November 5 behind it. By 9 A.M. the Thirty-second Division was in Favril, in touch with the Twenty-fifth on their left. Late on November 6 Cartignies was occupied. The advance rolled forward without serious interruption, though there was some bickering round Avesnes, and on November 8 the Thirty-second Division was established upon the high ground east of that town. At this time, as already recorded, the operations of the Fourth Army were confined to the single mobile column commanded by General Bethell, which was all that could be sent forward on account of the want of every sort of supply. Two days later came the sudden news of the signing of the Armistice. Never was there so sudden and wonderful a change. From dark cloud to bright sunshine seemed to have been the work of an hour. The long hurricane had blown out at last and left only the weals across the country which marked its passage. British officers have recorded how they sped eastwards in motor cars, and noted as far as the eye could range the white flags of joy and enfranchisement flying from the farm-houses and the village spires. The only signs of the invaders were the litter of abandoned equipment, lorries, and guns along the roads. For many a week, however, they left terrible marks of their passage in their delay-action mines, which, with their usual ruthless and reckless brutality, they had left in railway stations and other crowded points along the line of their operations, and which exploded long after the Armistice had been declared. This also was weighed against them in the day of doom, but indeed the scale was already overfull, and nothing which they could do could add to the horror and detestation with which they were regarded by the world, or to the absolute determination that they should never again raise their heads—or at least that those heads should never be crowned by the helmet of war. Such was the ultimate result of the doctrine of the Superman, of might is right, and of the whole material philosophy which had emanated from Frederick, miscalled the Great, and poisoned all Central Europe.

So ended the splendid work of Braithwaite's Ninth Corps. Its total advance since September 18 had been 50 miles, during which time it had captured nearly 17,000 prisoners and 318 guns.

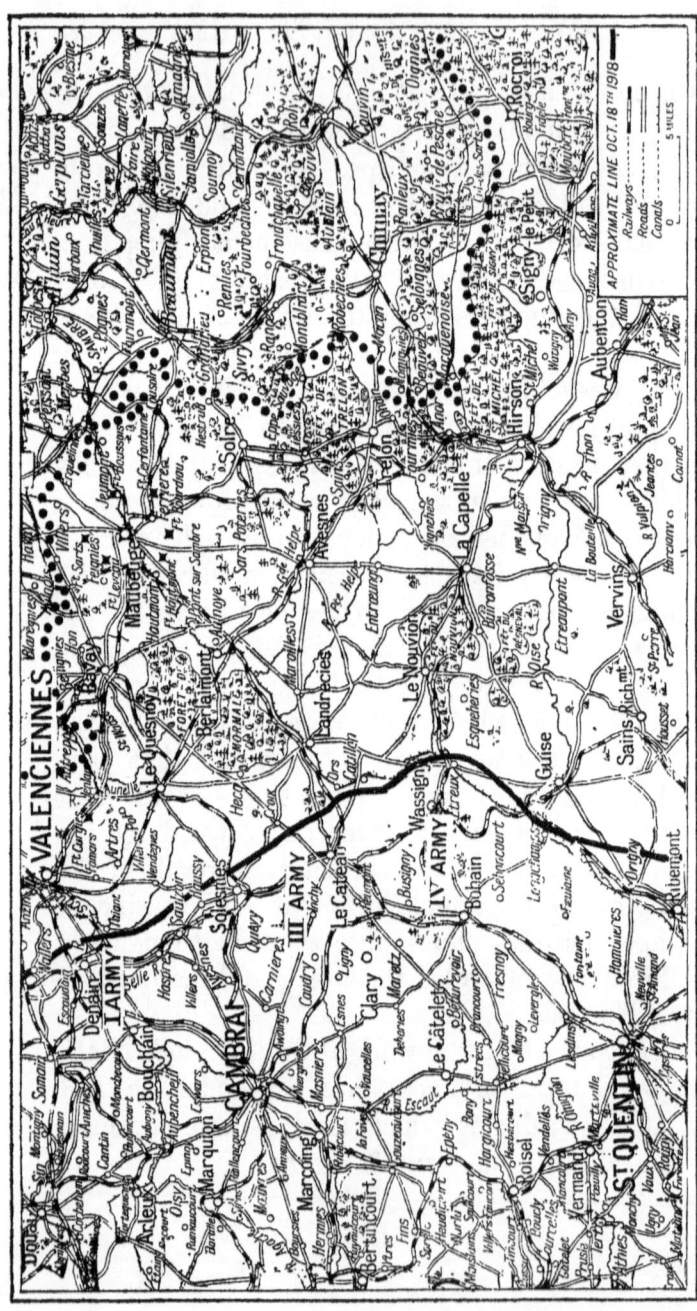

The Attack on the Selle.

CHAPTER VIII

OPERATIONS OF BYNG'S THIRD ARMY

From the Battle of the Hindenburg Line (September 29) to the Battle of the Selle (October 17)

Fighting at L'Escaut Canal—Dash of the New Zealanders—The Guards in a hot corner—Crossing of the Canal—Back on the old ground—Great work by all four Corps of the Third Army.

HAVING for the sake of continuous narrative carried the Fourth Army to the end of its labours, we shall now return to the Third Army, which we last saw on September 18 and following days, when it made good its way through the outposts of the enemy, and closed with the Hindenburg Line. We shall begin with the Fifth Corps on the right of the line, which was acting in close liaison with the Third Corps on the left of the Fourth Army.

On September 27 there was no particular action on the front of the Fifth Corps, save that the Twenty-first Division, that hard-bitten old scrapper, had a prolonged fight in front of African Trench, which it alternately took and lost, until on September 28 it got its iron claws fairly fastened in it. On this day it also pushed patrols to the east of Gouzeaucourt.

On September 29, the day of general battle

Chapter VIII. Operations of Byng's Third Army. Sept. 27–30.

along the line, the Thirty-third Division (Pinney) and the Twenty-first (Campbell) attacked at half-past three in the morning, advancing upon the Hindenburg Line on the front Honnecourt—Bantouzelle, while the Welsh Division operated to the north of that point. There was some progress at first and Villers-Guislain was occupied, but the enemy was strong and aggressive, so that the advance was first held and then forced back to its starting-point. It was not a successful day, and there seemed no choice but to settle down and subject these powerful lines to a renewed bombardment. On the morning of September 30 it was found, however, that the enemy had withdrawn his immediate front on account of the success in the south, and the Corps was able to push forward to the western bank of the Canal de l'Escaut. The Germans were still standing on guard on the eastern side. All bridges were destroyed, and for three days General Shute prepared for the difficult task of forcing this broad waterway — a formidable obstacle, it is true, but not one which was likely to stop the men who had carried the line of the Ancre. We shall now pass to the Fourth Corps on the left and bring them to the same point.

On September 27 Harper's Fourth Corps had been given the task to capture Beauchamp Ridge and Highland Ridge, and clear the front system of the Hindenburg Line as far as the Couillet valley. The assault was launched at 5.20 in the morning. The Fifth Division on the right was from the outset sadly hampered by the fire from African Trench, which struck upon its flank and inflicted heavy losses. The division showed its usual gallantry, but the position was an impossible one until the Fifth Corps got farther forward. The left of the division, however, and the Forty-second Division made good progress, though the fighting was very severe about Beauchamp, which was taken but could not be held, as a fresh German division, advancing about 7 o'clock in the evening, drove the defenders back to the west of it. The success of the Sixth Corps in the north, however, at Flesquières, had an encouraging effect upon the whole line, and about 2.30 P.M. of September 28 both the Fifth and Forty-second Divisions came on once more, the latter being particularly successful in getting prisoners and guns. The Fifth Division got Beauchamp and Highland Ridge, but was still held up on the right. By evening the line was well forward on the western slopes of Welsh Ridge, and some 1700 prisoners had come in. It was clear that the German line was sagging, so in order to press the advantage General Harper ordered up Russell's New Zealanders to carry the battle on through the night. There could be no more stringent test of the quality and discipline of troops, for the advance had to be made over unknown country covered with trenches and wire entanglements, with only a fitful, sinking moon to guide them. At 3 A.M. of a dark, cold night the splendid Colonials passed through the ranks of the Forty-second Division and, driving forward, thrust the enemy off Welsh Ridge and Bonavis Ridge beyond it, captured 1600 prisoners, and made good the line of the Canal de l'Escaut. North and South Island brigades kept line in the advance. More than thirty guns were among the trophies of this magnificent achievement. The Fifth Division on their right swept forward at the same time near La

P

210 THE BRITISH CAMPAIGN, 1918

CHAPTER VIII.
Operations of Byng's Third Army.
Sept. 27-30.

Vacquerie, but as Gonnelieu upon their flank had not yet been captured by the Fifth Corps, their attack was limited on that side. This was remedied shortly after dawn, when the Fifth Division, weary as it was, cleared their own right flank, captured Gonnelieu, and finally took Banteux with 250 prisoners. The indefatigable New Zealanders had also gone forward after dawn as blithely as though it was their first attack, clearing the whole of the west bank of the Canal, and penetrating at one time into Crevecœur, where, however, they were unable to remain. They did great work here, however, by holding and partly saving the bridge, all others having been destroyed, and establishing some sort of bridgehead.

The total result of these attacks since September 27 on the front of the Fourth Corps had been the capture of the whole front system of the Hindenburg Line from Havrincourt Wood to the Canal, and the capture of 40 guns with 4000 prisoners. Beyond the Canal, however, lay formidable dangers. Only the Crevecœur bridge remained British. Beyond was a strongly-wired line of trenches known as the Beaurevoir—Masnières line, which ran roughly southwards from Crevecœur. On October 1 the New Zealanders had got a footing, however, in Crevecœur, and had begun to push troops over the bridge, but it was desperate work, and the attacking brigade suffered heavy losses. It was, however, work of the first importance, as it turned the whole of the Beaurevoir line. There we may leave them, level with the Fifth Corps on their right, while we turn to follow the progress of the Sixth Corps to the north, which completes our survey of the Third Army.

BYNG'S THIRD ARMY

The old Third Division—the "Iron" Division, as its admirers had begun to call it—attacked on the right, and the Guards on the left. Deverell's men went forward in splendid form, the 8th and 9th Brigades overrunning the first objectives, and the 76th passing through them to the further positions. They captured Flesquières, the village which had held us up in the Cambrai battle, and by the afternoon they were east of Ribecourt, with 1000 prisoners trailing back to the rear. The Guards meanwhile, with the 2nd Brigade in front, had some very tough work at the onset, but fought their way forward, and were succeeded by the 1st Brigade who had reached by the afternoon the old British front line. Continuing from here they captured Orival Wood, and reached Premy Chapel, though this farthest point could not be maintained, as the party which had won it had lost touch with the main body. The whole advance represented a notable gain of ground. The losses were heavy, and were partly due to the fact that the flank of the Guards passed Graincourt before the Fifty-seventh Division in the Seventeenth Corps had captured that place, so that they were exposed to heavy fire. Even the Guards have seldom been in a hotter corner or shown more conspicuous examples of personal courage than during this long and trying day, which brought three Victoria Crosses to the battalions engaged. Lord Gort, who commanded the 1st Grenadiers, the leading unit of the 3rd Brigade, was wounded as the troops formed up, but took no notice of his injury, led on in the advance upon the Canal, was wounded again, lay for a time half unconscious upon a stretcher, struggled once more to his feet, and continued to lead his victorious

Chapter VIII.

Operations of Byng's Third Army. Sept. 27–30.

Guardsmen through a hellish fire with the final result of large captures of the men and guns who were opposing them. The crossing of the Canal was signalised also by a remarkable exploit by Captain Frisby and Corporal Jackson, who, with two other Coldstream Guardsmen, climbed down one side and up the other of the dry Canal in order to capture a machine-gun with a crew of nine who were lying amid the broken end of a bridge on the farther bank. Jackson unhappily did not survive to receive the Cross which he had won.

In the meantime the Sixty-second Division, now under General Whigham, passed through the Third Division, and continued their victorious career. Two companies of the 8th West Yorkshires got forward as far as the north-west outskirts of Marcoing and Nine Wood, but were exposed to a raking fire from the high ground on the south side of the Ribecourt valley, so had finally to fall back. That night the Sixty-second continued to hold its advanced line while the Second Division took the place of the Guards, and all was ready for the further advance next morning.

On September 28 the Sixty-second dashed forward as soon as it was light, and were soon in possession of Marcoing. There was no severe resistance. The Second Division on the left kept well in line with the Yorkshiremen, and were soon the masters of Nine Wood. By 10 o'clock the steady flow of the British infantry had enveloped Marcoing Copse, and the 186th Brigade had reached the Canal, where several bridges were found to be still intact. Noyelles had fallen to the Second Division, who were now fighting over the ground which they had held in the old Bourlon days, only nine months ago in time, and yet seeming so far off on account of the great succession of events which had elapsed. Some attempts were made to get across the Canal, but the Germans were there in strength, and nothing could be done without deliberate preparation. In the evening the Sixty-second extended its boundaries, and consolidated what it held. A small party of the Second Division got across the Canal during the night, but were unable to establish any permanent bridge-head. In the morning of September 29, however, one brigade of this division made a lodgment upon the farther side, and remained there, though with wire and machine-guns before them. Pontoons were brought up during the day and many bridges thrown across. The Sixty-second meanwhile had cleared Les Rues Vertes and Masnières and was well to the east of those villages.

No progress was made on September 30, and the day was mainly spent in strenuous preparations by General Harper for his renewed advance. The Sixty-second Division cleared some more ground, and the Second Division failed in a village attack, but neither movement was important. During the evening the Third Division was brought forward on the right and took the place of the Sixty-second, so that they might advance next morning in conjunction with the New Zealanders on their right. This was duly carried out, the 5th Brigade leading on the left, and the 76th on the right. It was a day of heavy fighting and of stout resistance. The immediate object was the capture of Rumilly, which was entered, but could not be entirely cleared by the 76th Brigade. The 5th Brigade found Mont sur l'Œuvre, which

CHAPTER VIII.

Operations of Byng's Third Army.
Sept. 27–30.

CHAPTER VIII.

Operations of Byng's Third Army.
Oct. 1.

faced them, a particularly tough proposition, and could make no headway. Altogether the losses on this day were greater than the gains, but the troops were undismayed and eager to get forward again on the morrow.

In the morning of October 1 they came back to their work, the 5th Brigade still carrying on, while the 8th Brigade took the place of the 76th. By 10 o'clock Rumilly had fallen, which gave the British a most important point as regards the passages over the river and canal. It took a great deal of clearing, for it was honeycombed with cellars and dug-outs, and there were continual outflames of unexpected fire. Before evening it was solidly British. No action of importance took place during the next few days, and the 4th of October found the Sixth Corps in the same position as the rest of Byng's Army, solidly established upon the western bank of the Escaut Canal and River, and with some bridge-heads on the farther side.

Sept. 27–30.

On September 27 Fergusson's Seventeenth Corps, which had done such splendid work in breaking a section of the main Hindenburg Line on September 2, was called into vigorous action once more. Its rôle was to advance in the general attack which was made on that date by the First and Third Armies in order to drive the enemy over the Canal de l'Escaut. The Fifty-second Lowland Scottish Territorial Division was on the right of the Seventeenth Corps, and the Sixty-third Naval Division on the left, while the Fifty-seventh Lancashire Territorials had been assigned the duty of following up the initial advance, and passing through the Sixty-third Division to reach the final objective. On the immediate right of the Corps were the Guards Division of the Sixth Corps, while on the left were the Fourth Canadians. The first line of objectives was the Hindenburg support line, the second included the villages of Anneux and Graincourt, while the third, if it could indeed be attained, would include Fontaine, Cantaing, and the west edge of La Folie Wood.

Chapter VIII. Operations of Byng's Third Army. Sept. 27–30.

A very desperate day of fighting lay ahead of the Seventeenth Corps before this ambitious programme could be carried through, and yet the fire and ardour of the troops carried them eventually to the farthest limit. The 156th Brigade crossed the Canal du Nord on the right of the Sixty-third Division, in spite of clouds of gas and very heavy shelling upon their places of assembly. The 4th Royal Scots led the advance, and were soon in the first objective. Here they were heavily attacked, however, and there was no further forward movement until the 7th Scottish Rifles came up to thicken the line. Meanwhile the 157th Brigade was dealing with that portion of the Hindenburg Line which was west of the Canal, their operations being on the extreme right flank of the Corps in close liaison with the Guards. This heavy work fell upon the 6th Highland Light Infantry aided by three tanks, and they got well forward, but the 7th Highland Light Infantry on their left were badly held up by thick wire and impossible conditions. The 7th Scottish Rifles in the north had more success, however, and they now worked south, which gave invaluable help to their comrades in that quarter. Before midday all the ground east of the Canal attacked by the 156th Brigade, between the Mœuvres — Graincourt Road and the Bapaume — Cambrai Road, was in the possession of the Scottish infantry.

On the left of the Fifty-second Division the Sixty-third had got off in excellent style, with the 190th Brigade leading, and the 188th immediately behind it. They were encouraged by constant good news from the north, where the Fourth Canadians were in Bourlon Wood. In front of the Sixty-third Division lay an important point called the Factory, an old bone of contention in the days of the Cambrai battle of 1917. This point was reached by the Anson Battalion, but they were driven out of it again, and the Germans put in a heavy garrison. It was then methodically bombarded, and shortly after 4 o'clock it was again attacked by the 188th Brigade with complete success, 11 guns and many prisoners being taken. Shortly afterwards both Graincourt and Anneux were overrun by the advancing waves of the Sixty-third Division. About 5 o'clock the Fifty-seventh Division was ordered up to take the place of the Sixty-third, moving round their north flank with the intention of attacking Cantaing. The German resistance had very much stiffened, however, and there was a menace of counter-attack, so that this final movement did not fully develop. The night fell with the 171st and 172nd Brigades in the advanced line which represented the farthest east of the Sixty-third Division. A thousand prisoners were taken during the day. Of the eleven tanks employed no less than nine were knocked out by the German fire—a proportion which shows how great the risks are which are taken by the brave men who form the crews. Each had done splendid work before it met its fate, and ever more and more the infantry learned, when at the last extremity before impassable wire and death-dealing trenches, to look behind them in the hope of catching sight of one of these lumbering ironclad monsters who had so often been their salvation.

On the morning of September 28 the two brigades of the Fifty-seventh Division were ordered to continue their advance and to force the passage of the Canal de l'Escaut, while the Sixty-third were to follow up and exploit any success which was gained. The immediate task of the 171st Brigade was to clear the ground between Anneux and Fontaine, and to establish touch with the Canadians on their left. This they had done while the day was still young. From about midday, however, the attack slowed up in this section of the line. The Marcoing position was very strong, and it held the 171st Brigade. By 2 o'clock a small force from the Fifty-seventh Division had got across the Canal, and at about the same hour the Drake Battalion of the 189th Brigade advanced upon Cantaing. The orders were to push on and cross the Canal, thrusting forward as far as was possible, while the cavalry were held in leash at the south end of La Folie Wood. It was soon clear, however, that the line of the canal and river could not be easily rushed, for all the possible crossings were swept by a deadly fire. The 171st Brigade was held under fire upon the spur east of Fontaine, and the Canadians on the left had not yet made good the Marcoing line. Two battalions of the 189th Brigade, the Drake and Hood, were in Folie Wood, endeavouring to force a crossing, but the night fell before it could be accomplished. Before morning two companies of Drakes had established posts upon the farther side, others getting across the river as well, over a broken bridge. Farther to the right the Sixth Corps had

CHAPTER VIII.

Operations of Byng's Third Army. Sept. 27–30.

three companies of the Second Division also across the Canal. A thousand more prisoners had been taken during the day.

On September 29 all three brigades of the Sixty-third Division were across the Canal. Before midday the Fifty-seventh Division had managed to clear the Marcoing line from the Bapaume—Cambrai Road to the Canal. The men were getting terribly worn, but it was reckoned that the Germans were even more so and that, at all costs, the long-drawn fight should continue. Therefore on September 30 both the Fifty-seventh and Sixty-third Divisions made some advance east of the Canal de l'Escaut. On October 1 the Fifty-seventh Division pushed out to the north and north-east of Proville, but the advance was not successful. Later in the day there was a renewed advance, but again it was not pushed, and did not get very far. The nearest enemy post, the Faubourg de Paris, was strongly held, and there were several small counter-attacks, one of which overwhelmed a British trench containing 40 men and 2 machine-guns. There followed a considerable pause while fresh dispositions and reorganisations were made along the whole line of the Army. These changes included very radical alterations in the Seventeenth Corps, which lost the Fifty-second Division, while it was strengthened by the addition of the Nineteenth (Jeffreys), the Twenty-fourth (Daly), and the Sixty-first (Duncan). With this strong reinforcement General Fergusson turned with confidence to his next task.

We shall now return to the operations of the rest of Byng's Third Army from the time that they fairly settled down to the crossing of the Escaut Canal, and the final occupation of the whole of the Hindenburg Line. We shall begin as before with Shute's Fifth Corps on the right. The attack of this Corps on October 4 was largely dependent upon the success of the Second American Corps, and as this was only partial some modifications had to be made. The immediate result of the American operations was that Morland's Thirteenth Corps, which was on their left and on the right of the Fifth Corps, had to undertake an advance against Le Catelet and Gouy on October 3. During this movement the Fiftieth Division on the left of Morland's Corps was to take possession of the high ground 1500 yards north of Le Catelet, and were then to be relieved by the Welsh Division of the Fifth Corps. This was duly carried out by the evening of October 4. The rôle of the Welsh Division was afterwards to attack northwards across the front of the Fifth Corps so as to clear the Hindenburg Line as far north as Rancourt Farm. It was found, however, on October 5 that as a result of the operations of the Fourth Army the enemy had withdrawn and crossings were effected by the Twenty-first and Thirty-third Divisions along the whole Corps front, while the Welshmen east of Vandhuile found that the line to the north of them had been abandoned. They pushed on, therefore, and took possession of the Nauroy—Le Catelet line, finishing up to the east of the village of Aubencheul, while the 64th Brigade of the Twenty-first Division moved forward and occupied the same line on their left. So far all had gone splendidly, but it was soon found that the enemy's retreat was not unlimited, for the Masnières—Beaurevoir line was strongly held, and the

<small>CHAPTER VIII.

Operations of Byng's Third Army. Oct. 4.</small>

Welsh Division on October 6 was unable to penetrate it, though the Twenty-first gained a limited footing at one point, which gave good hopes for the future. After a day of reorganisation the attack was vigorously resumed on October 8, the objectives being Malincourt on the right and Walincourt on the left. The troops were now in green and virgin country unscarred by any previous battles, and a most pleasant contrast to that terrible wilderness in which they had marched and fought so long. The attack of October 8 was made by night, the zero hour being 1 o'clock in the morning. All three brigades of the Welsh Division were concerned in the advance on the right, and all had heavy fighting and some setbacks, but persevered with fine valour, and succeeded before evening in piercing the Beaurevoir line, driving in the strong German rearguards and establishing their final position to the east of Malincourt. The Twenty-first Division on the left also came away with great dash and made rapid progress in their moonlight advance. By dawn most of the high ground in front of them, including Angles Château and Hurtebise Farm, had been taken and the 62nd Reserve Brigade moved forward to continue the operation, which resulted in the capture of the whole Beaurevoir line on that front. Before evening, after several temporary checks, the Twenty-first Division had reached a line 500 yards west of Walincourt, though the left of their advance had not passed the Sargrenon River. Nearly 1000 Germans were taken during this long day of battle. That night the Seventeenth Division took over from the Twenty-first, while the Thirty-third moved through the ranks of the Thirty-eighth, so as to be all

BYNG'S THIRD ARMY

ready for a continuation of the pressure in the morning.

On this October 8, when the enemy was reported to be withdrawing from the front of the Fifth and Fourth Corps, and it was probable that the movement would spread across the face of the Sixth and Seventeenth Corps, it was very necessary, if possible, to catch them in the very act. An attack was therefore ordered in which the Third Division to the south should move, supported by the Guards, upon Wambaix, while the Seventeenth Corps should take Niergnies as its general objective. The Sixty-third Division made the actual attack on a front of about a mile, with seven tanks in the van. The 188th Brigade on the right had Niergnies in front of it, approaching it from the north-east, while one battalion of the 189th Brigade attacked from the south, the rest forming a protective flank. The Fifty-seventh Division was at the same time to make a subsidiary attack. The advance started at 4.30, but by 6.30 the Fifty-seventh Division had made little progress, its tank being ditched and its 170th Brigade held up by an obstinate trench. By 8 o'clock the line had got forward, and all the first objectives were gained, but the Germans were still firing from the edge of the Faubourg de Paris. A little later a very spirited counter-attack was launched by the enemy from the direction of Awoingt, which was supported by seven British-made tanks, captured in the March operations. For a time the 188th Brigade and the Second Division on the right were thrown back, but by 10 o'clock they were going forward once again, and at that hour, or shortly afterwards, a very welcome pigeon message arrived from the Hoods of the 189th Brigade to say that they were

CHAPTER VIII.

Operations of Byng's Third Army. Oct. 8.

through Niergnies. By the late afternoon every objective had been captured, but the evening saw another strong German advance which struck upon the right of the Seventeenth Corps and upon the front of the Second Division. The Naval men stood fast, however, and not only cleared their own front, but by their enfilade fire were of great assistance to their neighbours in the south. Nearly a thousand prisoners had been captured during the day, and the little flags had moved eastwards once more upon the war maps.

On October 9 the troops were going forward shortly after dawn. It was soon found that the Germans had retreated, leaving only a few devoted machine-guns to impede the pursuit. Gard Wood and Clary were occupied by the Thirty-third Division, who came on so rapidly that they picked up a battery of field-guns near the village and captured the officers drinking in an estaminet, quite unconscious that their enemy was upon them. Bertry was occupied by the 19th Brigade, and before evening Troisvilles had also been captured. On the left without any opposition at all, the 51st Brigade of the Seventeenth Division passed through Malincourt, Selvigny, and Caullery. The German machine-guns made some show at Montigny, but the place was soon occupied, as was Tronquoy. There was no barrage this day in front of the Fifth Corps, and the advance was one long cross-country chase of six or seven miles, with an occasional skirmish. Early on the morning of October 10, the Thirty-third Division crossed the Inchy—Le Cateau Road, and with the mention of the latter name that huge circle seemed at last to be nearing completion, the line of which had begun to

BYNG'S THIRD ARMY 223

describe its strange curve in August 1914. The soldiers knew that the graves of their comrades were at last within their reach. The Seventeenth Division on this day flowed through Audencourt and Inchy, and the 7th East Yorkshires actually got up to Neuvilly in a fine attack, but had to be withdrawn. The Selle River in its shallow valley lay right across the Corps front, and this, as was clear from the increasing artillery fire, marked the new German front. Here we may leave the Fifth Corps while we hark back to bring up their comrades of the Third Army. On the evening of October 11, the situation was that the Thirty-third Division on the right had established one strong post upon the farther river bank, the Seventeenth on the left were lining the western bank of the Selle, while the enemy were reported to be holding the line of the Le Cateau–Solesmes railway in strength, and especially the village of Neuvilly to the east of the river.

CHAPTER VIII.

Operations of Byng's Third Army. Oct. 10–11.

Turning now to Harper's Fourth Corps on the left, and harking back to October 5, it became evident on that morning that the enemy was withdrawing from that point, as a result of the success of Rawlinson's Army to the south, and even more so to the possession of Crevecœur by Russell's New Zealanders. The retreat was closely followed by the Thirty-seventh and the New Zealand Divisions, and Vaucelles, with a portion of the Masnières line south of Crevecœur, was occupied without resistance. The Masnières line was still strongly held, though the glow of great fires in the east at night seemed to proclaim a coming retreat. October 6 and 7 were spent in preparing for a great attack upon the 8th, in which it was hoped that the Masnières line would be forced.

Oct. 5-10.

CHAPTER VIII.

Operations of Byng's Third Army.
Oct. 5-10.

This assault made by the Thirty-seventh and New Zealanders was completely successful, in spite of belts of wire which were often thirty yards wide and had to be crossed in the dim light of dawn. There was hard fighting round Briseaux Wood, but everywhere the attack prevailed and the Germans were beaten out of their positions. Lesdin fell to the New Zealanders and Rifle Brigade. Once the enemy tanks advanced, and there was a short check, but the forward movement was soon resumed. Over 2100 prisoners were taken in this successful day.

On the 9th and 10th the advance was as swift and successful as in the case of the Fifth Corps already described. The Thirty-seventh occupied Caudry, Bethencourt, and Viesly, while the New Zealanders, men of Otago and Canterbury, took Esnes, and finally crossed the Cambrai—Le Cateau Road. Up to now this district of France might have been a land without inhabitants, a mere stage for the drama of war; but now considerable numbers of the French civilians were liberated, no less than 2500 at Caudry, all with the same tales of German bullying and violence. In the early morning, the Thirty-seventh and their comrades of New Zealand were opposite the Selle River and had passed some elements across on each side of Biastre. We may leave them here on the eve of the battle of the Selle River and extend our view so as to take in the work of the Sixth Corps to the north of them.

In the case of Haldane's Sixth Corps there was a general German withdrawal on October 5, which did not prevent a very firm front being shown upon the general line which was held on October 8. The attack upon that day was made by the 9th Brigade

BYNG'S THIRD ARMY

of the Third Division on the right, and by the 99th Brigade of the Second Division on the left. The village of Seranvillers was the immediate objective of the 9th Brigade, which was strengthened by the 2nd Suffolk Battalion. Both the 9th and 99th Brigades got well forward at the start, but had very hard fighting, and at one time were driven back by a German counter-attack supported by tanks. The village had been taken, but the cellars were still full of Germans. La Targatte, the other village on the front, repulsed two attacks and was vigorously defended, the 2nd Suffolk having heavy losses in front of it. Later in the day, however, it was taken by a fine advance of the 8th Royal Lancasters and the 1st Gordons of the 76th Brigade. On the left flank both the 99th Brigade and the Sixty-third Division upon their left had encountered strong opposition from the village of Forenville and had suffered from the counter-attack already mentioned, but three of the German tanks were destroyed, and the advance was resumed with the result that before evening Forenville had been taken, and the whole line of the original objective secured. It was only attained, however, after a day of very desperate battle and heavy losses. During the evening the Guards came up, with their 1st and 2nd Brigades in the line, and early in the morning, supported by the fire of nine brigades of field artillery, they reached the line of railway along the whole Corps front, and took the village of Wambaix. News from the north now showed that the enemy was retreating upon a broad front and in no half-hearted manner. Patrols of the Seventeenth Corps were reported to have passed through Cambrai, while north of that the

CHAPTER VIII.

Operations of Byng's Third Army. Oct. 5–10.

CHAPTER VIII.

Operations of Byng's Third Army.
Oct. 5-10.

troops of the First Army had crossed the canal at Ramillies with little opposition. Previous experience had shown that such a retreat would certainly be conducted in an orderly fashion, and would be covered by rearguards composed mainly of machine-gun units. The main thing, however, was to sustain the pressure and keep as close to the retiring masses as possible. Led by that veteran body, the Oxfordshire Hussars, acting as advanced scouts, the infantry of the Sixth Corps hurried forward in pursuit with much the same general experience as the two Corps on their right. Estourmel, Igniel, and Boistrancourt marked the main line of the advance, and were occupied by the Guards, who were in touch with the New Zealanders of the Fourth Corps on their right and with the Twenty-fourth Division of the Seventeenth Corps on their left. On October 10 the Guards were through St. Hilaire, and up to St. Vaast, which latter village was cleared after a stiff local skirmish on October 11. The Germans still seemed inclined to fight in this quarter to the west of the Selle River, especially at St. Aubert and Solesmes. They were brushed aside, however, and on October 13 the Guards gained that portion of St. Python which is west of the Selle, a stream about thirty feet across and of some depth. It was evident that an organised full-scale attack would have to be made at this point, so the Sixth Corps waited for the general signal.

Returning to the Seventeenth Corps: On the morning of October 9 the attack was renewed by Daly's Twenty-fourth Division, a unit which has always been in the heart of the fighting in the past, and now was in the line once more. It was a great day, for early in the morning, as is recorded elsewhere, the Canadians and the Fifty-seventh Division had entered Cambrai. The situation seemed fluid, and the enemy disorganised, so the 6th Dragoon Guards were ordered forward to work towards Cagnoncles, while the 72nd Brigade, having taken Awoingt, gave way to the 73rd Brigade, who advanced towards Cauroir and west of Romilly. The Germans, however, were in a strong line of rifle-pits behind triple wire, so that the cavalry could gain no ground. The infantry were also unable to get forward very far on that day, but evening saw them in close touch with the German covering rearguards, the Twenty-fourth Division touching the Guards on the right, the Canadians on the left. In the morning of October 10 the screen had dissolved and the leading lines of the Seventeenth Corps, consisting of the 17th Brigade, were soon to the east of Cagnoncles, which fell to the 7th Northamptons, while the Dragoon Guards were pushing ahead once more. Rieux and Avesnes were both taken by the Twenty-fourth Division during the day, and before evening the line was well to the east of Cambrai, General Daly pushing the advance with great vigour.

On October 11 it was found that the Germans were in strength and apparently meant to make a serious stand. At about ten o'clock they counter-attacked with tanks, and pushed back both the Canadians on the left and the Twenty-fourth Division on the right. The former had taken Iwuy in the morning. No further advance was made during the day, but general orders were issued that the way should be cleared up to the Selle River, and that the high ground over the river should be secured in order

CHAPTER VIII.

Operations of Byng's Third Army. Oct. 9.

Oct. 11.

CHAPTER VIII.

Operations of Byng's Third Army. Oct. 11.

to safeguard the crossings. On October 12 the Canadian Corps on the left was drawn out of the line, and the Seventeenth Corps found themselves with the Forty-eighth Division of the Twenty-second Corps as their northern neighbours. On this day the Germans again began to retreat, and the Corps front was advanced down to the Selle River, between Haussy and Saulzoir. There was hardly any opposition. All day the Twenty-fourth Division was advancing with the Forty-ninth on their left and the Guards on their right. That evening the 17th Brigade of the Twenty-fourth Division made progress over the river, entering Montrecourt and securing the undamaged bridge. The posts on the farther side were swept by machine-gun fire and driven back next morning, that portion of the bank being commanded by rising ground on the east.

We have thus traced all four Corps of the Third Army from the date August 21, when it started from the line of Albert, until October 13, when it found itself after seven weeks of immense and continuous exertion and of uninterrupted victory upon the western bank of the Selle. In the compressed narrative of this chronicle it might seem no more complex than the forward movement of pieces upon a board, but no detailed account could ever make real the problems, the anxiety, the organisation, the unwearied heroic efforts which such an advance must entail when the great German army, now composed of veterans deeply skilled in every wile of modern warfare, were beaten out of position after position, and could find no safe refuge anywhere from the nation whose military weakness had for so long been its standing jest.

CHAPTER IX

OPERATIONS OF BYNG'S THIRD ARMY

From the Battle of the Selle, October 12, to the end

The battle of the Selle River—Reversion to open warfare—The valour of Lancashire—Haig's incessant blows—Weakening of the German morale—The battle of Mormal Forest—New Zealanders and the mediaeval fortress—Capture of the great forest—The Sambre bridged—A grand Division—Advance of Fergusson's Seventeenth Corps—The last phase.

THE River Selle is a small stream, only thirty feet across but of some depth, and it ran right athwart the course of the Army, with every indication that the enemy had built up a line of resistance behind it. How far this was a strong rearguard or how far it was a do-or-die line of battle could only be determined by actual assault. The river runs through swampy meadows from Neuvilly past Biastre to Solesmes. On the far bank the ground slopes up uniformly to a hog-backed ridge, with a road and railway running between Neuvilly and Solesmes, rather more than half-way up the slope. The railway joined other lines south of the latter town, forming a triangular embankment of great strength strongly defended by machine-guns, as was the whole railway line and the string of villages across the Army front, which was the northern prolongation of that described previously.

230   THE BRITISH CAMPAIGN, 1918

CHAPTER IX.

Operations of Byng's Third Army. Oct. 12.

It was a position of great natural strength, made more awkward by the presence of civilians in the villages, and by a damming of the river which broadened it in parts into a lake. The first move of General Byng was to endeavour to seize the high ground on the east of the river, so as to make a strong point which would cover the bridge-building operations. We shall describe the successive operations from the south or right, beginning with Shute's Fifth Corps, still working in close liaison with Morland's Thirteenth Corps on the right, the flank unit of the Fourth Army. It may be premised that the warfare from now onwards was very different from that which had preceded the capture of the great German lines. The trench, the bomb, and the wire all played subsidiary parts. An officer of pre-war Aldershot experience, or even the great Duke himself with his Peninsular prejudices, would have found himself able to appreciate the situation. That great shade, could he have ridden Copenhagen in the heart of this wonderful army, would have seen, as of yore, shells which burst over the enemy's position; he would have seen cavalry scouts who were the advanced posts of the marching army; he would have seen lines of skirmishers behind them; he would have seen mounted officers who carried personal reports; and he would have seen columns of route marching in fours down every road, and breaking up into small clumps of artillery formation as they came under fire. All this would have been familiar, and all this he would have seen had he been present in these later phases of the great war.

The attack was launched at 5 A.M. on October 12, when the advanced guard of the Thirty-third and

Seventeenth Divisions, under Generals Pinney and Robertson, advanced upon the high ground which faced them. They were working in close liaison with the Thirty-seventh on the left, and with the Sixty-sixth Lancashire Territorials on the right, these being the flank units of the Fourth and Thirteenth Corps respectively. The line of the advance was to the north of Montay, and it went very well at first, so that by 7.45 Pinney's men were far forward and consolidating on the left, though on the right they were unable to penetrate beyond the railway line. The attack of the Seventeenth on the left reached the high ground 1000 yards north-east of Neuvilly, but on the south side of that village could not get past the line of the Montay—Neuvilly Road, where the 9th West Ridings of the 52nd Brigade were heavily engaged. Neuvilly was gained, but while the troops were mopping it up a strong German counter-attack drove down from the Amerval direction, dashed up against the left of Pinney's Division and threw it back to the line of the railway. So great was the pressure and so continuous, that the Thirty-third could not hold any of its gains, and found itself in the afternoon on the west of the Selle River once more, save for the right-hand battalion, who held tight all day along the line of the road between the railway and the river.

The Seventeenth Division on the high ground north-east of Neuvilly was now in a very dangerous position, as the Thirty-seventh had not come up on its left, so that both its flanks were in the air. The 12th Manchesters stood firm, however, with little support, until about 3 p.m., when a creeping barrage with an infantry attack behind it drove them west

CHAPTER IX.

Operations of Byng's Third Army. Oct. 12.

of the railway, with serious losses, to a point 200 yards east of the river. The result was that the final line, when night fell upon this long and trying day, was across the river at both extreme flanks, but west of the river in the middle.

From the point of view of the Fourth Corps on the left the 12th had not been a very satisfactory day either. The Thirty-seventh had reached the crest of the opposite hill, but the New Zealanders on their left had not taken Bellevue, while Neuvilly on the right had never been thoroughly cleared. About 5 P.M. the German counter-attack, made in four waves, came down upon the Thirty-seventh, supported by flank fire from both villages. It reached Neuvilly in the Seventeenth Division sector, and then turned right so as to enfilade the Thirty-seventh, with the result that the latter were forced to evacuate both the hill and the railway line, but still held on to the east bank of the river, where a steep escarpment gave some protection. Thus ended this weary day, which had not involved the Sixth Corps on the north, but had exposed both the southern Corps of the Third Army to heavy losses with barren results.

A week now elapsed, which was marked by very heavy artillery work on both sides, the Germans endeavouring to prevent the British from assembling, while the British tried to break down the machine-gun nests and strong points which faced them, especially in Neuvilly. There were several daring minor engagements in which patrols endeavoured to widen or strengthen the front, so keen being the contest that sometimes posts were taken and retaken several times in one night. There was, it must be admitted, no obvious local sign of any failure in German morale. It was not until October 20 that the offensive was resumed upon a large scale by the Fifth and Fourth Corps, in conjunction with a full-dress attack by the whole of the Fourth Army in the south.

CHAPTER IX.

Operations of Byng's Third Army. Oct. 20.

The Fifth Corps advanced with Cubitt's Thirty-eighth Welsh on the right, and the Seventeenth Division on the left. Neither line had far to go before clashing with the enemy, for the outposts were almost touching each other. The attack began in the dark at 2 in the morning, the British having indulged in previous heavy shoots at night, in the hope, which was justified by the result, that the real barrage would be taken as being of a similar temporary nature. The Welshmen had a desperate experience at first, a quarry, a farm, and the old railway embankment all forming difficult obstacles. In the case of the quarry, every man of the original storming party became a casualty, but it was taken by their successors. The rain was heavy, the slopes slippery, the mud deep, and the whole of the conditions about as bad as they could be, which was the more serious as the tanks were put out of action thereby.

The 50th Brigade of the Seventeenth Division, with the 7th East Yorks and 6th Dorsets in the lead, had been launched upon Neuvilly with instructions to avoid a frontal attack, but to endeavour to get round to north and south so as to pinch it out; while the guns bombarded it and kept the machine-gunners in their lairs. South of the village the attack advanced rapidly through the mirk of a most inclement night. The first lines of machine-guns were overrun and destroyed. The wave of men then fought their way through some wire, and got as far as the embankment, which was thickly garnished with light artillery. Before dawn the 10th West Yorkshires closed in upon Neuvilly, and in spite of several obstinate machine-guns cleared the place and took the survivors prisoners, most of them being dragged out of cellars. Pushing on, the Seventeenth Division after several vicissitudes captured the village of Amerval, but were pushed out of it again by a counter-attack, finally regaining it after dark. The 7th Borders took this village, but lost both their commander and their adjutant in doing so. The Thirty-eighth had kept its line all through, so that by evening the whole objective was practically in the hands of the British after a very prolonged and stubborn fight, in the course of which the Corps had taken four guns and 600 prisoners.

Meanwhile Harper's Fourth Corps on the left had also gone forward at 2 A.M., their objective being the high ground to the south of Solesmes. The plan was that the Sixth Corps should take the ground to the north of the village, but the whole operations were made very difficult by the knowledge that the civilian inhabitants were still there, and that the guns had therefore to be used sparingly. When once the points on both sides had been occupied it was hoped that the Sixty-second Division of the Sixth Corps would be able to capture the place. The advance of the Fourth Corps was made with the Fifth Division on the right and the Forty-second on the left. The line of the railway and the high ground east of it were successively occupied, though the fire was heavy and the finest qualities were needed in the soldiers who breasted the hill with lines of machine-guns flashing at them from the hawthorn hedges of the embankment. In the attack upon the hamlet of Marou the 127th Brigade of the Forty-second Division showed the usual Lancastrian gallantry. There are no finer, tougher soldiers in the world, either in attack or defence, than these North Countrymen. On one occasion on this day, a company of the 5th Manchesters being pinned down, it was essential to convey news of their position to their supports. Four volunteers started in succession across the open bullet-swept plain, and all four were shot down. None the less Private Wilkinson volunteered as the fifth and actually got through unscathed and saved the situation. For this and other exertions during the day he received the Victoria Cross. The 1st and 3rd Guards Brigade had gone forward on the front of the Sixth Corps, with the 2nd Brigade in immediate support, and these magnificent troops, taking St. Python in their stride, beat down all opposition and by 7.30 were in their appointed place to the north of the village. The two flanks being thus secured, the Sixty-second went in between them with their usual vigour and, according to plan, assaulted the place from the west, fighting their way into it and out at the other side, the 186th Brigade taking the village while the 185th passed through it for a fresh advance. The 2/4 York and Lancaster aided in mopping up the village, which entailed some very severe fighting from house to house, as dangerous often as entering a cave in which lurks some wounded beast of prey. It was on this occasion that Corporal Daykins won his Cross, leading the twelve men, who were the only survivors of his platoon, with that mixture of wile and courage which is the ideal combination. He not only cleared

CHAPTER IX.

Operations of Byng's Third Army Oct. 20.

the front of his own platoon, but perceiving that his neighbours were held up he started out alone to their assistance, with such success that he brought back a machine-gun and 25 more prisoners as the prize of his own unaided effort.

The 3rd Guards Brigade on the extreme left attempting to make good the Solesmes—Valenciennes Road, were checked for a time by very heavy fire, but overcame the difficulty, and soon the Guards had their full objective, and were in touch with the Nineteenth Division on the flank of the Seventeenth Corps on their left at Maison Blanche. The Forty-second Division on the right had got well forward, but was checked at last on the line of the Beart brook, which caused the Sixty-second on their left to throw out a defensive flank and put limits to their advance. The Fifth Division on the extreme right had also been held, and were finally driven off the high ground south of Marou by a sharp counter-stroke of the enemy. By evening the Fifth and Forty-second had secured almost their full objectives, the Manchester battalions having borne the brunt of the fighting. The Fourth Corps had taken over 1000 prisoners. The Sixth Corps had also gone to its full limit, the Guards and Sixty-second having cleared everything in front of them and sent back 700 prisoners. It had been a most successful day; but the hardest work had fallen upon the Fourth Corps, both divisions having been badly knocked about. It was determined to spend a day therefore in consolidating the gains, and to continue the advance on October 23.

On that date the Fifth Corps on the right went forward once again, with the Thirty-third Division on the right and the Twenty-first on the left. If we attempt to describe the action from the broad point of view of the whole Corps front, the order of battle from the right was the Thirty-third, Twenty-first, Fifth, Forty-second, Third, and Second. On the front of the Sixth Corps there was a sudden outburst of artillery fire during the assembly of the troops, which unhappily caught the Third Division and caused many casualties. It is a hard test even for the most veteran troops to be under a hurricane of shells in the dark and cold of an autumn night, but the men of the Iron Division came into the battle as blithely as ever. The Harpies River, and a whole screen of villages and of woods, with the great Forest of Mormal at their back, were the immediate obstacles which confronted the Army. On the right the village of Forest was soon secured, though an obstinate pocket held out for some time to the north-east of it. The enemy in this quarter could be seen retiring in small parties towards Vendegies and the wood near that village. The Thirty-third Division on the flank had a greater volume of fire to contend with and was rather slower than the Twenty-first, which never halted until it was close to Vendegies, reaching it at 10 A.M. The defence was thickening, however, and both divisions had very heavy going in the afternoon, though the 19th Brigade of the Thirty-third Division fought its way along the north of Vendegies Wood, and reached its allotted line, while the 98th Brigade was held up by the fire from Bousies. As the farther line was reached the two reserve brigades of each division—the 62nd and the 100th Brigades— were pushed up to take the burden from those who

CHAPTER IX.

Operations of Byng's Third Army. Oct. 23.

238   THE BRITISH CAMPAIGN, 1918

CHAPTER IX.

Operations of Byng's Third Army. Oct. 23.

were wearied out by the long and strenuous day. Nearly 800 prisoners had fallen to the Fifth Corps.

The Fourth Corps had the preliminary task of clearing the south side of the St. Georges River, and taking the village of Beaurain. This was allotted to the Fifth and Forty-second Divisions, but the leading brigade of the former was caught in the artillery attack already alluded to, with the result that it sustained losses which seriously crippled it. None the less the attack started up to time and was successfully carried out, save that Beaurain could not be cleared—a fact which necessitated a change in barrage, no easy matter after a great action is launched. The 125th Lancashire Fusilier Brigade of the Forty-second Division did particularly fine work. The Thirty-seventh Division and the New Zealanders, Canterbury and Otago in the van, had now passed through the ranks of their comrades, and as there were signs of German disorganisation the pressure was strenuously maintained. As a result the New Zealanders captured the crossings over the Ecaillon River before they could be destroyed, and reached the edge of Le Quesnoy, while the Thirty-seventh seized Ghissignies with its bridge. It was a great day's work for Harper's Corps.

On the left the Third and Second Divisions had advanced on single-brigade fronts, the 76th and 5th being in the lead. The 1st Gordons of the 76th advancing rapidly, cleared the village of Romeries after a very sharp tussle. A battalion commander and 600 men were taken. The rest of the brigade then passed through it and carried the line forward. It was evident this day that the Germans, though hard in patches, were really becoming demoralised under the pounding of the British, and that they had lost all stomach for the fray. Several well-placed machine-guns were abandoned by their crews without a shot being fired, and serious opposition seemed at places to be at an end. Both the 8th Royal Lancasters and the 2nd Suffolks went through every defence like paper. The 8th Brigade then took up the running, and the 2nd Royal Scots carried Vertain with 200 more prisoners, while the 1st Scots Fusiliers took Escarmain also with 200 Germans. Patrols were sent forward as far as the Ecaillon River and few of the enemy appeared to be left upon the southern bank.

Chapter IX.
Operations of Byng's Third Army.
Oct. 23.

Meanwhile the 5th Brigade on the left had passed to the north of Vertain and swept forward, keeping level with the Nineteenth Division on their left. They co-operated in the capture of Escarmain, and the rest of the Second Division made its way through Capelle, and lined the Capelle—St. Martin Road, the latter village having been taken by the Nineteenth Division. So demoralised did the Germans appear on this flank, with their gun-teams all out in the open ready to limber up, that it appeared as if unlimited progress could be made by Haldane's Corps, but it was known that the enemy were in a sterner mood to the south and that the Fourth and Fifth Corps, though victorious, had no assurance of an easy advance. It was determined therefore to renew the battle next morning before daylight.

At that hour the Thirty-third and Twenty-first Divisions again went forward on the right, but the opposition in this quarter was still very stiff. Poix du Nord was captured by the Twenty-first and some 3000 inhabitants were found cowering in the cellars. Englefontaine was at the same time attacked by the 100th Brigade of the Thirty-third Division, but the machine-guns were busy and it was some time before they could get a lodgment. The Twenty-first was at the same time held up on the road north of the village. About 4 P.M. the line moved forward again behind a fresh barrage, that refreshing shower which revives the exhausted infantry. The men of the 100th Brigade got half-way through Englefontaine and remained there at close grips with their tenacious adversaries, while the Twenty-first fought their way forward to the south-east of Ghissignies, where they were again pulled up. The resistance on this southern section of the Corps front was certainly very different from that experienced by Haldane's Corps in the left flank. Meanwhile the Fourth and Sixth Corps were waiting for the Fourth Army and the Fifth Corps to swing into line, but they made a short forward movement on October 24, the Third Division passing through Ruesnes, while the New Zealanders on their right kept pace with them. Both the Fifth Corps on the right and the Seventeenth Corps on the left were for the time rather behind the general line, so that a long defensive flank had to be formed by each of the Corps between them. The Sixty-first Division had come in on the right of the Seventeenth Corps, but it had at once run into a sharp attack which drove it for the time out of Vendegies-sur-Ecaillon. During this day some attempt was made by the Sixth Corps to push cavalry through, but every horse of two strong patrols of Oxfordshire Hussars was shot, so that it was impossible to persevere.

BYNG'S THIRD ARMY

The village of Englefontaine had not yet been cleared, so after a breathing-space of one day the Thirty-third Division attacked once more, while its neighbour to the south, the Eighteenth Division, co-operated by advancing upon Mount Carmel. This attempt was entirely successful, the 100th Brigade flooding over the village and capturing 450 prisoners. The Twenty-first Division at the same time advanced its line on the north.

The Army had now outrun its communications and a halt was necessary. It was Haig's policy, however, to continue raining down hammer blows upon his reeling antagonist, so that all was ready for a big fresh advance on November 4, which should be on an immense scale, involving the fronts of the Fourth, Third, and First Armies.

The immediate objective in front of the right of the Third Army was the formidable bulk of the Mormal Forest, after which the action may well be named. The advance on the front of the Fifth Corps was made by the Thirty-eighth Welsh on the right and the Seventeenth Division on the left, each brigade succeeding the other, as the various objectives were reached. The edge of the Forest was strongly held, but when once it had been penetrated the progress along the sides was rapid and the enemy freely surrendered. So fair were the prospects that the troops were ordered not to confine themselves to the allotted objectives but to push on as far as they could. The ultimate aim was to gain a passage over the Sambre, though this seemed to be more than one day's work could possibly accomplish.

The Thirty-eighth Division attained its full objectives, but the Seventeenth met with a lively

CHAPTER IX.

Operations of Byng's Third Army. Nov. 4.

R

resistance in Locquignol, and was held up for a time. The weather had broken and the rain was falling, but in spite of the depressing surroundings the fighting line pressed on. The 13th Welsh Regiment moving forward with great dash pushed patrols into Sarbaras, where many rifles scattered over the ground pointed to the German demoralisation. All night the Welshmen pushed forward, and Berlaimont was taken in the early morning. At the same hour the Seventeenth Division, having overcome their difficulties, were nearly as far forward on their left. The Forest had been expected to form a greater obstacle than was really the case, for when once it was entered it was found that the clearings were so extensive that save in patches it was hardly an obstacle at all.

The Fourth Corps had gone forward on November 4 with the Thirty-seventh Division on the right and the New Zealanders on the left. The latter were to advance upon either side of Le Quesnoy, which was to be encircled and taken. The town, which was an old-fashioned walled fortress, was not shelled on account of the inhabitants, but smoke- and oil-drums were fired on to the ramparts.

The attack was a complete success and swept over every obstacle without a check, save for some short delay caused by a strong point missed by the barrage in front of the Thirty-seventh Division. Louvignies and Jolimetz were taken by the Thirty-seventh, which pushed on to establish itself within the Forest. The New Zealanders left Hart's Brigade to invest Le Quesnoy and also advanced rapidly into the Forest, capturing many prisoners and guns. Le Quesnoy was now completely isolated, but the ancient walls and gateways were strongly defended by all modern

BYNG'S THIRD ARMY 243

devices, and a machine-gun clattered through the slit where a bow may once have been bent. An officer with a flag of truce got no response. An aeroplane was then sent over, which dropped the message that our troops were in the Forest far to the east, and that a surrender would be the wisest course. The enemy, however, would have none of it. A forlorn hope of New Zealanders then approached with a scaling-ladder in the good old style, and swarmed up the walls. There was only one ladder and three successive walls, but in some miraculous fashion the whole of the 4th New Zealand Battalion reached the top of the rampart, with the loss of one man. This was accomplished by sweeping the walls round with such a fire that the defenders could not even peep over. On seeing that they had reached the rampart the German commander at last hoisted the white flag. The garrison consisted of about 1000 men.

The Sixth Corps advanced with the Sixty-second on the right and the Guards on the left, each on a two-brigade front. Both divisions went forward from the beginning without a hitch, prisoners streaming back. As they advanced, however, they came into heavy machine-gun fire from the orchards southwest of Frasnoy and south of Wargnies, where for a time the Guards were held up. The country here was very enclosed and thickly hedged, which made progress slow. By evening, however, the objectives had been reached, the orchards cleared, with Frasnoy, Preux-au-Sart, and 1000 prisoners to show for their day's work. Altogether this battle of Mormal Forest had been a day of triumph for the Third Army, and especially for the Fourth Corps in the centre. It was a great victory, in which on this front alone some

Chapter IX.
Operations of Byng's Third Army. Nov. 4.

CHAPTER IX.

Operations of Byng's Third Army. Nov. 4-5.

7000 prisoners and about 100 guns were taken, while the Germans had been beaten, with great loss, out of a position which, in their old form, they would have held for a month. So complete was the German break-up that several batteries were taken by the Fourth Corps, with horses, mounted officers, and all complete, and were then despatched in full working order to the rear. When one recalls how their papers and critics had clamoured for open warfare against the untrained British levies the result must have surprised them. At the end of the fight the British line was well up to the great forest.

In the evening the old Fifth Division, now at last reaching the end of those labours which had lasted for more than four terrible years without a break, came into the field once more. It would be interesting to know whether there was a single man left in the ranks of those who had skirted Mormal Forest in August 1914 among the eager battalions which now faced the same obstacle. It is of course true that even the units had been largely altered in the interval, and yet some of the grand old battalions still marched in their honoured formations, changed in all save that eternal spirit which has made and kept them famous. The Fifth Division was ordered to pass through the ranks of the Thirty-seventh after dawn at the western edge of Mormal Forest, and to push onwards to the east. General Oldman of the 15th Brigade on the left advanced on a one-battalion front, and kept the 1st Bedfords, 1st Norfolks, and 1st Cheshires leap-frogging through each other as often as possible in order to minimise the difficulties of the Forest. General Norton of the 95th Brigade on the right of the line attacked with the 1st East Surreys and

1st Cornwalls in the van, and the 1st Devons in reserve. All day the Fifth Division clove its way through the great forest, the British front, like a line of beaters, putting up the game as it went. For the most part it was but a faint-hearted quarry, but here and there it stood fiercely at bay, and trench mortars had to be rushed up and strong points blown down, before the infantry could get forward. The 3rd Hussars kept pace and connected up with the New Zealanders on the left. Pelting rain, deep mud, and broken tracks delayed, but could not stop, the ardent advance, which continued until the leading line was down on the bank of the Sambre, where they were joined next day by the van of the Forty-second Division, which had relieved the New Zealanders. One bridge at Quartes was found intact and was ready for demolition, but Major Cloutman of the Sappers, commanding the 59th Field Company, with extraordinary gallantry rolled across the tow-path, swam the river, and cut the leads of the charge, all under very heavy fire. It was a most daring deed, which was rewarded by a V.C., but unhappily a small party of the enemy with equal gallantry succeeded in repairing the leads and destroying the bridge.

CHAPTER IX.

Operations of Byng's Third Army. Nov. 4-5.

The operations on the right and centre of the Third Army front now took the form of an advance to complete the possession of the Forest of Mormal. On November 5 the Thirty-third and Twenty-first Divisions were back in line, and, working in close liaison with the Eighteenth Division on the left of the Fourth Army, they pushed the advance up to the bank of the Sambre. Here it was found that all bridges had been destroyed, and there was a check while the Twenty-first to the north were making

Nov. 5.

good the rest of the Forest and breaking out in little groups of khaki from the eastern edge. That night they threw light bridges over the Sambre and got some infantry across, the line running from north of Leval to east of Berlaimont. The left of the Twenty-first Division was still west of the river. Next day, November 6, the remorseless advance still went on. Transport was failing, for the roads through the Forest were impossibly bad, but nothing could stop the eager infantry, who were in full cry with their quarry in the open. A number of villages were taken, each of which was full of machine-guns, and showed some fight. By dusk the line of the Avesnes—Bavay Road had been made good. On November 7 the German retreat still continued, but the British had still to fight their way and their progress was far from being a walking-tour. Both the Thirty-third and Twenty-first had a sharp fight before they could dislodge the rearguards from the Bois du Temple, Ecuelin, and Limont-Fontaine. Campbell's men had a particularly hard task with the latter, which was strongly garrisoned and stoutly defended, while the neighbouring village of Eclaises also presented a bold front. There was a real close infantry battle, with some savage house-to-house fighting, before these points could be cleared. 130 prisoners were taken. The war had now left the open arable country and come into the country of small enclosed orchards with high hedges, which blinded the German observers, since they had already lost command of the air. This was a very vital point. On November 8 the Welsh and Seventeenth were in the front line once more, and the enemy was found to be still very organised and resolute on this sector, fighting hard and with some success to hold the line of a watercourse. Finally this opposition weakened, or it might be more fair to say that the brave rearguard, having done its work, was withdrawn. On November 9 the Fifth Corps got along rapidly, gaining the eastern edge of the Bois du Temple and the high ground east of Beaufort. For a time all contact was lost with the enemy, who were rapidly retreating, and they were not located again until they were on the line of the River Thure. The roads had been blown up, and pursuit was much retarded. The difficulties of the advance were much aggravated by the impossibility of getting the supplies forward. Many delay-action mines had gone up in the railways in the rear, which prevented rail-heads from being rapidly advanced. It is a fact, which is typical of the ghoulish humour of German methods, that after several explosions in the Le Cateau station it occurred to some one to dig up the graves which were marked in German as covering the remains of some unknown British soldiers and were placed near the line. In each case a delay-action mine was discovered all set for different dates. It was determined, therefore, in order to economise supplies, that a single Corps, the Sixth, should form the whole front of the Third Army from this time onwards. This change was accomplished, and the vanguard had just got in touch with the Germans on the River Thure, when the historic November 11 came to end the hostilities.

The troops of the Fourth Corps had moved forward from November 4 onwards in close liaison with the advance just recorded. The Fifth Division captured Pont-sur-Sambre, Boussières, and St. Remy, while the Forty-second occupied Hautmont, so that on Novem-

Chapter IX. Operations of Byng's Third Army. Nov. 9.

ber 9 the Corps line was the Avesnes—Maubeuge Road. There they found themselves when the bugles sounded the final "Cease fire." The record of Harper's Corps since August 21 can be tersely summed up in a few figures. They had lost 30,000 men. They had captured 22,500 prisoners and 350 guns, fighting for ten weeks without rest or break, and often in the worst of weather. The record of all the divisions was splendid, but this is perhaps the place to say a special word about the New Zealanders, which, in the judgement of many soldiers, was, if it be not invidious to say so, equal to the very best division in France. When it is stated that during the war they lost 57,632 men, and that the total number of prisoners taken from them is reported to have been 45, these extraordinary figures make all further comment superfluous. But what was particularly remarkable was their appreciation of a military situation which more than once altered the whole strategic situation. Thus it was their discovery that the Crevecœur bridge was intact, and their rapidity in seizing it and tenacity in holding it and the village, which threatened the whole Beaurevoir line and helped to reduce to nullity one of the greatest defences ever created by German engineers. These men return to their island homes bearing with them the deep admiration of their comrades and the gratitude of the Empire. They joined discipline in peace to valour in war, and England was the poorer when the last red hat-band was seen in the streets of her cities.

The Sixth Corps, after the battle of Mormal Forest, pushed on to the east, and was rather impeded by the water-logged country than by the German resistance. On November 6 there was a counter-attack upon the Sixty-second Division, which made no headway and had heavy losses. Bavisaux, Obies, and many other villages were taken, the church in the latter place containing thirty machine-guns. The Guards on the left took Buvignies, while the Twenty-fourth Division upon their north held the line of the Hongnau River. On November 7 the resistance was still negligible, but the continuous rain and the wooded nature of the country made rapid progress almost impossible. That evening General Haldane received the surprising news that it was probable that the enemy would send emissaries through the Allied lines with a view to negotiating an armistice, his instructions being that if they approached his front they should be detained pending instructions from higher authority. In the evening it was learned that they had actually reached the French lines. The fighting still continued, however, and on November 9 the Sixty-second Division had reached the Sambre. The Guards on the same day pushed forward rapidly and entered the citadel of Maubeuge in the afternoon. It was difficult to get touch with the enemy, who were reported to be standing at Boussois. At this period, as already told, the Sixth Corps took over the whole Army front, and was advancing upon the Maubeuge—Charleroi front when the fateful hour struck.

 The record of the Sixth Corps during their ten final weeks of work had been a magnificent one, and was strangely parallel to that of the Fourth Corps on their right. Their losses had been almost identical, about 30,000 men. Their prisoners came to over 20,000 and their captured guns were 350. The Fifth Corps, on the other hand, had endured more than its

Chapter IX.

Operations of Byng's Third Army. Nov. 4–9.

neighbours, having lost no less than 34,000 men. It had captured 13,000 prisoners. Altogether the losses of the Third Army during the final ten weeks had been 100,000 men, while they had taken about 60,000 prisoners with nearly 1000 guns.

We have considered the advance of the three southern Corps of the Third Army. In order to complete the record it is necessary to return to October 13, and to trace the operations of Fergusson's Seventeenth Corps, which were left on that date in front of the Selle River. On October 14 the 72nd Brigade of the Twenty-fourth Division, which was in the van, gained a footing at the edge of Haussy village, which straddles the river. On October 16 this same brigade took the whole village on either bank. The left of the line was held up, however, by a particularly heavy gas screen. Later in the day the Germans were into Haussy once more, but again were pushed out from the western section of it, on which they gas-shelled it, to the destruction of a number of unfortunate civilians who had been unable to get away. 400 prisoners were taken during the day. October 17 saw the British line where it had been on the 15th, as the gas clouds hanging low over the river valley made the position down there untenable.

On October 20, a rainy and tempestuous day, the general advance of the whole Third Army was resumed. The Nineteenth Division having relieved the Twenty-fourth, carried out the advance on the front of the Seventeenth Corps, having in touch with it the Fourth Division of the Twenty-second Corps on the left, and the Guards of the Sixth Corps on the right. The attack of the Nineteenth

BYNG'S THIRD ARMY

Division had for its first objective the bridging of the Selle, the capture of the railway and high ground beyond, and of the village of East Haussy. The second stage should be the ridge to the east. Two brigades advanced—the 57th on the left and the 58th on the right—behind a fine barrage from eleven brigades of artillery.

CHAPTER IX.
Operations of Byng's Third Army.
Oct. 20-25.

The attack was started at 2 in the morning, and before 4 A.M. the 57th Brigade were in the whole of Haussy, the resistance having been slight. At 6 o'clock the 8th Gloucesters, on the extreme right, had reached their final objective, where they were endeavouring to get touch with the Guards in the neighbourhood of Maison Blanche. The 10th Warwicks were held up on the left, but soon cleared out the obnoxious pocket. By 9 o'clock the 58th Brigade was also on its extreme limit, and an obstinate strong point was surrounded and destroyed. In this brigade the 2nd Wiltshires had the worst ordeal, but they won through at last. Patrols on the right had reached the banks of the Harpies. The blow had, as must be admitted, been delivered in the air, but the river line had been won, and that was the essential.

On October 23 the part played by the Seventeenth Corps was subsidiary to that of the Corps to the north and to the south. On this date the Nineteenth Division was ordered to protect the left flank of the Sixth Corps in its advance on Romeries and Escarmain. This was duly carried out by the 8th Gloucesters and 10th Warwicks, and contributed greatly to the victory in the south. That night the Sixty-first South Midland Division took over from the Nineteenth Division, with an ambitious programme for next day, October 24. In the course of

252   THE BRITISH CAMPAIGN, 1918

CHAPTER IX.
Operations of Byng's Third Army.
Nov. 1–4.

this attack the 183rd Brigade advanced on the right and the 182nd on the left, their objectives including the villages of Bermerain, Vendegies, and Sommaing. There followed a confused day of hard fighting, the general movement being always from west to east. All three villages were most hotly contested. Vendegies proved to be a special centre of resistance, but on the morning of October 25 it was found to be unoccupied, and the whole resistance had relaxed to such an extent that the front of the Army flowed slowly forward with hardly a check, submerging fresh areas and villages until it had reached the Rhonelle River, where a bridge-head was established on the front of the Twenty-second Corps.

On November 1 the advance was resumed, when Maresches was attacked by the Sixty-first Division, the Warwicks and Worcesters of the 182nd Brigade being in the lead. The village was taken with about three hundred of the garrison. Preseau on the left had fallen. This was the centre of a violent counter-attack in the afternoon, which involved the right of the Fourth and the left of the Sixty-first Divisions. Four German tanks co-operated, two of which were destroyed by the British guns. This attack pressed back the advance from its furthest point, but made no material change in the situation, though Preseau was regained by the Germans, with the effect that their machine-guns from this point held up the left flank of the 184th Brigade in their further advance. Nearly 800 prisoners were made during the day.

The advance was renewed next morning, November 2, and again the resistance seemed to wane, so that by midday the full objectives planned, but not attained, on the previous day had been reached with little loss, the Sixty-first moving onwards in close touch with the Fourth on their left and the Second on their right. The Sixty-first were now drawn out of the line, and the Nineteenth and Twenty-fourth each sent up a brigade to take their place.

Chapter IX. Operations of Byng's Third Army. Nov. 3–4.

November 3 found the front of the Corps still pushing forward without undue opposition. In the late afternoon the 9th Cheshires of the 56th Brigade were in Jenlain in touch with the Eleventh Division upon their left. The whole of the Jenlain—Le Quesnoy Road had been reached along the Corps front, and once again it seemed as if the cavalry might get their long-sought opportunity. Next morning, however, November 4, found the stubborn German still standing grimly on the defensive, and the infantry went forward once more to pitch-fork him a little farther to the east. It was a great general attack in which the three Armies, First, Third, and Fourth, all moved forward against the Avesnes—Maubeuge—Mons line. On the front of the Seventeenth Corps there was no very outstanding objective, and yet it was of course essential that they should keep well up with the line, if only in order to cover the flanks of their neighbours.

The right of the Corps when the advance began consisted of the 73rd Brigade of the Twenty-fourth Division. On its left was the 56th Brigade, and to the left of that the 58th, both of the Nineteenth Division. Both infantry and artillery had to find their battle stations in pitch darkness, but all were in their places at zero. At 6 o'clock the line went forward, faced in the first instance by a small stream, the Petit Aunelle, which was safely crossed, though its banks were in places 30 feet deep. At 10 o'clock both divisions had gained the higher ground beyond the stream. By midday the Twenty-fourth Division had reached the Great Aunelle River, and a party of the 7th Northamptons drove away with their accurate rifle-fire the German sappers who were endeavouring to destroy the bridge, but could not themselves cross on account of the heavy German fire. The 2nd Wilts of the Nineteenth Division had their patrols in Eth. To the north the Eleventh Division was over the river, and the German position was rapidly becoming impossible, though they were counter-attacking with great valour upon the farther bank of the stream. Before evening Wargnies had fallen to the 9th Cheshires, and the whole British front was up to or over the Aunelle. The advance was carried on in pouring rain on November 5, a further area being gained up to the Hongnau River and the position strengthened, though the amount of ground on the farther side of the river was still limited and varied with the German counter-attacks which occasionally swept back the intrusive bridge-heads, but only to have them re-established once more. The troops were soaked, the ground was sodden, the infantry were over the ankles in mud, and every one was exhausted.

On the morning of November 7 this line of the Hongnau had been abandoned by the Germans and the advance was resumed. It must surely have been at this period of the war one of the most impressive sights in the whole history of the world, could one with a single sweeping glance have seen that gigantic line from the left wing of the Belgians on the Dutch frontier to the right wing of the French within view of the Swiss, moving forward every day, millions of

BYNG'S THIRD ARMY 255

men advancing together, with the flash of their bayonets before them and the red glare of their shells in front of them, while along that whole front of four hundred miles the grey cloud, like some visible thing of evil, rolled slowly back in front, leaving bare the ground which it had blighted and poisoned. It was clear to all men that the end was near, and yet few dared to hope how near it actually proved to be.

On November 7 the Twenty-fourth Division took over Bavay, which had just been captured by the Guards. The weather conditions were more serious than the German opposition, and the advance was held back by the dreadful roads. None the less a long succession of villages were wrenched from the enemy—Taisnières, Feignies, and others—while on November 9 the Guards were in Maubeuge on the right. From this time there was practically no more fighting, and only a slow advance on the one side and a slow retreat on the other until the fateful November 11. To quote the memorandum of a General Officer upon the spot: "The moral effect of retirement upon the enemy was very marked, and it was found that even his machine-gunners, who had fought very well all through our advance, were beginning to feel the effect, and would not stand once a field-gun was brought up to deal with them."

Chapter IX.
Operations of Byng's Third Army.
Nov. 7-9.

CHAPTER X

THE ADVANCE OF HORNE'S FIRST ARMY

From September 27 to the end

The Canadians at the Canal du Nord—Hard fighting at Bourlon—Strong counter attack at Abancourt—Canadian valour—Godley's Twenty-Second Corps—The Ecaillon valley—Forcing of the Rhonelle—General Heneker's attack—Capture of Douai.

<small>CHAPTER X.
The Advance of Horne's First Army.
Sept. 27–29.</small>

ON September 27 the Canadian Corps, with the Eleventh British Division, attacked once more, the advance joining the left flank of that huge movement in which the First, Third, and Fourth Armies were all engaged. The Twenty-second and Eighth Corps to the north were not engaged, but made a vigorous demonstration in support. The Canadian attack, which began at early dawn, was on a 6000-yard front, from Mœuvres in the south to the Arras—Cambrai Road. In this advance the First and Fourth Canadian Divisions were, in the first instance, to cross the Canal du Nord, and to capture Bourlon Wood and village, with the high ground about Pilgrim's Rest. This attack was in conjunction with one upon the right made by the Seventeenth Corps, where the Fifteenth and Sixty-third Divisions stormed the line of the Canal du Nord east and south-east of Mœuvres, as already recorded. This movement was entirely successful, though there was

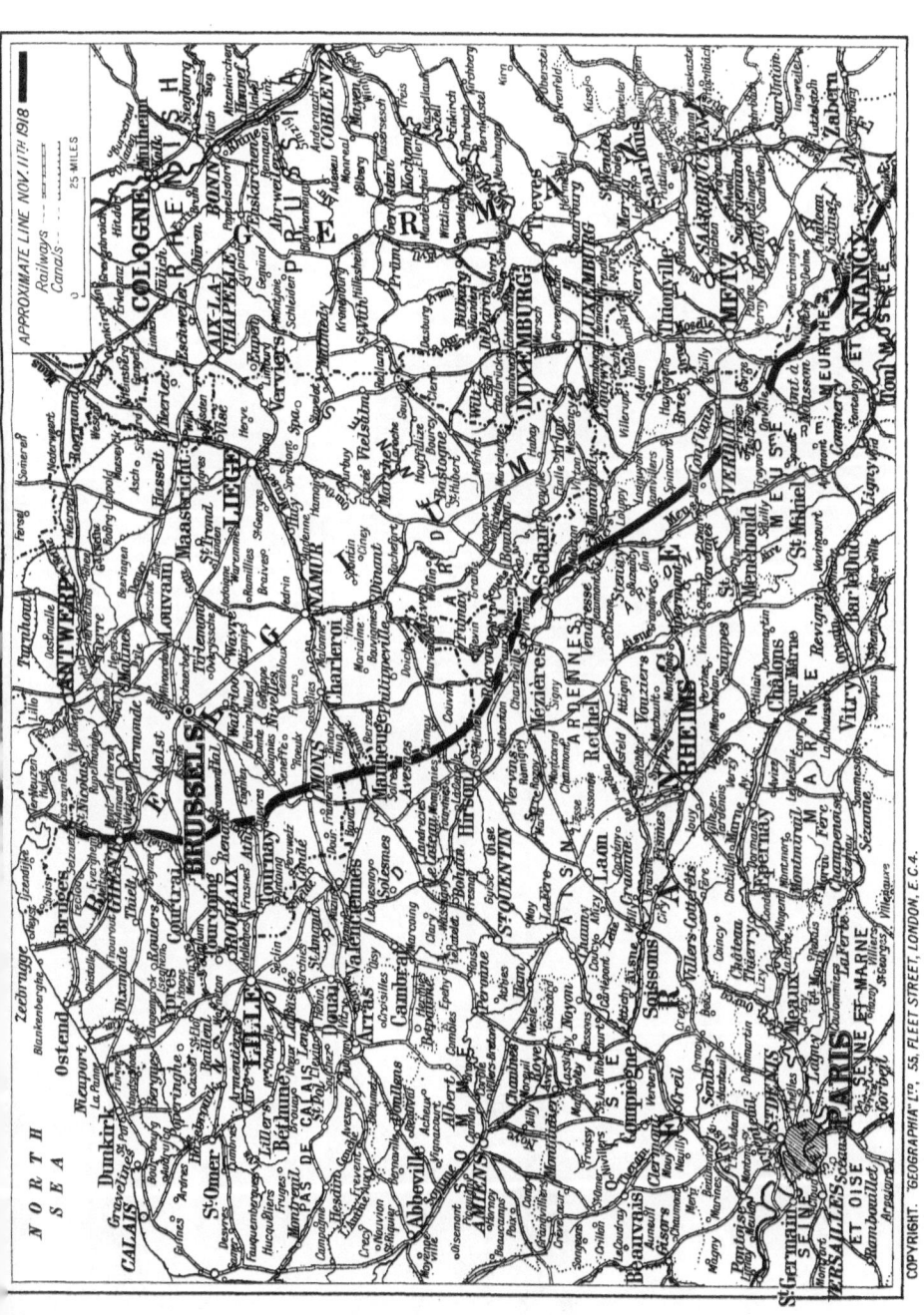

very obstinate resistance at Graincourt, which held up the advance for a time. The Fifty-seventh Division passed through, however, to the north of this village and gained Cantaing and Fontaine, so that the defenders of Graincourt, finding British troops behind them, were forced to surrender.

CHAPTER X.

The Advance of Horne's First Army. Sept. 27-29.

The Canal du Nord had been emptied by the blowing up of sluice-gates, and was quickly passed by the Canadian troops, who scrambled down one side and up the other, with or without the aid of scaling-ladders. At the other side they found much less resistance than had been expected, which was greatly the result of a barrage which has seldom been equalled for accuracy and intensity. Captured German officers declared that nothing could live under it. The German guns were slow and feeble in their reply, and the whole work of the enemy artillery at this period showed how nervous it had become through the recent heavy captures, and how much they appreciated the necessity of keeping well to the rear. The Canadian line poured on with little loss and did not halt until it had seized its whole objective, including the ground about Bourlon, which had been the scene of such bitter and fruitless fighting ten months before. Guardsmen and Highlanders, men of Surrey and of Yorkshire, all who had fallen upon and still lay within the soil of that sinister grove, were finally justified and avenged that day. The whole manœuvre, by which a large part of the German line was taken in the rear, elicited expressions of surprise and admiration from captured German officers.

In the second stage of the Canadian attack the First Canadian and the Eleventh British Divisions—

S

CHAPTER X.

The Advance of Horne's First Army.

Sept. 29.

the latter on the extreme left—took up the running, and carried the line forward in the direction of Raillencourt and Haynecourt. In the afternoon the 169th Brigade of the Fifty-sixth Division also came in upon the left, near the Arras—Cambrai Road, to clear the area between the Eleventh Division and the Canal du Nord, the latter division having taken Oisy-le-Verger. There was constant fighting during the day in this quarter, the 168th Brigade coming into action to the left of the 169th, and next morning the 8th Middlesex took Palluel. They also crossed the River Sensée and captured Arleux, but a strong barrage, followed by an infantry attack, drove them out again at 3.30 on the morning of September 29. All these attacks, both of the Eleventh and Fifty-sixth Divisions, were made, after crossing the Canal du Nord, from south to north, so as to extend the left flank of the Canadians.

One of the predominating factors in these operations was the great flood caused by the blocking of the Trinquis and Sensée rivers by the Germans, which created wide lakes shown upon no map, across the front of the Twenty-second Corps. As a matter of fact this development was regarded with some complacency by General Godley, for there had always been a chance that the Germans, by driving a really strong counter-attack along the line of the Scarpe, might checkmate the whole British advance to the south. The effect of the inundations was to free the British higher command from any fears of the kind and to enable them to hold that part very lightly, while they thickened their line elsewhere.

We have left the Canadian line on September 28. On this date the Third Canadian Division, which had relieved part of the Fourth British on the right of the Corps front, attacked with the 7th and 9th Brigades in the van. On its left was the 10th Canadian Brigade, which in turn had the 2nd Canadian Brigade to the north of it. The Third Canadian Division made good progress and pushed through as far as Raillencourt, but the First Canadian Division remained motionless, as it was already rather in front of the general line. The Eleventh British Division was doing continuous good work in the north, but on the morning of September 29 its 32nd Brigade was held up by a strong field of wire, and the advance was checked in that quarter, but later in the day the whole line pushed on once more, the order of brigades from the north being 32 (British), 2, 12, 7, 9 (all four Canadian). A mist covered the front, and from the heart of this impenetrable cloud came the constant rattle of the German fire, while their bullets swept every avenue of approach. The progress was irregular, but by 9.45 in the morning the 12th Canadian Brigade had taken Sancourt and had entered Blecourt, where some fierce bludgeon work was going on. At 10 A.M. the 2nd Brigade had reached Abancourt station, but the Eleventh Division were again held up in the north, which exposed the left flank of the Canadians. South of the Bapaume Road the 9th Brigade was making steady progress, while the 7th had reached Neuville St. Remy. For a moment the 12th Canadian Brigade was staggered by a heavy counter which broke upon it, but the ranks soon rallied and the ground was regained. It was desperately hard fighting, however, and it was to continue day after day until all the northern grit of General Currie's Corps was needed to sustain it.

Chapter X.

The Advance of Horne's First Army. Sept. 28.

CHAPTER X.

The Advance of Horne's First Army.

Sept. 30.

Early in the morning of September 30 they were at it again, the immediate objects of the operations being the capture of the bridge-heads on the Canal de l'Escaut by the Third and Fourth Canadian Divisions, and secondly, that the high ground over the River Sensée should be secured by the First Canadians and Eleventh British.

The attack began well, as the Third Canadian Division got Tilloy and the Fourth got Blecourt. There was some progress also along the Cambrai Road, when the 3rd Canadians got Petit Fontaine. It was "do or die" with the Germans, however, who were keenly alive to the fact that at all costs they must hold the bridge-heads of the Canal. They had put out a great effort, and had brought up three new fighting divisions, making seven in all between Cambrai and the Sensée River. Counter-attacks rolled one after the other from the east, but the Canadians showed themselves as stiff in defence as they were ardent in attack. They might well be in high heart, for since September 27, 200 guns and 5500 prisoners were visible signs of their victory.

Oct. 1.

On October 1 the Fifty-sixth Division relieved the Eleventh and both reverted to the Twenty-second Corps. At 5 A.M. on that date the Canadian attack was renewed, synchronising with that of the Seventeenth Corps in the south and the Twenty-second in the north. The order of brigades on the Canadian front was, from the north, 1, 3, 11, and 9. The advance was made under a heavy barrage, but it met with a most desperate resistance. In this and the following day the Canadians experienced as heavy fighting as any in their great record. By 8 o'clock the general line had got as far as Canal bank—

Morenchies Wood—Cuvillers—Bantigny—Abancourt. Shortly afterwards a very heavy German attack struck the whole Corps front, rolling chiefly up the Bantigny valley, the hostile infantry emerging from Paillencourt and thence pouring forward with great determination in several lines. The 1st Canadian Brigade in the north was bare upon its left flank and was in sore straits, but the 3rd Brigade held on fast to the slope which leads down to the Canal. While swarms of men attacked the British line a number of pockets developed in all the ground which had been taken that day, so that the troops were shot at from all sides. The British artillery came to the rescue, however, and caught the German masses as they advanced with murderous results—one battery of heavies firing 1600 rounds. None the less the enemy won back Abancourt, and gained some ground along the whole front, the battle centring upon Blecourt.

CHAPTER X.

The Advance of Horne's First Army Oct. 1.

That night the British line, which was already much weakened by prolonged fighting, and which was clearly opposed by superior forces, halted for a time for reorganisation and reinforcement. It has since been proved that no fewer than thirteen German divisions were thrown in upon this section of the line.

The work of the Canadian Corps in crossing the Nord Canal, following upon their splendid work in breaking the Quéant—Drocourt line, reasserted the fact, so often demonstrated before, that there are no better soldiers in the world than those of the Dominion. It has been impossible to specify the innumerable acts of valour performed by these brave men, but looking at the highest record of all, as chronicled during these few days of battle, one finds that the Victoria Cross was awarded to Captain

CHAPTER X.

The Advance of Horne's First Army.

Oct. 2.

MacGregor and Lieut. Kerr of the 1st Central Ontario Regiment, the first, after being himself wounded, having killed four and taken eight of the enemy, while the latter rushed a strong point single-handed and captured four machine-guns with thirty-one prisoners. Lieut. Gregg, of the Nova Scotians, killed or wounded eleven of the enemy and took twenty-five prisoners on September 28. Lieut. Honey, of the 78th Manitobas, captured a whole nest of guns single-handed, with ten prisoners, dying of wounds on the last day of the attack, while Sergeant Merisfield of the 4th Central Ontarios cleared out two posts by his own initiative, and fought after being wounded until a second wound left him senseless upon the ground. Such were the iron men who have made the name of Canada great in the battlefields of Europe.

For the sake of connected narrative we may carry on the story of the Canadians from October 2, when their weakened ranks, after their great and continuous exertions, were held by the strong German array in front of Abancourt. For the next few days, while gathering for a fresh spring, the Canadians saw heavy palls of smoke over Cambrai, while at night the dull red glow from great fires hinted at an approaching retreat. During the week which followed, the Seventeenth Corps was, as has been told in their own chronicle, making splendid progress to the south. On October 7 the Second and Third Canadian Divisions, rested and strengthened, renewed their advance. On that date they advanced with the old design of securing the bridge-heads over the Canal, Pont d'Aire and Ramillies being their objectives, the latter a name of good omen for any

British operation. Rapid progress was made, and it was soon evident that, be the machine-guns ever so numerous and spiteful, it was still only a rear screen which faced the attack. The light of day had hardly come before the 5th Brigade, after a short, sharp tussle, had possession of Pont d'Aire, while the 6th Brigade got Ramillies. The 8th Brigade, to its own amazement, crossed the Canal without opposition, and pushed its patrols into Cambrai. It seems that at the moment of the attack the Germans were caught in the confusion of their changes. On October 8 Cambrai was cleared, huge fires were extinguished, and wires, by which the destruction of the town might be completed, were traced and cut. An air reconnaissance at dawn on October 9 showed that the enemy had cleared away from the whole area between the Sensée Canal and the Canal de l'Escaut, having destroyed all the Sensée bridges. The Seventeenth Corps sent the Twenty-fourth Division into Cambrai to take it over, while there was an immediate pursuit of the retreating enemy, in which General Currie pushed forward a mobile column, called Brutinel's Brigade, which contained light guns and the Canadian Light Horse. Villages fell rapidly all along the line both to the Canadians and to the British Eleventh Division on their left.

On October 10 a fresh line of resistance was reached, and the Canadian Corps instantly attacked it, in conjunction with the Eleventh Division. The 4th Canadian Brigade advanced swiftly and got Naves with little opposition. The 6th Canadian Brigade took Thun St. Martin. The Eleventh Division got Estrun and reached the edge of Hem Lenglet.

Chapter X.
The Advance of Horne's First Army.
Oct. 7.

On October 11 the Second Canadian Division, together with the Forty-ninth Yorkshire Territorials, who had relieved the Eleventh, continued their advance. The Canadians met with heavy opposition from Iwuy, and in the forenoon there came a heavy counter-attack, led by seven tanks, six of which paid the penalty. On October 12 the First Canadian Division in the north found that their front was apparently clear, so they swiftly advanced and took Arleux and Estrées, while the Twenty-second Corps attacked on their right and reached Hordain. On this day was the fine attack, recorded elsewhere, of the Fifty-sixth British Division, which got across the Canal at Aubigny. On October 17 the whole line of the Canal was clear, and the First Canadian Division advanced towards Douai, which was occupied by the Eighth British Division from the north.

No further important services were exacted from the Canadian Corps, which had done its share, and more than its share, of the work, so that it retired from the line with the warm admiration and respect of every British soldier who had had experience of it. From its first dreadful baptism of fire, when it faced without masks the unknown horrors of the poison gas, down to the campaign in which it broke the great Quéant switch line, and forced the Canal du Nord, there was never one single occasion upon which the Canadians did not rise to the highest point of military virtue in actual battle. Their record will be fully set out in many a book which will deal fully and in detail with their great deeds. Such a chronicle as this can only hope to help the reader to fit that fuller and more worthy record into the general plan.

We shall now follow the work of Godley's Twenty-second Corps from the time that its right flank crossed the Canal du Nord in the Marquion sector, taking its operations consecutively, and linking them up with the Canadians on the south, who were now, as already recorded, advancing upon Cambrai, bursting through every obstacle as they went. Early in October Hunter-Weston's Eighth Corps extended down to the Scarpe. There was great preparation for the future, but no actual fighting, save for some outpost bickerings between the 12th Brigade of the Fourth Division and the Germans on the north of the Trinquis brook, in the course of which the British posts were attacked —one of them as many as eight times—but remained untaken. On October 7 the guns of the Twenty-second Corps co-operated in the attack made on that day by the Eighth Corps in the north which captured Biache St. Vaast, and a portion of the Fresnes—Rouvroy line. On October 9 there was a reconnaissance of the northern part of the Drocourt — Quéant line by strong patrols, but it was found that it was still strongly held. It was at this period that the Canadian Corps was brought across to the left of the Twenty-second Corps, while the latter moved south, so that it now lay between the Cambrai—Saulzoir Road and the Canal de l'Escaut. Whilst this considerable movement was in progress, on October 11 the Eighth Corps on the north captured the portion of the Drocourt line which was opposite to it. The Fifty-sixth Division and First Canadians, who were on the immediate south, took some part in the fray, the Londoners capturing Fresnes, and the Canadians the high ground which faced them. After the change was carried out, the front east of Cambrai was held by

CHAPTER X.

The Advance of Horne's First Army

Oct. 12.

CHAPTER X.

The Advance of Horne's First Army.
Oct. 11.

the Forty-ninth Yorkshire Division on the right and by the Fifty-first Highlanders on the left.

Immediately before these fresh dispositions were carried out in the south, there was a sharp action in this sector, in which, under the direction of General Currie, the Second Canadians and the Forty-ninth British attacked Iwuy and the ground south-west of it. This was on October 11. The attack gained ground and some hundreds of prisoners, but the losses were in excess of the gains, especially in the case of the Yorkshire Territorials, who suffered considerably in a counter-attack which was urged with the help of tanks. On the morning of October 12 the Fifty-first Highlanders had taken over from the Canadians and carried on the operation. All day there was sharp fighting in front of the British divisions. The Forty-ninth made good progress and followed up the retreating enemy, but the Fifty-first found a stiff opposition on the left, where the Germans held fast to Lieu St. Amand, powerfully supported by their guns on the north bank of the Canal de l'Escaut. The right of the Highland Division captured Avesnes-le-Sec, and so came level with the left of the Forty-ninth. This latter division had continual fighting at Haspres and Saulzoir on to the line of the Selle.

On October 13 the action was renewed, both the British divisions striving hard to push through the German rearguards, which were very strong and were backed by powerful artillery from north and east. Progress was slow, for the country was an open plain without a vestige of cover. The enemy were holding the Canadians to the north of the Escaut Canal, and so were able to keep their guns well forward on that side, to enfilade the advance to the south, and to support their position on the Selle. The British had come into the region of the civil population, so that they had to be chary and discriminating in the use of their guns, while gas shells could hardly be used at all. The Third Army had now got so far ahead that it was compelled to pause for supplies, and the First Army was forced to conform.

Cameron's Forty-ninth Division was much exhausted by its exertions, so the Fourth British Division came up about October 15 to relieve it. It met with a sad misfortune immediately after it had taken its place in the line, as its commanding officer, General Lipsett, was killed while carrying out a reconnaissance in front of the line. He had recently been transferred from a Canadian division, and had a great war record, extending back to near the beginning. It is indeed tragic when one who has played a great part in the drama leaves before the final curtain falls. General Lucas took over the division.

There was no change in the situation so far as the Twenty-second Corps was concerned until October 19, when the enemy began to retire in front of the Highland Division, in conformity with a movement which had already begun north of L'Escaut, and which spread down to the front of the Fourth Division. The Germans had prepared a line of defence upon the Ecaillon River in the rear, and were now letting go of the Selle in order to reassemble their forces upon this even stronger front. The withdrawal was irregular, so that some parts of his array remained hard when others had almost ceased to exist. Thus at Haspres and the part of the Selle

CHAPTER X.

The Advance of Horne's First Army. Oct. 11.

CHAPTER X.

The Advance of Horne's First Army. Oct. 20.

to the north of it, there was still some stiff fighting. He abandoned Saulzoir, however, and the Fourth Division promptly established a bridge-head which should be the base for a future advance. On the Fifty-first Divisional front the pursuit was so rapid, both by the Highlanders and by the Corps Cavalry, that there was not much time for reorganisation.

During October 20 and 21 the Germans were slowly pressed back from the high ground east of the Selle into the Ecaillon valley, and artillery was pushed up to prepare for a further attack upon the new line. The sappers did some great work in throwing, under fire, many bridges over the Selle. Noyelles and Douchy were occupied on the morning of October 20. The river was found to be strongly wired, and there were scattered lines of trenches on the farther side, which made up a strong, fortified position, called by the Germans the Hermanstellung. It was clearly a more elaborate position than that of the Selle. None the less the infantry was not to be denied and the troops crossed the river by wading, the water in many cases being up to the armpits of the men. The 10th and 11th Brigades of the Fourth Division fought their way half-way up the north-eastern slope of the valley, past the villages of Verchain and Moncheaux. The 1st Somersets and 1st Hants occupied the latter and pushed through it, securing the high ground east of the villages, but they found that their comrades of the 2nd West Riding and 1st Warwicks were held up by the German main line upon the crest of the hill, and that the Sixty-first Division, the nearest unit on their right, were temporarily checked at Vendegies. The 2nd West Riding got forward, however, and occupied a position on the crest called "The Pimple," whilst the Fifty-first Division on the north of the 11th Brigade also got well forward up to the village of Maing. In the morning of October 25 the 12th Brigade took up the task in this sector, the 1st King's Own on the right and the 2nd Essex on the left advancing without any very serious opposition, being in touch with the left of the Seventeenth Corps. In the late afternoon the Germans reacted strongly, and there was a counter-attack upon the front of the 2nd Lancashire Fusiliers and upon the Highlanders to their left, but it had little effect. The 154th Brigade of Highlanders was very heavily engaged during this strenuous day, and the 6/7th Argyll and Sutherlands, among others, had serious losses. Among many brave deeds that of Lieut. Bissett is conspicuous, for he won the V.C. by repeated acts of gallantry, leading his men in a desperate bayonet charge, after all their ammunition was expended, and so saving the line. Before evening the village of Querenaing had been occupied and the line of the Artres—Famars Road; 1200 more prisoners were in the Corps cage.

The attack upon the Ecaillon position was a difficult military operation, and one which showed very clearly the marked ascendancy which the British soldier had gained over his German rival. Every factor was in favour of the defence, and yet the line was rapidly shattered by the determined advance of the two divisions concerned. The object of the action was not merely the gain of ground, though that was considerable, but it was to cover the left of the Third Army and also to assist in the advance of the Canadian Corps towards Valenciennes, all of which aims were fully carried out. The action of the infantry was all the finer because they entirely lost the time-table barrage, and had to depend upon their own fine courage and the tactical skill of their leaders. In the actual crossing of the river all ranks showed great gallantry and determination. The method in which the advance was pressed and the victory followed up by very weary soldiers was remarkable, and resulted, among other things, in the capture of the bridge-head of Artres by the Fourth Division, which proved of great value both to the Seventeenth and to the Twenty-second Corps.

A railway from Valenciennes to Le Quesnoy ran across the front of the Corps, and this was made the forming-up point for the renewed attack next morning, when the Fourth and the tireless Fifty-first went forward again under a heavy barrage. Having lost the successive lines of the Selle and the Ecaillon, the Germans were now lining up on the east bank of the Rhonelle, prepared to make a resolute defence. A party of the 2nd Lancashire Fusiliers got across, however, on the morning of the 26th, and established a bridge-head, and joined hands with a party from the Sixty-first Division on their right, who had also forded the stream. This point held firm, but when the 2nd Essex on the left attempted also to cross, there was a stubborn resistance. With field-guns in the face of them and a raking fire from machine-guns at Gaumont Farm on their left flank, this brave battalion had a bad half-hour. The Germans then counter-attacked, falling upon both the Highlanders and the Essex men, but both stood firm, though the gas with which the whole position was drenched made the defence difficult.

In this action the leading battalion of Highlanders at the point attacked, the 6th Argyll and Sutherlands, dashed forward with the bayonet at the advancing Germans and drove them pell-mell back; 212 more prisoners were secured.

The situation on October 26 was that the Corps front was well up to the River Rhonelle, that the Fourth Division had taken Artres and established a post across the river, and that the Fifty-first had got as far as Famars, which it had occupied. Attempts of the Fourth Division to enlarge their holding on the east of the stream had no good result, but the bridge-head was still held against all attacks. On the 27th the Germans attacked the Highlanders and forced their way into Famars, but were again met with the cold steel, this time by the 4th Gordons, and thrown out of the village. Next morning, October 28, the Fifty-first advanced its line, making a lodgment upon Mont Houy on its left flank, and capturing Poirier station. Here they were stopped by a strong German attack. It must be admitted that, considering the incessant retreats and the heavy punishments which they had received, the German troops showed a fine constancy in these numerous but useless efforts to throw back the advance. On October 30 the Fifty-first Division was drawn into reserve and the Forty-ninth took their place in the line. Although there had been no eastward movement during the last few days, the Highlanders had spent them in an incessant pressure to the north-east, to aid the advance upon Valenciennes. By this means a good jumping-off place was secured, from which a Canadian brigade was to attack Valenciennes from the south, in conjunction

CHAPTER X.

The Advance of Horne's First Army.
Nov. 1.

with the main attack upon the Rhonelle line. The Highlanders withdrew from the line in great heart but very exhausted by a long spell of ceaseless work.

On November 1, under a tremendous artillery barrage, the Twenty-second Corps advanced to the forcing of the Rhonelle, the third river front within a fortnight. If the operation were successful it would be decisive of the fate of Valenciennes. The men were very weary, and their ranks had been thinned by the influenza microbe as much as by bullets, but they were cheered by victory and the visible signs of progress in the virgin country all around them. The Fourth Division were still on the right, and the Forty-ninth Yorkshire Territorials on the left. The 11th Brigade held the all-important bridge-head, and across it went the 1st Rifle Brigade, while the 1st Hants forded the river on their left. The crossing was accomplished with no great difficulty, and once across the advance was rapidly pushed. Preseau village was the first objective on this wing of the attack. The resistance was unequal and was soon disposed of, and the village was taken, together with the line of the Preseau—Marly Road. About ten o'clock there came a strong German counter-attack, which got round both flanks of the Rifle Brigade and practically surrounded them, so that the leading companies were hard put to it to fight their way back into the village and out to the west of it. The machine-gun fire was very severe. This attack was purely local, and did not affect the Hampshires or the Forty-ninth Division. Low-flying aeroplanes aided the German infantry, but were more alarming than dangerous. Eventually the Rifle Brigade dug in about 400 yards west of the village ; 1700 prisoners were taken during the day.

Following the policy of giving the Germans no rest, both divisions attacked again next morning. The 2nd Seaforths of the 10th Brigade were on the right and the 1st King's Own of the 12th Brigade on the left of the Fourth Division's front. The German resistance, which was expected to be strong after the counter-attacks of the day before, suddenly collapsed, and Preseau was taken once more. So was the dangerous high ground 700 yards to the east, which was bristling with machine-guns. The Yorkshiremen on the left had advanced with equal bravery, and had taken the steel works south of Marly. Altogether about 1000 more prisoners were taken. That night the Eleventh Division relieved the Fourth, while the Fifty-sixth took the place of the Forty-ninth. The latter division was very weak in numbers, so Blacklock's Sixty-third Naval Division was transferred to the Twenty-second Corps in order to help cover the widening front.

It is worth recording that in all this recent fighting, with its approximation to open warfare, the youths who now made up the bulk of the fighting divisions were found to acquit themselves manfully. Their only deterioration from the older type was in their power of endurance and of resistance to weather, so that after two rough days there was a distinct weakening of their powers. They were trained to use their individual minds in the assault, advancing in small independent sections in single file. " In open country the employment of waves in the attack is criminal "—such was one of the last military notes of the war.

Early on the morning of November 3 the enemy showed clear signs of having had enough, and was withdrawing along the whole front, closely pursued by mounted troops and by infantry. Curgies and Saultain were taken, and the line rapidly extended. On November 4 the pace accelerated, and the crossings of the River Aunelle were forced, the Eleventh Division having a sharp fight at Sebourg. On November 5 the Belgian frontier was crossed and the villages of Mesaurain, Boisin, and Angre were occupied. There was some fighting on this day, the 168th Brigade having a sharp skirmish at Angre. Three tanks of British pattern were captured during the day. On November 6 the Grande Aunelle River had to be crossed, and the Germans made a resistance which at one time was both strenuous and successful. There was a great deal of gas, and all troops had to wear their masks. The Eleventh Division was unable to reach the river on account of the long open slope down which any advance must be made. The Fifty-sixth Division got across south of Angre, and reached the high ground to the east, the 2nd London and London Rifle Brigade in the lead. The former battalion was heavily counter-attacked in the Bois de Beaufort and was driven back to the river, while the London Rifle Brigade also suffered heavy casualties from machine-gun fire from Angre. Forty men of the 2nd Londons were entirely cut off but held on in a deep ditch in the wood, and were surrounded by the enemy. None the less they managed to cut their way out and rejoin their battalion.

On the left of the attack the Kensingtons and London Scottish crossed the river and got possession of Angre. They found themselves involved in a very fierce fight, which swayed backwards and forwards all day, each side attacking and counter-attacking with the utmost determination. Twice the Londoners were driven back and twice they regained their objectives, ending up with their grip still firm upon the village, though they could not retain the high ground beyond. Late at night, however, the 168th Brigade established itself almost without opposition upon the ridge.

Chapter X. The Advance of Horne's First Army. Nov. 7.

On November 7 the opposition had wilted away and the Twenty-second Corps advanced with elements of three divisions in front, for the naval men were now in line on the left, "on the starboard bow of the Second Canadians," to quote their own words. The river was crossed on the whole front and a string of villages were occupied on this and the following days. The rain was pouring down, all bridges had been destroyed, the roads had been blown up, and everything was against rapidity of movement. None the less the front flowed ever forward, though the food problem had become so difficult that advanced troops were supplied by aeroplane. The 16th Lancers had joined the Australian Light Horse, and the cavalry patrols pushed far ahead. Bavay was taken on November 10, and the Corps front had reached one mile east of Villers St. Ghislain when, on November 11, the "cease-fire" was sounded and the white flag appeared.

The general experience of the Twenty-second Corps during these last weeks of the war was that the German rearguards consisted mainly of machine-guns, some of which were fought as bravely as ever. The infantry, on the other hand, were of low

CHAPTER X.

The Advance of Horne's First Army.
Sept. 21.

morale and much disorganised. Need for mounted troops who could swiftly brush aside a thin line and expose a bluff was much felt. The roads were too muddy and broken for the cyclists, and there was no main road parallel with the advance. Owing to his machine-guns and artillery the enemy was able always to withdraw at his own time. 3200 prisoners had been taken by the Twenty-second Corps in the final ten days.

In dealing with the advance of Horne's First Army we have examined the splendid work of the Canadian Corps and of the Twenty-second Corps. We must now turn to the operations of Hunter-Weston's Eighth Corps on the extreme north of this Army, linking up on the left with the right of Birdwood's Fifth Army in the neighbourhood of Lens. Up to the end of September, save for local enterprises, neither the Eighth Division on the right nor the Twentieth on the left had made any serious movement. The time was not yet ripe. At the close of September, however, when the line was all aflame both to the south and in Flanders, it was clear that the movement of the British Armies must be a general one. At that date the Eighth Division extended its flank down to the Scarpe, where it was in touch with the Forty-ninth Division, forming the left of Godley's Twenty-second Corps. Before effecting this change Heneker, on September 21, carried out a spirited local attack with his own division, by which he gained important ground in the Oppy and Gavrelle sectors. It was a hard fight, in which the 2nd Berks had specially severe losses, but a considerable area of important ground was permanently gained.

Early in October General Heneker proceeded to carry out an ambitious scheme which he had meditated for some time, and which had now received the approbation of his Corps Commander. This was an attack by his own division upon the strong Fresnes—Rouvroy line, to the north-east of Arras. His plan was to make a sudden concentrated assault upon the south end of this formidable deeply-wired line, and then to work upwards to the north, avoiding the perils and losses of a frontal advance. This enterprise was begun at 5 A.M. on October 7, and was carried through with that mixture of dash and skill which marks the ideal operation. The 23rd and 25th Brigades supplied the storm-troops, who were drawn from the 2nd Middlesex, 2nd West Yorks, and 2nd Devons, and attacked on a front of 3500 yards. The gain of ground was nearly two miles; the line was broken and Biache was taken. On the next day, October 8, the northward turning movement was carried through, the 1st Worcesters, 1st Sherwood Foresters, and 2nd Berkshires pushing into the front line, the work being mainly carried out by bombing. Altogether 37 machine-guns and 250 prisoners were taken, together with the villages of Fresnes and Neuvireuil, so that the divisional front was now brought opposite the Drocourt—Quéant line.

This strong triple system of the Hindenburg type was attacked in the early morning of October 11 in this sector by Grogan's 23rd Brigade, and by 7 A.M. both the 2nd Middlesex and 2nd Devons were through it, holding the whole front before them, with the exception of the town of Vitry on the Scarpe. The Twelfth Division had taken the place of the Twentieth on the left of the Eighth, and it had also fought its

CHAPTER X.

The Advance of Horne's First Army.
Oct. 11.

way forward, but it was still short of striking distance and could not take part in the attack. The chief danger was from the south, as the floods in the Trinquis River were holding up the First Canadian Division in that quarter, so that the German guns could all swing their muzzles to the north. This was obviated by a free use of smoke and gas, so that the British infantry were shrouded on their right flank. The barrage, by a very ingenious device, was not put down in such a fashion as to pin the Germans to their positions and make it more dangerous to fly than to stand, but it was poured upon one spot, and then moved slowly up the line at the rate of 100 yards in eight minutes, giving the garrison plenty of time to see and to avoid it by a timely flight, which most of them preferred to do. When the new position, which soon included Vitry, had been occupied, some of the 2nd Middlesex scrambled across the Scarpe by a broken bridge and took Mont Metier, the strong point on the left front of the Canadians, in the rear, so as to help their future advance. The total gain was not less than an average of three miles, with Cuincy in the centre as the most advanced point. The German line was now shattered, and though there were sporadic bickerings and resistance, with a constant resource to the ignoble warfare of land mines and booby traps, there was no serious battle. In a single day the Tunnelling Companies, which were always ready for any desperate service, removed 300 mines. On October 14 the Twelfth Division, after a spirited attack, captured Auby on the left, while the Canadians on the right had got up to the Douai Canal. On the 17th the German line was clearly recoiling, and a personal reconnaisance by Colonel

Roberts of the 1st Worcesters showed that there was hope for an advance over the canal. At 2 p.m. accordingly the 2nd Rifle Brigade went forward, and their patrols, with those of the 2nd Middlesex, entered the historic old city of Douai, taking down the German flag which was still flying from the town hall. "The town was found to be fairly intact," says a general officer on the spot, "but the inside of every house had been stripped of everything of value, and what had not been removed had been smashed to atoms. . . . The inside and reeds of the beautiful organ in the Cathedral had been torn out, and lay in a heap on the floor." There is no doubt that President Wilson's note on this subject had an effect in preventing the destruction of towns from this time onwards, and that it was the salvation of Douai. No inhabitants had been left in the town.

From this period the advance on this front was a slow but steady triumphant progress. By the end of October the Eighth Division had gone forward more than thirty miles since it started, and had captured thirty-five towns and villages, including Douai, Marchiennes, and St. Amand. Beyond being greatly plagued by murderous explosive traps, 1400 of which were discovered, and being much incommoded by the destruction of roads and bridges and by the constant canals across its path, there was no very serious resistance. Great floods early in November made the situation even more difficult. On November 5 the Eighth Division was relieved by the Fifty-second, and quitted the line for the last time.

This splendid division has had some injustice done to it, since it was the one Regular division in France

CHAPTER X.

The Advance of Horne's First Army. Oct. 17.

CHAPTER X.

The Advance of Horne's First Army.

in 1914 which was somewhat invidiously excluded from the very special and deserved honours which were showered upon "the first seven divisions." But even in 1914 it had done splendid work, and as to its performance in the following years, and especially in 1918, when it was annihilated twice over, it will live for ever, not only in the records of the British Army, but in that of the French, by whose side it fought in the direst crisis and darkest moment of the whole campaign. There were no further movements of importance on the front of the Eighth Corps, and the completion of their history covers the whole operation of Horne's First Army in this final phase of the war. It was indeed a strange freak of fate that this general, who commanded the guns of the right wing at Mons in that momentous opening battle, should four and a half years later be the commander who brought his victorious British Army back to that very point.

ALLIED ADVANCE IN THE NORTH

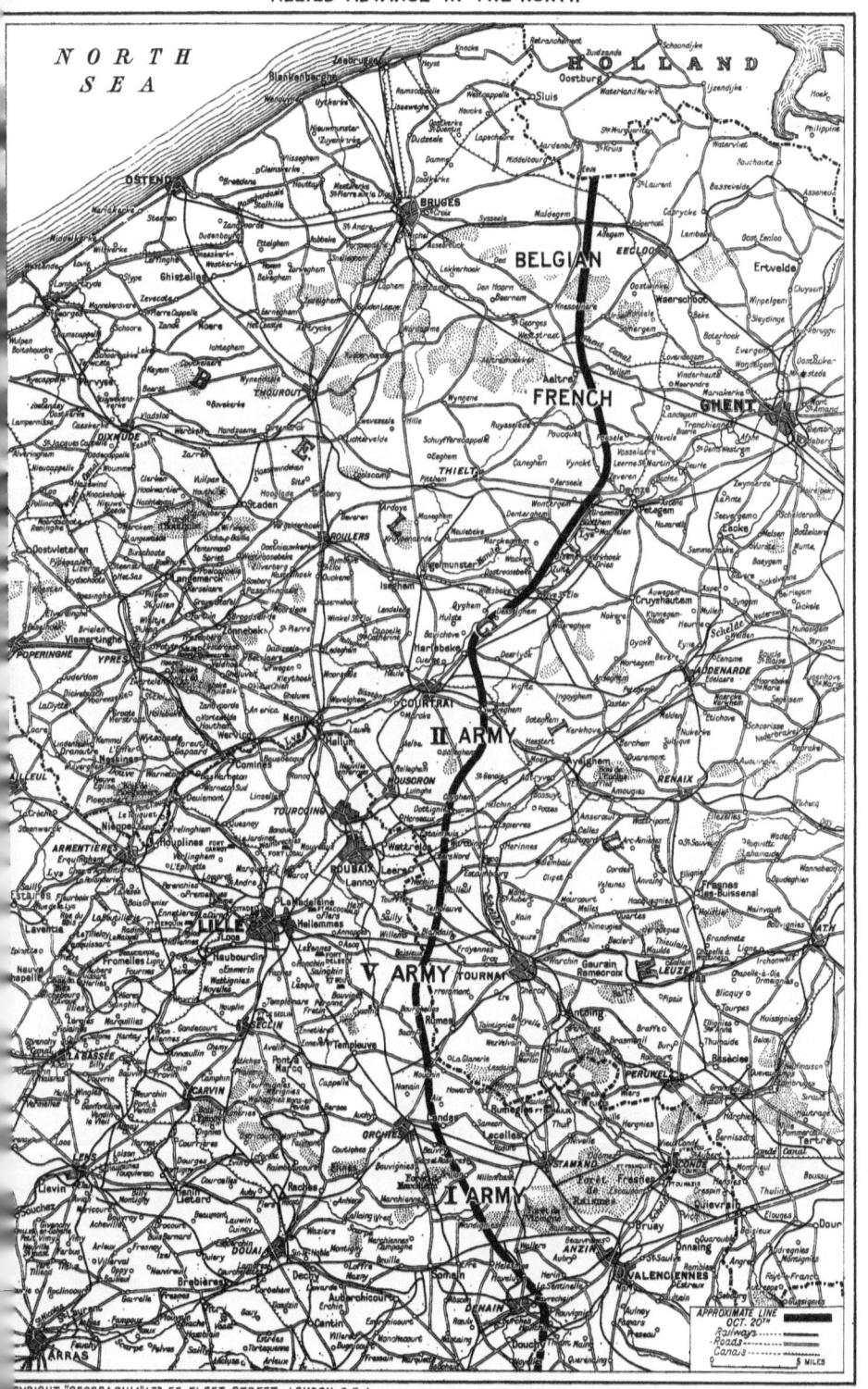

CHAPTER XI

OPERATIONS OF THE SECOND AND FIFTH ARMIES

September 28–November 11

King Albert in the field—Great Belgo-Franco-British advance—The last act on the old stage—The prophet of 1915—Renewed advance—Germans desert the coast—Relief of Douai and Lille—The final stage of the subsidiary theatres of war.

WE have followed the operations of the three southern British Armies from the first blow on August 8—a blow which Ludendorff has stated made him surrender the last hope of ultimate victory—through all their uninterrupted progress of victory until the final armistice. We shall now turn to the northern end of the British line, where the two remaining Armies, the Fifth in the Nieppe district and the Second in the area of Ypres, were waiting impatiently for their share in the advance. Flanders was a convalescent home for divisions, and there was not a unit there which was not stiff with half-healed wounds, but these Armies included many of the grand old formations which had borne the stress of the long fight, and they were filled with the desire to join in the final phase. Their chance came at last, though it was a belated one.

There were many indications in the third week of July that the Germans had planned one of their great attacks upon the front of Birdwood's Fifth Army in the Nieppe district. The succession of blows which rained upon Hindenburg's line in the south made it impossible, however, for him to attempt a new offensive. There was considerable activity along the British line, and a constant nibbling which won back by successive ventures much of the ground which had been gained by the Germans in April. Early in July the Fifth Division, forming the left unit of the Fifth Army, advanced from the edge of Nieppe Forest, where they had lain since their return from Italy, and gained a stretch of ground—the first sign of the coming recoil in the north. To the left of them lay De Lisle's Fifteenth Corps, which moved forward in turn, effecting a series of small but important advances which were eclipsed by the larger events in the south, but reacted upon those events, since they made it impossible for the Germans to detach reinforcements. On July 19 the Ninth Division with a sudden spring seized Meteren with 453 prisoners, while on the same date the First Australian Division occupied Merris to the south of it. On August 9 the movement spread farther south, and the Thirty-first Division took Vieux Berquin. There was a slow steady retraction of the German line from this time onwards, and a corresponding advance of the British. On August 30 the ruins of Bailleul passed into the hands of the Twenty-ninth Division. On September 1 Neuve Eglise was submerged by the creeping tide, while on the 3rd Nieppe also was taken. Finally on September 4 two brigades of the Twenty-ninth Division, the 88th under Freyberg and the 86th under Cheape, captured Ploegsteert by a very smart concerted movement in which 250 prisoners were taken. Up to this date De Lisle's Fifteenth Corps had advanced ten miles with no check, and had almost restored the original battle line in that quarter—a feat for which M. Clemenceau awarded the General special thanks and the Legion of Honour.

All was ready now for the grand assault which began on September 28 and was carried out by the Belgians and French in the north and by Plumer's Second British Army in the south. The left of this great force was formed by nine Belgian and five French infantry divisions, with three French cavalry divisions in reserve. The British Army consisted of four corps: Jacob's Second Corps covering Ypres, Watts' Nineteenth Corps opposite Hollebeke, Stephens' Tenth Corps facing Messines, and De Lisle's Fifteenth Corps to the south of it. The divisions which made up each of these Corps will be enumerated as they come into action. To complete the array of the British forces it should be said that Birdwood's Fifth Army, which linked up the First Army in the south and the Second in the north, consisted at that date of Haking's Eleventh and Holland's First Corps covering the Armentieres—Lens front, and not yet joining in the operations. The whole operation was under the command of the chivalrous King of the Belgians, who had the supreme satisfaction of helping to give the *coup de grâce* to the ruffianly hordes who had so long ill-used his unfortunate subjects.

The operations of the Belgians and of the French to the north of the line do not come within the scope of·this narrative save in so far as they affected the British line. General Plumer's attack was directed from the Ypres front, and involved on September 28 two Corps, the Second on the north and the Nineteenth on the south. The order of divisions from the left was the Ninth (Tudor) and the Twenty-ninth (Cayley), with the Thirty-sixth Ulsters (Coffin) in reserve. These constituted Jacob's Second Corps, which was attacking down the old Menin Road. South of this point came the Thirty-fifth (Marindin) and the Fourteenth Division (Skinner), with Lawford's Forty-first Division in support. These units made up Watts' Nineteenth Corps. On the left of Jacob's was the Belgian Sixth Division, and on the right of Watts' the British Tenth Corps, which was ordered to undertake a subsidiary operation which will presently be described. We shall now follow the main advance.

This was made without any bombardment at 5 in the morning of September 28, behind a heavy barrage which swept eastwards at the rate of 100 yards every three minutes. The Germans had clearly sent away reinforcements to the south and were weak in numbers as well as in spirit. The result was a very complete victory all along the line, and before evening Plumer's men had passed over all the ground which had been previously contested. For the last time the roar of battle went down the old Menin Road and rose from historic Gheluvelt. The Ninth and Twenty-ninth Divisions swept everything before them, and before evening it was not only Gheluvelt but Zandvoorde, Kruiseik, and Becelaere which had passed into their possession. The Belgians on the left had cleared the whole of Houthulst Forest, that lowering menace which had hung so long before their line. Zonnebeke and Poelcappelle had also passed into the hands of the Allies. It was a great victory, and it was not marred by heavy losses to the victors. Those of Jacob's Corps were not more than 1100, while their prisoners were 2100. The total of prisoners came to 10,000, with more than 100 guns.

On September 29 the advance was resumed with ever-increasing success all along the line. The Scots of the Ninth Division, working in close liaison with the Belgians, got Waterdamhoek, and detached one brigade to help our Allies in taking Moorslede, while another took Dadizeele, both of them far beyond our previous limits. The Twenty-ninth Division still pushed along the line of the Menin Road, while the Thirty-sixth Ulsters fought their way into Terhand. In this quarter alone in front of Jacob's Second Corps fifty guns had been taken. Meanwhile the Nineteenth Corps on the right was gaining the line of the Lys River, having taken Zandvoorde and Hollebeke; while the Thirty-fourth and Thirtieth Divisions of the Tenth Corps were into Wytschaete and up to Messines, and the Thirty-first Division of the Fifteenth Corps was in St. Yves. In these southern sectors there was no attempt to force the pace, but in the north the tide was setting swiftly eastwards. By the evening of September 29 Ploegsteert Wood was cleared and Messines was occupied once again. The rain had started, as is usual with Flemish offensives, and the roads were almost impossible; but by the evening of October 1 the whole left bank of the Lys from Comines southward had been cleared. On that date there was a notable hardening of the German resistance, and the Second Corps had some specially fierce fighting. The Ulsters found a tough nut to crack in Hill 41, which they gained twice and lost twice before it was finally their own. The Ninth Division captured Ledeghem, but was pushed to the west of it again by a strong counter-attack. Clearly

Chapter XI.

Operations of the Second and Fifth Armies. Sept. 29.

a temporary equilibrium was about to be established, but already the advance constituted a great victory, the British alone having 5000 prisoners and 100 guns to their credit.

In the meantime Birdwood's Fifth Army, which had remained stationary between the advancing lines of the Second Army in Flanders and of the First Army south of Lens, began also to join in the operations. The most successful military prophet in a war which has made military prophecy a by-word, was a certain German regimental officer who was captured in the La Bassée district about 1915, and who, being asked when he thought the war would finish, replied that he could not say when it would finish, but that he had an opinion as to where it would finish, and that would be within a mile of where he was captured. It was a shrewd forecast based clearly upon the idea that each side would exhaust itself and neither line be forced, so that a compromise peace would become necessary. For three years after his dictum it still remained as a possibility, but now at last, within six weeks of the end, La Bassée was forced, and early in October Ritchie's Sixteenth Division, the Fifty-fifth West Lancashire Territorials, and the Nineteenth Division under Jeffreys, were all pressing on in this quarter, with no very great resistance. South of Lens the Twentieth Division (Carey) had been transferred from the left of the First Army to the right of the Fifth, and this had some sharp fighting on October 2 at Mericourt and Acheville. Both north and south of the ruined coal capital the British infantry was steadily pushing on, pinching the place out, since it was bristling with machine-guns and very formidable if directly attacked. The Twelfth Division (Higginson), fresh from severe service in the south and anaemic from many wounds, occupied 11,000 yards between Oppy and Lens from October 7 onwards. Their orders were to press the enemy at the first sign of retreat. All three brigades were in the line, each with its own artillery, to give greater independence. The German withdrawal was gradual but there was some hard rearguard fighting, especially at the strong line of the Haute Deule Canal. There was little cover for the troops at this point save where some ruined hamlets screened their ranks. These flat levels leading up to wire and water could have been made a Golgotha had the Germans been of the old temper, but they were oppressed by the general wilting of their line. The 1st Cambridge captured Auby on October 14 and so got to the edge of the Canal. On the 16th the 5th Berks got across the broken bridge at Pont-a-Sault, though they could hardly deploy upon the farther side. After this date the only obstacle to the advance was the supply question, for the villagers were all clamouring for food and sharing the scanty rations of the soldiers. On October 23 the Scarpe was crossed, Lieutenant Egerton of the 87th Field Company R.E. gallantly bridging the stream and losing his life in the effort. The 6th West Kents got across at Nivelle, but had the misfortune to lose their splendid commander, Colonel Dawson, who had already been wounded six times in the course of the war. Upon October 23 the Twelfth was relieved by the Fifty-second Division upon this front.

The attack in the north had been held partly by the vile weather and partly by the increased German

Chapter XI.

Operations of the Second and Fifth Armies. Oct. 14.

CHAPTER XI.

Operations of the Second and Fifth Armies.

Oct. 14.

resistance. The Twenty-ninth Division had got into Gheluvelt but was unable to retain it. The enemy counter-attacks were frequent and fierce, while the impossible roads made the supplies, especially of cartridges, a very serious matter. The worn and rutted Menin Road had to conduct all the traffic of two Army Corps. No heavy artillery could be got up to support the weary infantry, who were cold and wet, without either rest or cover. Time was needed, therefore, to prepare a further attack, and it was October 14 before it was ready. Then, as before, the Belgians, French, and British attacked in a single line, the advance extending along the whole Flemish front between the Lys River at Comines and Dixmude in the north, the British section being about ten miles from Comines to the Menin—Roulers Road.

Three British Corps were engaged, the Second (Jacob), the Nineteenth (Watts), and the Tenth (Stephens), the divisions, counting from the south, being the Thirtieth, Thirty-fourth, Forty-first, Thirty-fifth, Thirty-sixth, Twenty-ninth, and Ninth. The three latter divisions, forming the front of Jacob's Corps, came away with a splendid rush in spite of the heavy mud and soon attained their immediate objectives. Gulleghem, in front of the Ulsters, was defended by three belts of wire, garnished thickly with machine-guns, but it was taken none the less, though it was not completely occupied until next day. Salines had fallen to the Twenty-ninth Division, and by the early afternoon of October 15 both divisions were to the east of Heule. Meanwhile Cuerne and Hulste had been cleared by the Ninth Division, the 1st Yorkshire Cyclists playing a gallant part in the former operation. The net result was that in this part of the line all the troops had reached the Lys either on the evening of September 15 or on the morning of September 16.

The advance in the south had been equally successful, though there were patches where the resistance was very stiff. The 103rd Brigade on the left of the Thirty-fourth Division enveloped and captured Gheluwe and were afterwards held up by field-guns firing over open sights until they were taken by a rapid advance of the 5th Scottish Borderers and the 8th Scottish Rifles. The 102nd Brigade made a lodgment in the western outskirts of Menin, which was fully occupied on the next day, patrols being at once pushed across the Lys. These were hard put to it to hold on until they were relieved later in the day by the Thirtieth Division. Wevelghem was cleared on the 15th, and on the 16th both the Ninth and Thirty-sixth Divisions established bridge-heads across the river, but in both cases were forced to withdraw them. In the north the Belgians had reached Iseghem and Cortemarck, while the French were round Roulers. By the night of October 15 Thourout was surrounded, and the Germans on the coast, seeing the imminent menace to their communications, began to blow up their guns and stores preparatory to their retreat. On October 17 the left of the Allied line was in Ostend, and on the 20th it had extended to the Dutch border. Thus after four years of occupation the Germans said farewell for ever to those salt waters of the west which they had fondly imagined to be their permanent advanced post against Great Britain. The main tentacle of the octopus had been disengaged,

CHAPTER XI.

Operations of the Second and Fifth Armies.

Oct. 14.

U

and the whole huge, perilous creature was shrinking back to the lairs from which it had emerged.

Operations of the Second and Fifth Armies.
Oct. 20.

Events were now following each other in very rapid succession as the pressure upon the flanks increased. On the one side it was Ostend; on the other, as already recorded, it was Douai, which the Eighth Division had entered on October 17. Finally, on the morning of October 18, Haking's Eleventh Corps from Birdwood's Army held Lille in their grasp. The Fifty-seventh and Fifty-ninth Divisions were north and south of the town, which was occupied before evening, to the immense joy of the liberated inhabitants. Meanwhile De Lisle's Fifteenth Corps pushed on in the north and occupied both Roubaix and Tourcoing. There was little resistance to these operations, for the Flemish advance on one side and that to Le Cateau on the other had made the position of the German garrisons impossible. By October 22 the troops were on the line of the Escaut from Valenciennes to Avelghem.

Though the advance of Birdwood's Army was comparatively bloodless there was still some obstinate fighting in the north, and the divisions which forced the Lys had by no means a holiday task. This operation was carried out on October 20 and 21, and owing to some delay on the part of the French Seventh Corps in getting into position the flank of the Thirty-sixth Ulster Division was exposed to enfilade fire which caused great loss. As the Ulsters advanced across the river they had to throw back a defensive flank 6000 yards deep before evening of the 21st. On the 22nd the Germans were still fighting stoutly, and delivered at least one dangerous counter-attack by storm-troops, while on the 25th they brought a new division, the Twenty-third Reserve, an old opponent of early Ypres days, into the line, and held their ground well. There were changes in the British fighting line also, as the Thirty-first relieved the Twenty-ninth, while the Thirty-fourth, coming from the south, took the place of the Ulsters.

Chapter XI. Operations of the Second and Fifth Armies. Oct. 25.

These two divisions attacked once more on October 31, the Thirty-first surrounding Caster while the Thirty-fourth captured Anseghem, the 8th Scottish Rifles forcing their way into the town, and joining up with the French at Winterkan. That evening the enemy retired across the Escaut, and the line was definitely made good. The bridges over the river had been destroyed, but the French were advancing rapidly from the north, and on November 2 had reached Driesen and Peterghem. They then extended south and took over the whole front of the Second Corps, joining up with the left of the Nineteenth Corps. The Second Corps drew out from its last battle, having since the advance began captured 7500 prisoners and 150 guns, at a loss to itself of 11,000 casualties. At this period the operations of the north may be said to have reached their term.

The weight of the campaign never fell fully upon Birdwood's Fifth Army, but it was comprised of divisions which had been knocked to pieces elsewhere and which would not have been battle-worthy at all had they not been of splendid individual material. Some of them were actually called B divisions, but upon one of them doing thirty-three miles in thirty hours it was decreed by their General that such an invidious title must cease. The Portuguese troops accompanied the British in the Fifth Army. There was a good deal of discontent in the ranks of this contingent, largely due to the fact that it was impossible to grant the men the same privileges in the way of leave as were given to the officers. By a great concession they were broken up, however, among the British brigades, with the result that they did very well during the last phases of the fighting. The fact that General Birdwood with his depleted and inexperienced divisions was able to drive the Germans through Merville, Estaires, La Bassée, and on over the Aubers Ridge and out of Lille, forcing the Scheldt and reaching as far as Ath, will always be a memorable military exploit. It is on record that the last bag of prisoners by this Army was at 10.57 on the 11th November, three minutes before time.

On November 15 Marshal Foch visited the Headquarters of the Fifth Army, and his remarks on that occasion were meant, no doubt, to apply to the whole British line. "Your soldiers," he said, "continued to march when they were exhausted, and they fought, and fought well, when they were worn out. It is with such indomitable will that the war has been won. At the moment of ceasing hostilities the enemy troops were demoralised and disorganised and their lines of communication were in a state of chaos. Had we continued the war for another fortnight we might have won a most wonderful and complete military victory. But it would have been inhuman to risk the lives of one of our soldiers unnecessarily. The Germans asked for an armistice. We renounced the certainty of further military glory and gave it to them. I am deeply sensible of the fact that Lille was delivered without damage to the town, and I am grateful for the help given so generously to the inhabitants."

So ended the Great War in the northern sector. It need not be said that while the British had been attacking again and again in the manner described, taking no heed of their own losses and exhaustion so long as they could bring the tottering giant to his knees, the French and the Americans were advancing in unison. The work of the latter in the wooded region of the Argonne was especially difficult and also especially vital, as its effect was to cut in upon the German rear and to narrow the pass through which the great multitude must make their escape from the lands which they had so wantonly invaded. On September 12 the Americans had shown their quality by their successful attack upon the St. Mihiel salient. In the advance of the Argonne the American attack extended over several weeks, was often held up, and furnished more than a hundred thousand casualties, but General Pershing and his men showed a splendid tenacity which carried them at last through all their difficulties, so that the end of the war, which their exertions had undoubtedly helped to hasten, found them with their line in Sedan and biting deeply into the German flank.

Before entering upon the terms of the Armistice and describing the subsequent conditions of peace, representing the final fruits of all the terrible sacrifices of these years of alternate hope and fear, one last glance must be cast round at the other fields of the great struggle—Italian, Salonican, Syrian, and Mesopotamian—all of which were decided at the same moment. It could almost be believed that some final spiritual fiat had gone forth placing an allotted term upon the slaughter, so simultaneous was the hostile collapse on every front. In Italy General Diaz, who had succeeded General Cadorna after the disaster of Caporetto, made a grand and victorious attack on October 25. It was a great military achievement, and justified those who had always upheld the fine quality of the Italian Army. The Austrian forces were superior in number, being roughly a million against nine hundred thousand, but they were inferior in gun power. Diaz cleverly concentrated his forces so as to have a local superiority in the central sector, but his difficulties were still very great, since a stream a mile broad lay before him, shallow in parts but deepening to five feet even at the best fords. A long island, the Grave di Papadopoli, lay near the hostile shore, and this was seized on the night of the 24th October by the 1st Welsh Fusiliers and the 2/1st Honourable Artillery Company, who held on in spite of a severe shelling and so established an advanced base for the Army. Early on October 25 crossings were made at all points, and though the bridges were frequently shot away by the Austrian guns, and one corps was unable to get a single man across, none the less those who had reached the other side, including Babington's Fourteenth Corps, which had the Seventh and Twenty-third British Divisions in the line, with the Thirty-seventh Italian Division, made excellent headway. By the evening of October 29 this Fourteenth Corps, which had been held up by having its left flank exposed through the failure of the Eighth Corps to cross the river, found a brave comrade in the Italian Eighteenth Corps which lined up with it and crashed its way right through the Kaiserstellung position forming the battle zone of the Austrian line. It was a very complete victory, and broadened to such an extent during the next few days that by November 2 the whole Austrian army had ceased to exist, and 700,000 men with 7000 guns were in the hands of the victors. Not only had they regained by arms all the ground they had lost a year before, but Trieste surrendered on November 3 and was occupied from the sea. Trento had also been taken in the north, so that the two goals of Italian ambition had both been reached. Every part of the Italian line had been equally victorious from the Alps to the sea, and great valour was shown by every formation, as well as by the French and British contingents. The British Forty-eighth Division was engaged in the northern sector, far from its comrades, and carried through its complete objective in a manner worthy of so veteran a unit, which had learned its soldiering in the hard school of the Somme and of Flanders. On November 3 the final Armistice was signed by the Austrians, by which they withdrew into their own country and waited there for the final terms of the victors.

On September 12 began the great Franco-Serbian advance on the Salonican front—a front which had been greatly strengthened by the accession of the Greek forces. Under General Franchet d'Esperey and Marshal Misitch there was an advance on a front of sixteen miles, penetrating occasionally to a depth of four miles. By September 17 this had extended to a depth of twelve miles, and it was clear that a decisive movement was on foot. On

CHAPTER XI.

Operations of the Second and Fifth Armies.

September 18 the British and Greek troops joined in on the Lake Doiran sector, and the Bulgarians were retreating along their whole front of a hundred miles. General Milne's troops were the first to cross the Bulgarian border, after a very severe action in which some units sustained heavy losses. All the Allied nations were advancing swiftly, and it was clear that the end was near. On September 30 the Bulgarian nation, misled by its own unscrupulous ambitions and by its unsavoury king, sent in its surrender, retired from the conflict, and waited to hear what the final punishment of its misdeeds might be. Thus fell the first of the four pillars of the Central Alliance.

The fate of Turkey was not long delayed. On September 19 General Allenby, who had halted long upon the line of Jerusalem while he gathered his forces for a supreme and final effort, gave the word for a fresh advance. The victory which followed will perhaps be accounted the most completely scientific and sweeping of the whole war. With his mixed force of British, Indians, Australians and smaller Allied contingents, Allenby broke through the enemy's lines near the coast, and then despatched his splendid cavalry towards Damascus in a wild pursuit which can hardly be matched for calculated temerity. Some of the troopers in that wonderful ride are said to have accomplished seventy to eighty miles in the twenty-four hours. The result was that a strong force was thrown across the Turkish rear and that their Seventh and Eighth Armies were practically annihilated. In the final tally no less than 80,000 men and 250 guns were in the hands of the victors. · It was a shattering blow. Damascus was occupied, the Turks

SECOND AND FIFTH ARMIES 297

were driven pell-mell out of Syria, General Marshall advanced in Mesopotamia, and Turkey was finally brought to her knees after a battle on the Tigris in which her last army was destroyed. On October 30 she signed an armistice by which the Allied fleets might enter the Dardanelles and occupy Constantinople, while all Allied prisoners should at once be returned. As in the case of the Germans the feelings with which the Allies, and especially the British, regarded the Turks were greatly embittered by their consistent brutality to the unfortunate captives whom the fortune of war had placed in their hands. There can be no peace and no sense of justice in the world until these crimes have been absolutely expiated. The last spark of sympathy which Britain retained for her old Oriental ally was extinguished for ever by the long-drawn murder of the prisoners of Kut. It should be added that the small German force in East Africa still continued to dodge the pursuing columns, and that it was intact in Rhodesia at the time when the general collapse compelled it to lay down its arms. It was a most remarkable achievement, this resistance of four years when cut away from a base, and reflects great credit upon General von Lettow-Vorbeck, whose name should certainly shine among the future reconstructors of Germany.

As to naval matters there is nothing to be said save that the submarine trouble had been greatly ameliorated by the splendid work of the Navy, much assisted by the American destroyers. The blockade was still rigorously enforced, and had much to do with the general German collapse. There was some hope that the German fleet would come out and that a more decisive Jutland might adorn the finish

Chapter XI.

Operations of the Second and Fifth Armies.

Chapter XI.

Operations of the Second and Fifth Armies.

of the war, but the plans of the German officers were marred by the insubordination of the German men, and there was no heroic gesture to dignify the end of the great useless fleet, the most fatal and futile of all Germany's creations, for its possession led her to her ruin.

CHAPTER XII

THE END

BEFORE entering into the terms of the Armistice it may be instructive to give some short outline of the course of events at the German Headquarters which led to so sudden and dramatic a collapse. No doubt the political and economic state of Germany was very bad, but the disaster was primarily a military one, as is clearly shown by the subsequent White Book published after the declaration of peace. This compilation shows that the arrogance with which the military leaders spoke during their successful offensive, and down to the middle of July, had changed in the short space of ten weeks to such utter despair that on October 1 they were sending urgent messages to Berlin that the war was to be closed down at any cost, and that even such questions as the loss of the German colonies and the cession of Alsace-Lorraine were not to weigh in the balance against the imperative necessity of staving off a tremendous military disaster. The inclined plane seems to have taken an abrupt tilt on August 14, after the first successful British advance, when it was decided to take the opportunity of the next German success to ask for peace. No success arrived, however, but rather a long succession of disasters, and Hertling, the dotard Chancellor, was unable to make up his mind what to do, so that matters were allowed to drift from bad to worse. Early in October it was announced from General Headquarters that a break through might occur at any moment. Prince Max of Baden had been made Chancellor on the understanding that he would at once appeal to President Wilson for a cessation of hostilities, which was the more urgent as Bulgaria had already dropped out of the war and Austria was on her last legs. As might have been foreseen, President Wilson refused to treat without the concurrence of his Allies, and some improvement in the German defensive line enabled them to hold on until early November, when their needs once again became overpowering, and the great twin-brethren Hindenburg and Ludendorff finally admitted defeat. Then followed in quick succession events which are political and outside the scope of this record—the revolution in the Fatherland, the flight of the Kaiser and of the Crown Prince into Holland, and the advance of the Allied armies, under the terms of the Armistice, to the left bank of the Rhine.

Some account should, however, be given of the circumstances under which the Armistice was signed, and the drastic terms which were exacted by the Allies, the fit preliminaries to a peace founded upon a stern justice. It was at nine o'clock on the evening of Thursday, November 7, that the German delegates, led by the ambiguous and scheming Erzberger, travelling along shell-broken roads, under the glare of searchlights and signal-fires, entered within the French lines near La Capelle. The roar of the battle in their rear was a constant reminder of the urgency of their mission. They came no farther than Marshal Foch's travelling headquarters, where they were met

THE END

by the Marshal himself, with Admiral Wemyss to represent that British sea-power which had done so much to promote this interview. The proceedings were short and strained. A proposition for a truce was waved aside by the victors, and a list of terms was presented which made the German delegates realise, if they had failed to do so before, the abyss into which their country had been precipitated by two generations of madmen. Disgrace abroad, revolution at home, a fugitive monarch, a splitting empire, a disbanding army, a mutinous fleet—these were the circumstances under which Germany ended her bid for the dictatorship of the world.

At 5 A.M. on Monday, November 11, the Armistice was signed, and at 11 A.M., as already recorded, the last shot of the greatest war that ever has been, or in all probability ever will be, had been fired. London and Paris were at last relieved from their terrific strain, and none who witnessed them can forget the emotions and rejoicings of the day. Those who had not realised the complete collapse of the Colossus were surprised at the severity of the terms which had been accepted in such haste. All invaded territory had to be cleared within fourteen days. All Allied prisoners to be at once returned, while those of Germany were retained. The left bank of the Rhine, together with ample bridge-heads, to be handed over, as a temporary measure, to the Allies, the Belgians holding the north, the British the Cologne area, the Americans the Coblentz area, and the French, Strasburg, with all Alsace-Lorraine. All danger of a continuation of the struggle was averted by the immediate surrender of 5000 guns, 30,000 machine-guns, and 2000 aeroplanes, together with great numbers of locomotives, lorries, waggons, and barges. All Roumanian, Russian, and other forced treaties were abrogated. East Africa was to be evacuated. All submarines and a large portion of the German navy were to be handed over to the care of the Allies until peace terms should decide their ultimate fate. The blockade was to continue. Such were the main points of the Armistice which foreshadowed the rigorous peace to come.

It was not until January 11, 1919, that the delegates from the various interested nations assembled in Paris, and their deliberations, which seemed long to us, but may appear hasty and ill-considered to our descendants, terminated on May 7, a most dramatic date, being the anniversary of that sinking of the *Lusitania* which will always be recorded as the supreme instance of German barbarity. So stringent were the terms that the Scheidemann Government resigned and left the unpleasant task of ratification to a cabinet of nobodies, with Herr Bauer at their head. So long as the firm signed, it mattered nothing to the Allies which particular partner was the representative. There was higgling and wriggling up to the last moment, and some small concessions were actually gained. The final results were briefly as follows :

1. Two new countries shall be formed—Poland in the north and Czecho-Slovakia in the south, the former largely at the expense of Germany, the latter of Austria. Germany shall contribute to the building up of Poland the districts of West Prussia and Posen, both of which are historically Polish. The important district of Upper Silesia—the prized conquest of Frederick from Maria Theresa—was left indeterminate, its fate to be decided by the people's will.

THE END

2. The northern portion of Schleswig shall revert to Denmark, from which it was taken.

3. Alsace-Lorraine shall be returned to France, and that country shall receive for a time the produce of the Saar coal-fields as recompense for the destruction of her own coal-fields by the Germans.

Thus on each side, Germany was trimmed down to the lands inhabited by Germans, the Danes, the Poles, and the French borderers being emancipated. When next they march to war they will not swell their ranks by unwilling conscripts forced to fight against their own friends and interests.

4. Every effort was made by the treaty to disarm Germany, and to prevent her in the future from plotting the destruction of her neighbours. Those sudden irruptions of 1864, 1866, 1870, and 1914 were to be stopped once and for ever—if indeed we can place final terms upon a phenomenon which dates back to the days of the Roman republic.

The German General Staff—that dangerous *imperium in imperio*—was to be dissolved. The army should be only sufficiently powerful to keep internal order and to control the frontiers. Compulsory service was abolished, and the manhood of Germany — to the probable detriment of all trade competitors — was dedicated to the arts of peace. The import and export of war material were forbidden, and the great war-god, Krupp, lay prostrate in his shrine at Essen. All submarines were forbidden. The navy was limited to thirty-six vessels of mediocre strength. Zeppelins were to be handed over. German cables, fourteen in number, and all German oversea possessions passed into the hands of the Allies. With such terms, if the Allies continue to stand together and

CHAPTER XII.
The End.

guarantee their enforcement, the Frenchman may look eastward without a tremor, and the mists of the North Sea can cloud no menace for our islands. For many a long year to come the formidable military history of Germany has reached its close. A clause which dealt with the trial of all military offenders, including the Kaiser, concluded the more important items of the Treaty.

So at last the dark cloud of war, which had seemed so endless and so impenetrable as it covered the whole heavens from the Eastern horizon to the Western, passed and drifted beyond us, while a dim sun in a cold sky was the first herald of better times. Laden with debt, heart-heavy for its lost ones, with every home shaken and every industry dislocated, its hospitals filled with broken men, its hoarded capital all wasted upon useless engines—such was the world which the accursed German Kultur had left behind it. Here was the crop reaped from those navy bills and army estimates, those frantic professors and wild journalists, those heavy-necked, sword-trailing generals, those obsequious, arrogant courtiers, and the vain, swollen creature whom they courted. Peace had come at last—if such a name can be given to a state where international bitterness will long continue, and where within each frontier the bulk of mankind, shaken by these great events from the ruts of custom, contend fiercely for some selfish advantage out of the general chaos. In the East, Russia, like some horrible invertebrate creature, entangles itself with its own tentacles, and wrestles against itself with such intricate convulsions that one can hardly say which attacks or which defends, which is living or which already dead. But the world swings on the divine cycle. He who made the planet from the fire-mist is still at work moulding with set and sustained purpose the destinies of a universe which at every stage can only reach the higher through its combat with the lower.

Here the historian's task is done. It has occupied and alleviated many heavy days. Whatever its sins of omission it should surely contain some trace of the spirit of the times, since many a chapter was written to the rumble of the distant guns, and twice the author was able to leave his desk and then return with such inspiration as an actual view of the battlefields could afford him. The whole British line in 1916, the Soissons and Ardennes positions of the French, the Carnic Alps, the Trentino, and the Isonzo positions of the Italians were all visited in turn; while in 1918, as recorded, the crowning mercy of September 29 was actually witnessed by the writer. He lays down his pen at last with the deep conviction that the final results of this great convulsion are meant to be spiritual rather than material, and that upon an enlightened recognition of this depends the future history of mankind. Not to change rival frontiers, but to mould the hearts and spirits of men—there lie the explanation and the justification of all that we have endured. The system which left seven million dead upon the fields of Europe must be rotten to the core. Time will elapse before the true message is mastered, but when that day arrives the war of 1914 may be regarded as the end of the dark ages and the start of that upward path which leads away from personal or national selfishness towards the City Beautiful upon the distant hills.

x

APPENDIX

THE following account of some personal experiences on the day when the Hindenburg Line was finally broken—the most important day, perhaps, in the whole war—may possibly be worthy of the decent obscurity of an appendix, though it is too slight and too personal for the pages of a serious chronicle. It is appended for what it is worth, reprinted with a few additions from the columns of *The Times* :—

Mine eyes have seen the glory of the coming of the Lord,
He is trampling out the vintage where the grapes of wrath are stored.

The grand, sonorous, mystical lines of Julia Ward Howe rang in my head as I found myself by most unlooked-for chance an actual eyewitness of this, one of the historical episodes of the greatest of wars. Yes, with my own eyes I saw the rent while the men who made it were still pushing forward from the farther side of it.

Even now I can hardly realise that it was so. A kindly invitation from the Australian Government explains my presence on their front, while the energy and goodwill of a helpful soldier on the spot, a captain of Australian Artillery, brought about the rest. Let me try to transcribe what I saw.

It was about 11 o'clock when we reached the edge of the battle-field on Sunday, September 29. "We" refers to Sir Joseph Cook, Colonial statesman, Commander Latham, the Australian Naval Attaché, and myself, with Captain Plunket, a twice-wounded Australian officer, as our shepherd.

The programme of the day was already clear in our heads. American Divisions were to rush the front line. The Australian

Divisions were to pass through them, and carry the battle front forward. Already as we arrived the glad news came back that the Americans had done their part, and that the Australians had just been unleashed. Also that the Germans were standing to it like men.

As our car threaded the crowded street between the ruins of Templeux we met the wounded coming back, covered cars with nothing visible save protruding boots, and a constant stream of pedestrians, some limping, some with bandaged arms and faces, some supported by Red Cross men, a few in pain, most of them smiling grimly behind their cigarettes. Amid them came the first clump of prisoners, fifty or more, pitiable enough, and yet I could not pity them, the weary, shuffling, hang-dog creatures, with no touch of nobility in their features or their bearing.

The village was full of Americans and Australians, extraordinarily like each other in type. One could well have lingered, for it was all of great interest, but there were even greater interests ahead, so we turned up a hill, left our car, which had reached its limit, and proceeded on foot. The road took us through a farm, where a British anti-aircraft battery stood ready for action. Then we found open plain, and went forward, amid old trenches and rusty wire, in the direction of the battle.

We had now passed the heavy gun positions, and were among the field-guns, so that the noise was deafening. A British howitzer battery was hard at work, and we stopped to chat with the major. His crews had been at it for six hours, but were in great good-humour, and chuckled mightily when the blast of one of their guns nearly drove in our ear-drums, we having got rather too far forward. The effect was that of a ringing box on the exposed ear—with which valediction we left our grinning British gunners and pushed on to the east, under a screaming canopy of our own shells. The wild, empty waste of moor was broken by a single shallow quarry or gravel-pit, in which we could see some movement. In it we found an advanced dressing station, with about a hundred American and Australian gunners and orderlies.

There were dug-outs in the sides of this flat excavation, and it had been an American battalion H.Q. up to a few hours before. We were now about a thousand yards from the Hindenburg Line, and I learned with emotion that this spot was the Egg Redoubt, one of those advanced outposts of General Gough's Army which suffered so tragic and glorious a fate in that great military epic of March 21—one of the grandest in the whole war. The fact that we were now actually standing in the Egg Redoubt showed me, as nothing else could have done, how completely the ground had been recovered, and how the day of retribution was at hand.

We were standing near the eastward lip of the excavation, and looking over it, when it was first brought to our attention that it took two to make a battle. Up to now we had seen only one. Now two shells burst in quick succession forty yards in front of us, and a spray of earth went into the air. "Whizz-bangs," remarked our soldier-guide casually. Personally, I felt less keenly interested in their name than in the fact that they were there at all.

We thought we had done pretty well to get within 1000 yards of the famous line, but now came a crowning bit of good fortune, for an Australian gunner captain, a mere lad, but a soldier from his hawk's eyes to his active feet, volunteered to rush us forward to some coign of vantage known to himself. So it was Eastward Ho! once more, still over a dull, barren plain sloping gently upwards, with little sign of life. Here and there was the quick fluff of a bursting shell, but at a comforting distance. Suddenly ahead of us a definite object broke the sky-line. It was a Tank, upon which the crew were working with spanners and levers, for its comrades were now far ahead, and it would fain follow. This, it seems, was the grand stand which our young gunner had selected. On to the top of it we clambered—and there, at our very feet and less than 500 yards away, was the rift which had been torn a few hours before in the Hindenburg line. On the dun slope beyond it, under our very eyes, was even now being fought a part of that great fight where at last the children of light were beating down into the earth the forces of darkness. It was there. We could see it. And yet how little there was to see!

The ridge was passed and the ground sloped down, as dark and heathy as Hindhead. In front of us lay a village. It was Bellicourt. The Hindenburg position ran through it. It lay quiet enough, and with the unaided eye one could see rusty red fields of wire in front of it. But the wire had availed nothing, nor had the trench that lurked behind it, for beyond it, beside the village of Nauroy, there was a long white line, clouds of pale steam-like vapour spouting up against a dark, rain-sodden sky. "The Boche smoke barrage," said our guide. "They are going to counter-attack." Only this, the long, white, swirling cloud upon the dark plain, told of the strife in front of us. With my glasses I saw what looked like Tanks, but whether wrecked or in action I could not say. There was the battle—the greatest of battles—but nowhere could I see a moving figure. It is true that all the noises of the Pit seemed to rise from that lonely landscape, but noise was always with us, go where we would.

The Australians were ahead where that line of smoke marked their progress. In the sloping fields, which at that point emerged out of the moor, the victorious Americans, who had done their part, were crouching. It was an assured victory upon which we gazed, achieved so rapidly that we were ourselves standing far forward in ground which had been won that day. The wounded had been brought in, and I saw no corpses, though some friends who had reached the line to our left found eighteen American lads lying dead by the roadside. On that side the fight was very severe, and the Germans, who had been hidden in their huge dug-outs, were doing their usual trick of emerging and cutting off the attack. So much we gathered afterwards, but for the moment it was the panorama before us which was engrossing all our thoughts.

Suddenly the German guns woke up. I can but pray that it was not our group which drew their fire upon the half-mended Tank. Shell after shell fell in its direction, all of them short, but creeping forward with each salvo. It was time for us to go. If any man says that without a call of duty he likes being under aimed shell-fire, he is not a man whose word I would trust. Some of the shells burst with a rusty red outflame, and we were told that they were gas shells. I may say that before we were admitted on to the battle-field at all, we were ushered one by one into a room where some devil's pipkin was bubbling in the corner, and were taught to use our gas-masks by the simple expedient of telling us that if we failed to acquire the art then and there a very painful alternative was awaiting us.

We made our way back, with no indecent haste, but certainly without loitering, across the plain, the shells always getting rather nearer, until we came to the excavation. Here we had a welcome rest, for our good gunner took us into his cubby-hole of a dug-out, which would at least stop shrapnel, and we shared his tea and dried beef, a true Australian soldier's meal.

The German fire was now rather heavy, and our expert host explained that this meant that he had recovered from the shock of the attack, had reorganised his guns, and was generally his merry self once more. From where we sat we could see heavy shells bursting far to our rear, and there was a general atmosphere of explosion all round us, which might have seemed alarming had it not been for the general chatty afternoon-tea appearance of all these veteran soldiers with whom it was our privilege to find ourselves. A group of sulky-looking German prisoners sat in a corner, while a lank and freckled Australian soldier, with his knee sticking out of a rent in his trousers was walking about with four watches dangling from his hand, endeavouring vainly to sell them. Far be it from me to assert that he did not bring the watches from Sydney and choose this moment for doing a deal in them, but they were heavy old Teutonic time-pieces, and the prisoners seemed to take a rather personal interest in them.

As we started on our homeward track we came, first, upon the British battery which seemed to be limbering up with some idea of advancing, and so lost its chance of administering a box on our other ear. Farther still we met our friends of the air guns, and stopped again to exchange a few impressions.

APPENDIX. They had nothing to fire at, and seemed bored to tears, for the red, white, and blue machines were in full command of the sky. Soon we found our motor waiting in the lee of a ruined house, and began to thread our way back through the wonderfully picturesque streams of men, American, Australian, British, and German, who were strung along the road.

And then occurred a very horrible incident. One knew, of course, that one could not wander about a battlefield and not find oneself sooner or later involved in some tragedy, but we were now out of range of any but heavy guns, and their shots were spasmodic. We had halted the car for an instant to gather up two German helmets which Commander Latham had seen on the roadside, when there was a very heavy burst close ahead round a curve in the village street. A geyser of red brick-dust flew up into the air. An instant later our car rounded the corner. None of us will forget what we saw. There was a tangle of mutilated horses, their necks rising and sinking. Beside them a man with his hand blown off was staggering away, the blood gushing from his upturned sleeve. He was moving round and holding the arm raised and hanging, as a dog holds an injured foot. Beside the horses lay a shattered man, drenched crimson from head to foot, with two great glazed eyes looking upwards through a mask of blood. Two comrades were at hand to help, and we could only go upon our way with the ghastly picture stamped for ever upon our memory. The image of that dead driver might well haunt one in one's dreams.

Once through Templeux and on the main road for Peronne things became less exciting, and we drew up to see a column of 900 prisoners pass us. Each side of the causeway was lined by Australians, with their keen, clear-cut, falcon faces, and between lurched these heavy-jawed, beetle-browed, uncouth louts, new caught and staring round with bewildered eyes at their debonnaire captors. I saw none of that relief at getting out of it which I have read of; nor did I see any signs of fear, but the prevailing impression was an ox-like stolidity and dulness. It was a herd of beasts, not a procession of men. It was indeed farcical to think that these uniformed bumpkins represented the great military nation, while the gallant figures who lined the road belonged to the race which they had despised as being unwarlike. Time and Fate between them have a pretty sense of humour. One of them caught my eye as he passed and roared out in guttural English, "The old Jairman is out!" It was the only word I heard them speak. French cavalry troopers, stern, dignified, and martial, rode at either end of the bedraggled procession.

They are great soldiers, these Australians. I think they would admit it themselves, but a spectator is bound to confirm it. There is a reckless dare-devilry, combined with a spice of cunning, which gives them a place of their own in the Imperial ranks. They have a great advantage, too, in having a permanent organisation, the same five divisions always in the same Corps, under the same chief. It doubles their military value—and the same applies equally, of course, to the Canadians. None the less, they must not undervalue their British comrades or lose their sense of proportion. I had a chance of addressing some 1200 of them on our return that evening, and while telling them all that I thought of their splendid deeds, I ventured to remind them that 72 per cent of the men engaged and 76 per cent of the casualties were Englishmen of England. But this is a description of a day's adventure on the Hindenburg line, and my deep appreciation of the Commonwealth soldiers, of their officers, and of their Commander, must appear elsewhere.

Arthur Conan Doyle.

INDEX

Abancourt, 259, 261, 262
Achiet-le-Grand, 81, 102, 103, 106, 121, 123
Achiet-le-Petit, 121
Adams, Sapper, V.C., 202
Aisne River, 1, 5, 6, 21, 80
Albert, 26, 45, 47, 48, 82, 84, 85, 228
Allason, General, 86
Allenby, General Sir Edmund, 22, 296
American Army, co-operation of, with British Armies, 6, 25, 32, 37, 38, 39, 40, 41, 150-158, 161, 164, 166, 168, 169, 174, 175, 177, 178, 179, 181, 182, 183, 184, 185, 186, 187, 307-313; advance in the Argonne, 293; successful attack on the St. Mihiel salient, 293; in Sedan, 293
Americans reinforce the Allies on Western front, 2, 23
Amerval, 231, 234
Amiens, 26, 40, 45
Ancre River, 31, 33, 39, 47, 81, 82, 84, 85, 86, 87, 89, 103, 120, 122, 124
Angre, 274, 275
Anneux, 215, 216, 217
Ardres River, 6, 7, 9, 12, 14, 139
Argonne, American advance in the, 293
Arleux, 258, 264
Armistice, the, 204, 205, 275, 295, 297; signed, 301; terms of, 302
Arras, 139, 277
Artres, 270, 271
Atkinson, Major, 20
Auby, 278, 287
Aunelle, Petite, 253
Aunelle River, 254, 274

Austria, defeated on the Piave, 3, 22; collapse of, 294-295, 300
Avesnes, 204, 227
Avre River, 25, 27
Awoingt, 221, 227

Babington, General Sir J., 294
Baden, Prince Max of, 300
Bagdad, 22
Bailleul, 139, 282
Baku, 22
Banks, Colonel, 51
Banteux, 210
Bapaume, 60, 90, 91, 125, 126
Barastre, 93, 127
Barbow, Colonel, 20
Barker, General, 50
Barnes, General, 129
Bauer, Herr, 302
Bavay, 255, 275
Bazuel, 190, 191
Beaucourt, 81, 83
Beaufort, 29, 34, 35, 247
Beaulencourt, 89, 91, 92, 126
Beaurevoir, 162, 165, 168, 171, 172, 174
Beaurevoir Line, 152, 166, 167, 171, 210, 219, 220, 248
Behagnies, 105, 107, 108
Belgians, King Albert of, 283
Belgian Army, co-operation with British Armies, 283, 284, 288, 289
Bell, General (U.S. Army), 38
Bellenglise, 158, 160
Bellicourt, 66, 151, 153, 156, 310
Benstall, General, 28
Berlaimont, 197, 242, 246
Berthaucourt, 74, 75, 76
Berthelot, General, 13
Bertry, 176, 222

315

Bethell, General, 170, 204
Beugneux, 19, 20
Beugny, 126, 127
Biastre, 224, 229
Bickmore, Colonel, 10
Bihucourt, 120, 123
Billon Wood, 49, 50
Birdwood, General Sir W., 141, 276, 281, 283, 286, 290, 291, 292
Bissett, Lieutenant, V.C., 269
Blacklock, General, 273
Blanding, General (U.S. Army), 152
Blecourt, 259, 260, 262
Bligny, 6, 13, 14
Boiry Becquerelle, 103, 142
Bois du Temple, 246, 247
Bois l'Évêque, 192, 200
Bouchavesnes, 59, 60
Bouilly, 7, 8
Bourlon village, 256, 257
Bourlon Wood, 216, 256
Bousies, 192, 193, 237
Boyd, General, 75, 157
Braithwaite, General, 6, 8, 12, 64, 72, 98, 118, 119, 149, 150, 157, 161, 164, 185, 205
Brancourt, 178
Bray, 45
Brie, 63, 64
Brodie, Colonel, V.C., 106
Brutinel, General, 263
Bucquoy, 81, 82, 121
Bulgaria, surrender to Allies, 296, 300
Bullecourt, 131, 132, 133, 134
Burnett, General, 8
Burnyeat, Colonel, 194
Butler, General, 26, 40, 63, 68, 149
Buzancy, 14, 15, 17
Byng, General Sir Julian, 24, 43, 79, 80, 83, 98, 107, 109, 120, 126, 128, 129, 138, 170, 214, 218, 230

Cadorna, General, 294
Caix, 28, 34
Calvert, Sergeant, 118
Cambrai, 144, 225, 227, 260, 262, 263, 265
Cameron, General, 143, 267
Campbell, General, 6, 82, 84, 87, 88, 95, 97, 208, 246
Canal de l'Escaut, 150, 170, 208, 209, 210, 212, 213, 214, 217, 218, 219, 260, 263, 265, 266

Canal du Nord, 66, 94, 117, 118, 137, 142, 144, 147, 215, 256, 257, 258, 261, 264, 265
Cantaing, 215, 216, 217
Capelle, 239
Caporetto, 294
Carey, General, 286
Carter-Campbell, General, 12, 139
Cartwright, General, 204
Catillon, 194, 195, 200, 202, 203
Cayley, General, 284
Chaplin, General, 18
Charles, General, 170
Chateau-Thierry, 5
Chaumuzy, 12, 14
Cheape, General, 282
Chipilly, 31, 32, 33, 34, 37, 38, 39
Clarke, Sergeant, 201
Clemenceau, M., 3, 283
Cloutman, Major, V.C., 245
Cockhill, Captain, 9
Coffin, General, 284
Cojeul River, 104, 129, 130
Comines, 285, 288
Constantine, King, 22
Constantinople, 297
Cook, Sir Joseph, 307
Courcelette, 86, 89
Courcelles, 101
Coussmaker, Colonel, 105
Craigie-Hackett, General, 174
Cressaire Wood, 39, 40
Crevecœur, 166, 210, 223, 247
Croisilles, 105, 108, 109, 110, 111, 114, 129, 130, 131
Cross, Colonel, 106
Crown Prince of Germany, 300
Cubitt, General, 82, 84, 233
Cuitron, 7, 9
Currie, General Sir A., 26, 259, 263, 266

Daly, General, 218, 226, 227
Damascus occupied, 296
Damery, 35, 41
Dardanelles, 297
Dawson, Colonel, 70, 287
Daykins, Corporal, V.C., 235
Debeney, General, 25
De Lisle, General, 282, 283, 290
Delville, 50
Delville Wood, 91
D'Esperey, General Franchet, 295

INDEX 317

Deverell, General, 98, 112, 211
Diaz, General, 294
Dixmude, 288
Doake, Captain, 48
Dobson, Colonel, 21
Doiran, Lake, 296
Dompierre, 52, 198
Dooner, Colonel, 20
Douai, 144, 264, 279, 290
Douai Canal, 278
Drocourt-Quéant Line, 132, 135, 136, 143, 261, 265, 277
Dudgeon, General, 87
Duncan, General, 218
Dury, 144, 145

East Africa, 297
Ecaillon, 184
Ecaillon River, 238, 239, 267, 268, 269, 270
Ecoust, 107, 110, 113, 114, 132, 133
Egerton, Lieutenant, 287
Englefontaine, 193, 240, 241
Epéhy, 62, 66, 68, 97
Ervillers, 104, 105, 106, 107
Erzberger, Herr, 300
Escarmain, 239, 251
Escaufort, 176, 179
Estrées, 52, 157, 172, 174, 264
Eterpigny, 143, 161

Faison, General (U.S. Army), 153
Favreuil, 110, 125
Fergusson, General Sir Charles, 110, 114, 128, 138, 139, 140, 145, 214, 218, 250
Feuillaucourt, 54, 55, 57
Fisher, General, 101, 102
Flers, 89, 90, 91
Flesquières, 209, 211
Foch, Marshal, 3, 4, 21, 292, 300
Fonsomme, 162, 166
Fontaine, 215, 217, 257
Fontaine-les-Croisilles, 129, 131
Forest, 177, 237
Fortune, General, 16
Framerville, 34, 36
Frémicourt, 90, 126
French Army, co-operation of, with British Armies, 10-21, 27, 28, 78, 80, 161, 162, 165, 166, 178, 179, 180, 185, 186, 187, 194, 283, 288, 289, 291
Fresnes, 265, 277

Fresnoy, 73, 74, 75, 76, 77, 243
Fresnoy-le-Grand, 180
Freyberg, General, 282
Frisby, Captain, V.C., 212
Fryell, General, 174

Gagnicourt, 135, 136, 144, 145
Gauche Wood, 96
Gavrelle, 141, 276
General position on Western front in July, 1-4; survey of the various fronts at beginning of August, 21-23
George, Mr. Lloyd, 3
Germany, internal condition of, 2; collapse of resistance, 299
Gheluvelt, 284, 288
Gheluwe, 289
Ghisignies, 238, 240
Gillibrand, General, 29
Girdwood, General, 60, 66
Glasgow, General, 30
Godley, General Sir A. J., 6, 40, 63, 143, 258, 264, 276
Gomiecourt, 103, 104, 105, 106, 123
Gorringe, General, 32, 40
Gort, Lord, V.C., 211
Gough, General Sir Hubert, 71, 309
Gouraud, General, 4, 5
Gouy, 151, 154, 171, 172, 173, 219
Gouzeaucourt, 96, 97, 98, 127, 207
Graincourt, 211, 215, 216, 257
Grandcourt, 82, 87, 88
Grand Rozoy, 18, 19, 20
Greenland Hill, 141, 142
Greenwood, Colonel, 88
Gregg, Lieutenant, V.C., 262
Gricourt, 77, 78, 149, 159
Griffiths, Lieutenant, 85
Grogan, General, 277
Guémappe, 140
Gueudecourt, 89, 91
Guild, Major, 202
Guillemont, 51, 90
Guillemont Farm, 151, 154, 155, 163
Gwyn-Thomas, General, 86, 98

Haig, Field Marshal Sir Douglas, 21, 25, 80, 166, 241
Haking, General Sir R., 283, 290
Haldane, General Sir J., 80, 83, 98, 103, 105, 110, 114, 224, 239, 240, 249

Hamelincourt, 103, 104
Harper, General Sir G. M., 80, 83, 98, 120, 208, 209, 213, 223, 234, 238, 248
Harpies River, 237, 251
Harris, Sergeant, V.C., 40
Hart, General, 242
Hart, Colonel, 17
Hartennes Forest, 16, 17
Hartley, Colonel, 100
Haspres, 266, 267
Haucourt, 141, 143
Haussy, 228, 250, 251
Havrincourt, 118, 119, 120, 128
Havrincourt Wood, 210
Hendecourt, 131, 132, 133, 134, 145
Henderson, Colonel, 104, 116
Heneker, General, 141, 276, 277
Henin, 108
Henin Hill, 108, 129, 130
Herbert, Colonel, 114
Herting, Count von, 299
Hickie, General Sir W., 173
Higginson, General, 31, 51, 66, 287
High Wood, 90
Hill, General, 129
Hindenburg, General von, 48, 300
Hindenburg Line, the, 42, 43, 62, 65, 66, 69, 71, 72, 75, 77, 79, 83, 95, 98, 105, 106, 108, 109, 111, 118, 119, 127, 129, 130, 131, 132, 136, 137, 143, 149, 151, 152, 153, 155, 163, 166, 169, 207, 208, 210, 214, 215, 219, 282, 307-313
Hobbs, General, 30, 155
Holland, General, 141, 283
Hollebeke, 283, 285
Holnon, 74, 75
Honey, Lieutenant, V.C., 262
Hongnau River, 249, 254
Horne, General Sir H., 24, 41, 138, 141, 276, 280
Houthulst Forest, 284
Hull, General, 129
Hunter, General, 176
Hunter-Weston, General Sir A., 141, 170, 265, 276

Inchy, 137, 223
Incledon-Webber, General, 39
Irles, 120, 124
Irwin, Colonel, 59, 193

Italy, victorious on the Piave, 3, 22, 294; co-operation of, on Western front, 7
Iwuy, 227, 264, 266

Jackson, General, 170, 173
Jackson, Corporal, V.C., 212
Jacob, General Sir C., 283, 284, 285, 288
Jeffreys, General, 218, 286
Jerusalem, 296
Johnson, Colonel, V.C., 203
Joncourt, 156, 161, 162
Jourdain, Colonel, 20

Kaiser, the, 300
Kennedy, Colonel, 17
Kerr, Lieutenant, V.C., 262
Kruseik, 284

La Bassée, 286, 292
La Boiselle, 49, 85
La Capelle, 300
La Folie Wood, 215, 217
Lagnicourt, 115, 135
Lambert, General, 44, 72, 158
Landrecies, 195, 196, 197, 204
Latham, Commander, 307, 312
Lawford, General, 284
Le Cateau, 147, 177, 183, 187, 188, 190, 191, 247, 290
Le Catelet, 151, 154, 156, 157, 171, 172, 173, 219
L'Escaut, 267
Le Hamel, action of, 24, 25
Le Quesnel, 29, 34, 35
Le Quesnoy, 238, 242, 270
Le Tronquoy, 158, 161
Le Vergies, 161, 162
Le Verguier, 65, 72
Lee, General, 31, 46, 66, 170
Lempire, 66, 67
Lens, 27, 100, 276, 286, 287
Lettow-Vorbeck, General von, 297
Lewis, General (U.S. Army), 152
Lihons, 35, 36, 37
Lille, 290, 292, 293
Lipsett, General, 28, 267
Locquignol, 197, 242
Logeast Wood, 82, 121, 123
Longueval, 89, 90, 91
Lucas, General, 267
Luce River, 27

INDEX 319

Ludendorff, General, 30, 42, 281, 300
Lys River, 285, 288, 289, 290

M'Culloch, General, 87, 88
MacDonald, Captain, 192
Macdonell, General, 28
MacGregor, Captain, V.C., 262
MacGregor, Lieutenant R. R., 116
Maclagan, General, 30, 37
Macleod, Colonel, 17
Macquincourt Valley, 163, 164
Malincourt, 220, 222
Mametz, 49, 50
Mametz Wood, 89
Manchester Hill, 75, 78
Mangin, General, 5, 14, 18, 44, 80
Mannequin Hill, 165, 166, 180
Marcoing, 212, 217
Marden, General, 72, 73, 78, 157
Marfaux, 7, 9, 14
Marindin, General, 284
Marne River, 1, 4, 5, 6, 11
Maroilles, 195, 197
Marou, 235, 236
Marshall, General, 22, 297
Martin, General, 54, 167
Masnières, 171, 213, 223
Maubeuge, 197, 249, 255
Meaulte, 47, 48
Menin, 289
Menin Road, 284, 285, 288
Mennevret, 186, 187
Mericourt, 180, 286
Merisfield, Sergeant, V.C., 262
Merville, 292
Mesopotamia, 22, 297
Messines, 283, 285
Meteren, 282
Mezières, 28, 204
Milne, General, 296
Miraumont, 82, 83, 85, 87, 88, 120, 122, 123, 124
Misitch, Marshal, 295
Mœuvres, 117, 137, 256
Moir, Major, 12
Molain, 182, 184
Monash, General Sir John, 25, 26, 29, 36, 52, 63, 71, 169
Monchy, 140
Mons, 280
Mont St. Quentin, 53, 54, 55, 56, 57, 59, 63, 64
Montauban, 50
Montay, 177, 231

Montbrehain, 165, 168, 171
Morchies, 115, 135
Morcourt, 31, 34
Morlancourt, 25, 26, 31, 33, 34
Morland, General, 164, 169, 170, 171, 174, 179, 199, 200, 219, 230
Mormal Forest, 191, 195, 237, 241, 243, 244, 245, 246, 248
Morval, 51, 91, 92
Mory, 106, 107, 109, 110
Moyenneville, 81, 99, 100
Murman Coast, 23

Nagle, Captain, 116
Nauroy, 151, 154, 156, 157, 160, 161, 310
Neuve Eglise, 282
Neuvilly, 223, 229, 231, 232, 233, 234
Nicholson, General, 18, 19
Nicholson, Captain, 49
Nieppe, 281, 282
Niergnies, 221, 222
Nivelle, 287
Noreuil, 115, 134
Norton, General, 244
Noyelles, 212, 268
Nurlu, 61, 62, 94

Oise River, 3, 5, 80
Oldham, General, 244
Onions, Corporal, V.C., 123
Oppy, 141, 276, 287
Orr-Ewing, General, 16
Ors, 194, 195, 200, 201
O'Ryan, General (U.S. Army), 151
Ostend, 289, 290
Ovillers, 85
Owen, General, 62

Palestine, 22
Parvillers, 35, 41
Peace conference at Paris, 302; chief terms of settlement, 302-304
Peizières, 62, 66, 67, 94, 97
Pelves, 141, 142
Penet, General, 18
Percival, Colonel, 51
Pereira, General, 98
Peronne, 53, 54, 55, 58, 59, 60, 63, 64
Pershing, General, 293
Petit Camp Wood, 7, 8, 9

Piave, defeat of Austrians on, 3, 22, 294
Pierce, General (U.S. Army), 151
Pinney, General, 96, 208, 231
Ploegsteert, 282
Ploegsteert Wood, 285
Plumer, General Sir H., 283, 284
Plunket, Captain, 307
Ponchaux, 172, 173, 175
Ponsonby, General, 124
Pont d'Aire, 262, 263
Pontruet, 76, 77, 158, 159
Portuguese, 292
Pozières, 85, 86
Premont, 175, 176, 178
Preseau, 252, 272, 273
Priez Farm, 51, 59, 60
Pronville, 137, 146
Prospect Hill, 171, 172
Puisieux, 120, 122
Pys, 89, 124

Quadrilateral, the, 73, 74, 75, 76, 78
Quéant, 115, 116, 135, 136, 137, 146, 264
Quinnemont Farm, 151, 154

Raillencourt, 258, 259
Ramicourt, 163, 165, 166
Ramillies, 226, 262, 263
Ramsay, General, 31
Rancourt, 59, 60
Rawlinson, General Sir Henry, 24, 25, 34, 40, 41, 53, 59, 80, 82, 84, 90, 94, 96, 107, 138, 148, 149, 169, 223
Read, General (U.S. Army), 150, 184
Regiments:
  Artillery—
  Royal Field Artillery, 10, 21
  Honourable Artillery Company, 294
  Trench Mortar, 49, 60
  Cavalry—
  6th Dragoon Guards, 91, 227
  12th Lancers, 198
  16th Lancers, 275
  3rd Hussars, 245
  8th Hussars, 89
  20th Hussars, 89
  Northumberland Hussars, 33
  Oxford Hussars, 226, 240
  Australian Light Horse, 64, 275
  Canadian Light Horse, 263

Regiments (*contd.*):
  Guards—
  Coldstream, 100, 104, 110, 111, 212
  Grenadier, 100, 104, 109, 110, 211
  Scots, 100, 104, 107, 109
  Welsh, 107, 109
  Infantry—
  Argyll and Sutherland Highlanders, 10, 11, 20, 142, 269, 271
  Bedford, 48, 51, 192, 196, 244
  Berkshire, 49, 50, 51, 61, 62, 99, 107, 193, 276, 277, 287
  Black Watch, 10, 14, 15, 142, 159, 196
  Border, 94, 234
  Buffs (East Kent), 39, 47, 193
  Cambridge, 33, 62, 287
  Cameron Highlanders, 16, 17, 73
  Cameronians (Scottish Rifles), 16, 215, 289, 291
  Cheshire, 20, 244, 253, 254
  Connaught Rangers, 177
  Devon, 8, 119, 123, 245, 277
  Dorset, 86, 93, 98, 201, 233
  Duke of Cornwall's, 245
  Durham Light Infantry, 8, 9, 87, 97, 118, 177
  East Surrey, 47, 50, 59, 193, 244
  East Yorkshire, 87, 88, 97, 223, 233
  Essex, 48, 50, 62, 69, 192, 196, 269, 270
  Gloucester, 76, 77, 78, 159, 196, 202, 203, 250
  Gordon Highlanders, 10, 11, 12, 14, 15, 17, 101, 102, 103, 112, 113, 142, 225, 238, 271
  Hampshire, 7, 118, 268, 272
  Hereford, 20, 128
  Highland Light Infantry, 105, 106, 108, 215
  Inniskilling Fusiliers, 171, 198
  King's Liverpool, 100, 104, 106, 107, 113, 177
  King's Own Royal Lancaster, 101, 103, 225, 239
  King's Own Scottish Borderers, 16, 17, 134, 289
  King's Royal Rifles, 73, 74, 77, 107, 172, 190
  Lancashire Fusiliers, 201, 238, 269, 270

INDEX

Regiments (*contd.*):
 Infantry—
  Leicester, 156, 160
  Lincoln, 94, 97, 160
  London Rifle Brigade, 131, 274
  1st London, 108, 131
  2nd London, 49, 131, 274
  3rd London, 49
  4th London, 49, 105, 133
  6th London, 38
  10th London, 32, 38
  13th London (Kensingtons), 105, 133, 274
  14th London (Scottish), 105, 133, 274
  20th London, 119
  22nd London, 46
  23rd London, 46
  24th London, 46
  — London (Queen's Westminsters), 131
 Manchester, 231, 235, 236
 Middlesex, 108, 131, 258, 277, 278, 279
 Munster Fusiliers, 135, 136, 190
 Norfolk, 62, 244
 Northampton, 47, 51, 70, 76, 163, 227, 254
 North Lancashire, 20, 73, 158, 159
 North Staffordshire, 159, 160
 Northumberland Fusiliers, 100, 102, 114, 172
 Oxford and Bucks, 105, 106, 108
 Queen's (West Surrey), 48, 59, 193
 Rifle Brigade, 224, 272, 279
 Royal Fusiliers, 47, 48, 51, 67, 70, 99, 100, 105, 108, 113
 Royal Irish, 136
 Royal Scots, 10, 12, 16, 17, 101, 104, 115, 116, 120, 215, 239
 Royal Scots Fusiliers, 101, 115, 116, 120, 239
 Royal West Kent, 40, 48, 50, 60, 70, 192, 193, 196, 287
 Seaforth Highlanders, 10, 12, 14, 15, 17, 142, 273
 Sherwood Foresters, 160, 174, 177, 179, 185, 277
 Shropshire, 101, 104, 115
 Somerset Light Infantry, 268
 South Staffordshire, 106, 159, 160
 South Wales Borderers, 159, 202, 203

Regiments (*contd.*):
 Infantry—
  Suffolk, 101, 103, 112, 116, 225, 239
  Sussex, 20, 62, 73, 74, 76, 203
  Warwick, 196, 251, 252, 268
  Welsh, 77, 84, 85, 202, 203, 242
  Welsh Fusiliers, 294
  West Riding, 7, 8, 9, 93, 110, 118, 232, 268
  West Yorkshire, 13, 93, 98, 212, 234, 277
  Wiltshire, 190, 251, 254
  Worcester, 196, 252, 277, 279
  York and Lancaster, 7, 8, 118, 235
  Yorkshire, 177, 288
  Yorkshire Light Infantry, 7, 87, 97, 118, 172, 198, 269, 273

 Royal Engineers, 21, 104, 160, 201, 202, 245, 287
 Royal Naval Division, 101, 102, 121, 123, 124, 125, 135, 136, 137, 145, 146, 214, 216, 217, 218, 221, 222, 273, 275
 Tunnelling Companies, 196, 278
  Overseas Forces—
  Australians, 6, 12, 25, 29, 30, 31, 34, 36, 37, 38, 39, 40, 41, 42, 44, 45, 46, 52, 53, 54, 55, 56, 57, 58, 59, 61, 63, 64, 65, 67, 71, 72, 73, 74, 79, 149, 150, 152, 153, 154, 155, 156, 157, 162, 164, 165, 166, 167, 168, 169, 171, 172, 173, 174, 282, 307-313
  Canadians, 26, 27, 28, 29, 31, 34, 35, 36, 41, 42, 107, 110, 111, 116, 129, 130, 132, 134, 135, 136, 138, 140, 141, 142, 143, 144, 145, 146, 147, 148, 176, 215, 216, 217, 227, 228, 256, 257, 258, 259, 260, 261, 262, 263, 264, 265, 266, 269, 271, 276, 278
  New Zealanders, 6, 9, 83, 95, 122, 123, 124, 125, 126, 127, 128, 166, 209, 210, 213, 223, 224, 226, 232, 238, 240, 242, 243, 245, 248
  South Africans, 52, 170, 175, 188, 189, 190
Rheims, 3, 4, 6
Rhonelle River, 252, 270, 271, 272

Ribeauville, 184, 187
Ribecourt, 211, 212
Richemont River, 192, 193
Riencourt, 126, 131, 132, 134, 136, 145
Riqueval, 158, 159
Ritchie, General, 286
Roberts, Colonel, 279
Robertson, General (17th Division), 82, 87, 93, 97, 231
Robertson, General (5th Brigade), 57
Robinson, General, 196
Robinson, Mr. Perry, correspondent of *The Times*, quoted, 146, 147
Rollo, General, 172
Romeries, 238, 251
Ronssoy, 66, 67
Rosenthal, General, 54, 58, 63
Rosières, 34, 35, 36
Roulers, 289
Rumilly, 213, 214
Russell, General Sir A. H., 209, 223
Russia in revolution, 22, 23, 304

St. Benin, 177, 179, 188
St. Christ, 63, 64
St. Georges River, 238
St. Leger, 107, 109
St. Maurice River, 184
St. Mihiel, American success at, 293
St. Pierre, 186
St. Pierre Divion, 83, 84, 85
St. Pierre Vaast Wood, 61
St. Python, 226, 235
St. Quentin Canal, 54, 157, 158, 159, 160, 162, 163, 164, 165, 171, 172, 174, 175
St. Souplet, 179, 182, 183, 187
Sadleir-Jackson, General, 48
Sailly-Sallisel, 60, 92
Saint, Colonel, 33
Salonica, 22, 295
Sambre and Oise Canal, 191, 194, 195, 196, 199, 200, 201, 202, 203
Sambre River, 197, 241, 245, 246, 249
Sanders, General, 98
Sapignies, 105, 107, 108
Sassegnies, 195, 197
Scarpe River, 138, 139, 140, 143, 258, 265, 276, 277, 278, 287

Scheidemann, Herr, 302
Scheldt River, 292
Schwaben Redoubt, 86
Sedan, Americans in, 293
Selency, 74, 76, 78
Selle River, 175, 176, 177, 179, 182, 187, 191, 199, 223, 224, 226, 227, 228, 229, 231, 250, 251, 266, 267, 268, 270
Sensée Canal, 263
Sensée River, 105, 131, 144, 258, 260
Sequehart, 162, 163, 165, 166, 168, 171
Serain, 175, 176
Serre, 81
Shute, General, 80, 82, 84, 98, 173, 208, 219, 230
Skinner, General, 284
Smith, Colonel (Gordons), 17
Smith, Colonel (Seaforths), 14
Smith, Colonel Holroyd, 87, 88, 97
Smyth, General, 29
Soissons, captured by French, 21
Solesmes, 226, 229, 234
Solly-Flood, General, 83, 122
Someren, Colonel van, 51
Somme River, 1, 25, 26, 30, 31, 32, 34, 37, 38, 39, 40, 44, 45, 52, 54, 60, 80
Spicer, Captain, 88
Statton, Sergeant, 38
Stephens, General, 283, 288
Strickland, General, 64, 72, 157
Sugden, General, 171
Suthery, Captain, 49
Swindells, Colonel, 20
Syria, 297

Tadpole Copse, 117, 137
Tanner General, 188, 189
Tara Hill, 48, 82, 88
Tarleton, Colonel, 14
Templeux, 62, 67, 72, 308, 312
Thiepval, 82, 84, 85, 86
Thilloy, 125, 126
Thomas, Colonel, 93
Thomson, General, 14, 18
Thorpe, Colonel, 194
Thure River, 247
Tigris River, 296
Tortille River, 61
Tourcoing, 290
Trento captured, 295

INDEX

Trescault, 96, 118, 119, 127, 128
Trieste, surrendered to Italy, 295
Trinquis River, 147, 258, 265, 278
Trones Wood, 50, 90
Tudor, General, 284
Turkey, collapse of, 296
Turner, Colonel, 17
Tweedie, Colonel, 78

Usna Hill, 48, 84, 85

Valenciennes, 269, 270, 271, 272
Vandhuile, 66, 149, 150, 151, 163, 164, 171, 172, 219
Vaulx-Vraucourt, 110, 112, 113, 126
Vaux Andigny, 179, 181
Vaux Wood, 52
Vendegies, 237, 240, 252, 268
Venizelos, M., 22
Vesle River, 21
Vickery, Colonel, 117
Vieux Berquin, 282
Villers-Bretonneux, 29, 169
Villers-Cotterets, 3, 4
Villers-Guislain, 208
Villers-Outreaux, 175, 176
Villers St. Ghislain, 275
Vincent, General, 33
Vitry, 277, 278

Walsh, Colonel, 97
Walthall, General, 21
Wambaix, 221, 225
Wargnies, 243, 254
Warlencourt, 89, 124
Watson, General, 28
Watts, General Sir H., 283, 284, 288
Weeks, Captain, 20
Wemyss, Admiral Sir Rosslyn, 301
Whigham, General, 98, 212
Wiancourt, 165, 167
Wilkinson, Private, V.C., 235
Williams, General (37th Division), 83, 121
Williams, General (102nd Brigade), 18
Wilson, President, 279, 300
Wisdom, General, 167
Wood, General, 67, 192, 193
Woodcock, General, 18
Wytschaete, 285

Young, Lieutenant, V.C., 128
Ypres, 281, 283

Zandvoorde, 284, 285
Zonnebeke, 284

THE END

Printed in Great Britain by R. & R. CLARK, LIMITED, *Edinburgh.*

www.ingramcontent.com/pod-product-compliance
Lightning Source LLC
Chambersburg PA
CBHW030816190426
43197CB00036B/504